The Book on
VA LOANS

An Essential Guide to Maximizing Your
Home Loan Benefits

Chris Birk

Veterans United Home Loans

The Book on VA Loans:
An Essential Guide to Maximizing Your Home Loan Benefits

By Chris Birk
© 2014
ISBN: 0615458270
ISBN-13: 9780615458274

DEDICATION

*This work is dedicated to the tens of thousands of American service
members who have put their trust in us. To serve those who have
served is a duty — and a privilege — we will never take for granted.*

On the cover: James Roy, 16th Chief Master Sergeant of the Air Force, his wife, Paula, and their sons outside their new home. Veterans United Home Loans was honored to help Chief Roy and his family become first-time homeowners.

"They didn't tell me just sign at the bottom line," Chief Roy said. "They shared with me why it's important at any given time through the process. It's great that we could get associated with a company like Veterans United."

You can watch Chief Roy's homebuying story at VeteransUnited.com/ChiefRoy.

VETERANS UNITED HOME LOANS

Veterans United Home Loans is a national leader in VA home loans. We are a private company (NMLS #1907) and not a government agency.

We take great pride in serving our nation's veterans, service members and military families. We specialize in VA loans, and that dedication and focus has allowed us to streamline the homebuying and refinance process. We made available more than $4 billion in home financing in 2013 alone.

Leading the way is a team of more than 1,000 people dedicated to serving those who have served our nation.

Great communication and our expertise as VA loan specialists were cited as the top two reasons people chose Veterans United Home Loans, according to a recent survey of more than 10,000 borrowers.

The book you're holding is just one more way we're working to communicate with veterans, real estate agents and the community at large.

Our mission is to help veterans and military members take full advantage of the benefits earned by their service.

RESOURCES

Our VA mortgage specialists and service team are available day and night to answer your questions and keep the process rolling. Please don't hesitate to contact us with your questions or concerns.

We're committed to enhancing lives every day.
Let us know what we can do to help.

CONTACT VETERANS UNITED HOME LOANS

- **Call us anytime** at 800-884-5428

- **Start the loan process now** at VeteransUnited.com

- **Interact with us** at Facebook.com/vuhomeloans

- **Keep up with company news on Twitter** @veteransunited

- **Reach author Chris Birk** at chris@vu.com or Facebook.com/VALoansInsider

RESOURCES

- Watch video overviews and go deeper into The Book on VA Loans. **VeteransUnited.com/book**

- Need help boosting your credit score? Check out our Lighthouse Program, which works with veterans and active military for free to help them develop a plan to repair their credit and get on the path to loan prequalification. **Talk to a Lighthouse credit expert today at 888-392-7421**

- Get a sense of your purchasing power and what you can afford. **VA Loan Calculator.com**

- Learn more about the VA Funding Fee and whether you're exempt at **VA Funding Fee.com**

- We're not the VA nor are we affiliated with any government agencies. You can visit the VA's online home loans hub at **Homeloans.VA.gov**

FOREWORD

A young soldier once asked me how he could become Sergeant Major of the Army.

I told him to start by being a good soldier and to listen to your noncommissioned officers to learn everything you can about the Army and your career field. I told this soldier the lessons he would learn by being a good soldier and becoming an expert in his profession would set him up for success as a junior noncommissioned officer. To become a great noncommissioned officer you have to teach everything you learned as a young soldier to your soldiers, your little piece of the Army, and make them good soldiers and experts in their profession.

I told this soldier and the group of leaders standing with him to apply these same thoughts to each level of responsibility as you get promoted and move up through the ranks. Develop and teach your subordinates and leaders in each piece of the Army you're responsible for throughout your career. Finally, I told him that taking care of soldiers, developing them as good soldiers and experts in their profession, is more important and carries more responsibility than any job he will ever have in any career.

After more than 35 years in the military, including seven as the most senior enlisted member of the U.S. Army, I have seen the tremendous work and sacrifice our service members and military families make every day. We have thousands of service men and women forward deployed to more than 80 countries around the world, performing vital missions and facing new challenges in an effort to protect America.

Quality of life for all our service men and women and their families is an inseparable element of our readiness posture. To improve that quality of life I've made it my mission to implement initiatives and improve resources in areas that are most important to those most affected by change.

As Sergeant Major of the Army, I was part of a leadership team that created our Warrior Transition Units to support wounded, ill or injured soldiers, with a singular focus on warrior healing and support for Army families.

This Army leadership team also boosted family programs at installations where we committed more than $1.5 billion to enhance quality of life programs. They standardized family programs, upgraded troop and family housing, further developed youth and child care facilities and supported single soldiers by offering additional recreation and travel through the Better Opportunities for Single Soldiers program.

This team had the opportunity to hire more than 1,000 new Family Readiness Support Assistants to provide additional support to Family Readiness Groups in deployable units.

Following my retirement from the Army, I had the honor to serve as president of Homes for Our Troops, a national non-profit organization that helps build specially adapted homes for severely injured veterans. It's through my work with Homes for Our Troops that I came to know Veterans United Home Loans. The company and its philanthropic arm, Veterans United Foundation, teamed with us to help in the campaign to build 100 homes for veterans nationwide.

For those who seek it, homeownership remains one of those critical foundations of American life, especially for those who serve. Our military members sacrifice so much to safeguard our nation's security and prosperity. They deserve a fair and equitable path to the American dream, one that honors their service and acknowledges the debt we owe them.

Seventy years ago, our nation set out to do just that. Congress passed the sweeping GI Bill of Rights in 1944, a major provision of which established a home loan guaranty program. The government pledged to stand behind these mortgages, a promise that opened the doors of homeownership to a generation of returning veterans.

In fact, more than 2.4 million veterans sought out and secured VA-backed loans from 1944 to 1952.

Flash forward to today. A fledgling program created to help the Greatest Generation has now guaranteed more than 20 million loans. Veterans and active military members are turning to the safety, security and buying power of the VA home loan program in huge numbers.

That spirit of giving back, of serving all of those who have so proudly served our great nation, is stronger than ever.

I tell you all of this because it takes a team effort to make a real and lasting difference. I've come to trust Veterans United Home Loans as a genuine partner that's passionate about enhancing the lives of our nation's military members.

They understand how difficult it can be for military families to routinely move from installation to installation, both here in the U.S. and overseas, and how these frequent moves pose unique financial and emotional challenges. They realize that a stable home can provide service members and their families a much-needed sanctuary, especially when those warriors are deployed.

It's our duty as veterans to take care of our own, but we should never take for granted those who wish to help us in our endeavors to improve our quality of life. There will always be challenges in and out of service, but I know that Veterans United Home Loans will continue to take care of our military family.

Our benefit is their mission.

Ken Preston
13th Sgt. Major of the U.S. Army

TABLE OF CONTENTS

Introduction 1

Chapter 1: VA Loans in Today's Market 3

Chapter 2: Eligibility and Requirements 21

Chapter 3: Loan Prequalification and Preapproval............77

Chapter 4: Purchasing a Home with a VA Loan 127

Chapter 5: Loan Processing, Rates and Costs 181

Chapter 6: VA Refinance Loans 239

Chapter 7: The Future of VA Loans..255

INTRODUCTION

With the Second World War still raging in Europe and the Pacific, U.S. officials started planning to address the inevitable struggles American soldiers would face upon returning to civilian life.

The government created its concept of a home loan guaranty in 1944, part of a more widespread movement to shift from a wartime economy to a peacetime one. The idea was to provide those who proudly served our country with a simple and streamlined path to homeownership in the wake of the war.

Service abroad made it difficult for some soldiers and service members to build a solid financial profile. A home loan guaranty program would mitigate that concern and help level the playing field for those who spent months and even years fighting for American freedom.

Instead of providing loans, the Department of Veterans Affairs would guaranty a portion of every loan made to a qualified borrower. That layer of protection would spur lenders to issue loans to veterans and service members who might otherwise struggle to obtain financing.

Seventy years later, the Department of Veterans Affairs and its VA Home Loan Guaranty Program have helped millions of veterans and service members achieve the dream of homeownership.

Today, the financial flexibility and purchasing power behind the VA loan is more important than ever.

Mortgage lenders have ratcheted up requirements in the wake of the subprime mortgage meltdown. Industry experts and government officials are working to redefine the concept of sustainable homeownership in America. For some borrowers, that means securing a home loan is becoming more difficult than ever before.

But the VA loan program has helped ensure service members are in a prime position to succeed. VA loans feature flexible requirements and significant financial benefits, chiefly the ability to purchase a home with no money down. In an era of tight credit and cautious lending, that kind of opportunity seems anachronistic. But it's a cornerstone of the program.

So is reliability.

VA loans have weathered the subprime collapse and proved incredibly resilient in the face of foreclosure. In fact, given the fiscal tumult of the last few years, VA loans have emerged as "a model of stability," as Thomas J. Pamperin, a VA deputy undersecretary, told a Congressional subcommittee in spring 2010.

To the average service member, VA loans often represent the clearest and most cost-effective path to homeownership. They come with an array of benefits that no other lending program can match. They are, in many ways, a lifeline for scores of service members and military families.

C H A P T E R   1 :
VA LOANS IN
TODAY'S MARKET

Despite the recent economic freefall, homeownership remains a cornerstone of American society. Nearly 70 percent of citizens own a home, which most see as a path toward wealth creation and financial stability. Rates for homeownership among veterans are even higher, right around 82 percent, according to the Mortgage Bankers Association.

The last few years have proved a mixed bag for homebuyers and existing homeowners. Purchasing a home today looks a bit different than it did six or seven years ago. For many people it's increasingly difficult. Borrowers who qualify have reaped the benefits of government-sponsored tax credit programs and record-low interest rates. At the same time, the subprime mortgage meltdown and ensuing financial crisis created a restrictive credit environment and made it significantly tougher for some prospective borrowers to purchase homes or to refinance existing mortgages.

That relatively grim storyline isn't exactly the same for military members.

VA loans are consistently easier to qualify for than other loan products. Veterans and service members don't need to hit tough credit or income guidelines to participate in the program. In fact, credit history plays less of a role in determining homeownership for veterans than it does for non-VA borrowers.

These loans also come with significant financial benefits. Veterans routinely point to the program's signature benefit as its most powerful: Qualified borrowers can purchase a home with no money down.

Given the lending environment we now inhabit, it's almost difficult to believe anyone can buy a house today without shelling out a down payment. But it's true, it's incredibly powerful and it's a benefit that helps make homeownership possible for scores of borrowers who might otherwise struggle.

"Most people don't realize, especially younger people and first-time homebuyers, what a benefit it is," said Scott Dow, of Charleston, S.C., a former Coast Guard officer and Reservist who has purchased two homes using his VA benefit. "I would not have been able to purchase a home without a VA loan."

Neither would most military buyers.

About 8 in 10 VA borrowers could not have qualified for conventional home financing. Nearly 90 percent of VA homebuyers purchase a home without making a down payment.

Falling home prices and a watertight credit market have brought new attention to the long-cherished VA home loan program. VA loan volume has soared 372 percent since 2007, as military borrowers have flocked to the agency's more flexible and often less costly alternative.

Here's a look at the last seven years' worth of VA loan totals to give you a sense of the program's trajectory and its growing importance:

FY13: 629,312 loans
FY12: 539,884 loans
FY11: 357,592 loans
FY10: 314,011 loans
FY09: 325,690 loans
FY08: 179,670 loans
FY07: 133,313 loans

VA loans have more forgiving credit and debt-to-income requirements than some other loan programs. VA lenders are generally looking for a credit score of at least 620.

In comparison, the average credit score on a successful FHA purchase loan in March 2014 was 684, according to mortgage software firm Ellie Mae. Conventional lenders are looking for even higher credit scores. The average credit score for a successful conventional purchase loan that month was 755.

Foreclosures

The VA loan and military borrowers have also proved resilient in the face of foreclosure.

Default notices and foreclosure filings have fallen since late 2010, in large part because of questionable foreclosure practices on the part of lenders. But there are still hundreds of thousands of distressed properties in markets across the country.

In Nevada alone, one in every 33 homes was facing foreclosure. Foreclosure rates were slightly better in states like Florida, Arizona and California, but homeowners across the country continue to drown in "underwater" homes where they owe far more than what the property is worth.

Military borrowers certainly haven't been immune to foreclosure. More than 20,000 veterans, service members and reservists lost their homes in 2010. Communities located near military bases saw foreclosure filings increase 32 percent over 2008 levels, according to RealtyTrac.

Still, the damage could have been much worse.

Despite the harrowing numbers, VA loans have had the lowest foreclosure rate of any product on the market for nearly all of the last six years. Part of that success is due to the loan experts at the VA who work tirelessly to keep veterans and their families from losing their homes. The VA has multiple programs and options aimed at helping those who have served our country stave off foreclosure.

But service members and veterans themselves deserve much of the credit. Order, structure and obligation are deeply ingrained tenets for most service members. That conditioning tends to follow them throughout their lives, including when the time comes to follow through on structured loan payments.

Spreading the Word

Despite their wide-ranging benefits, VA loans have been utilized by only a fraction of the nation's 22 million veterans. Fewer than 15 percent have taken advantage of the program to purchase or refinance a home.

What's worse is that about a third of veterans are not even aware of the program's existence, according to the VA.

Thousands of service members have recently returned from Iraq and Afghanistan. Millions more who have proudly served our country in years past remain unsure or unaware of the benefits created to honor their service and sacrifice.

VA loans make more sense for some veterans than for others. That's something we'll address throughout these chapters. But it's important that those who have served are at least aware of the benefits and programs out there.

Please make sure the veterans, service members and military spouses in your life are fully aware of the VA's vast array of benefits, covering everything from medical and mental health assistance to job training and home lending.

Is a VA Loan Right For Me?

It's an important question and one that we'll evaluate as fully as possible. But there's an underlying question here that's probably more fundamental as a first order of business: Are you ready for homeownership?

Wanting to buy a home and being able to responsibly afford one are entirely different. As a homeowner, you're on the hook for repairs, maintenance, taxes, insurance and all the other hidden or often forgotten costs that come with owning a home.

There's something to be said for the freedom and relative autonomy of renting. At the same time, it isn't exactly a vehicle for building equity and net worth. What prospective homebuyers need to consider is their own unique economic situation.

Jumping from $600-per-month rent to a mortgage payment might be tough if your budget is already stretched drum-skin thin. Conversely, maybe you've got a great deal and are able to sock away a decent chunk of change each month.

Either way, you need to determine a baseline, an amount that you're able to afford each month for a mortgage payment and associated costs. At the outset, your best bet is to run some numbers using a legitimate online mortgage calculator (we maintain one at Veterans United.com/resources/calculators/mortgage). There are also calculators devoted to helping consumers determine whether it's better to rent or buy (both Ginnie Mae and The New York Times have helpful ones).

Homeownership is an investment. But it's probably not wise to think of it purely in those terms. A $250,000 mortgage is going to wind up costing significantly more after 30 years of taxes, insurance and maintenance costs. And there's no guarantee the equity will be there down the road. Just ask the thousands of American homeowners who saw housing values plummet in recent years.

But that's more exception than rule when we look at the long road of the American housing industry. Home equity continues to represent a larger share of household wealth than retirement savings or any other financial asset, according to the Federal Reserve.

There's also the undeniable, irreplaceable feeling of living in a space that's truly yours. This will be your home, your refuge. You can paint the walls or rip off the wainscoting without asking for permission. You'll also spend a chunk of your monthly income building equity for yourself instead of for your landlord.

Once you're reasonably confident you can afford to purchase and maintain a home, the next step is thinking more in-depth about the type of loan that might fit best. For the vast majority of military borrowers, a VA loan is far and away the most cost effective and advantageous path. Bank on it.

Types of Home Loans

Not all home loans are created equal. Some mortgage types will be more beneficial or costlier than others, depending on your unique financial situation and your homebuying goals.

Home loans are generally divided into two categories: non-conventional loans (including VA, FHA and USDA loans) and conventional loans (those that aren't insured by the government).

The VA loan program is often the most powerful mortgage option for military borrowers. Before you decide what type of loan is right for you, take time to explore each program's features. This is something your Veterans United loan specialist can help with, too. The goal is finding the right loan given your particular financial needs and homebuying goals.

VA Loans

The VA loan program has helped millions of service members, veterans and military families secure home financing since its creation in 1944. This flexible, no-down payment mortgage program was part of the original GI bill signed by President Franklin D. Roosevelt. The VA guarantied its 20 millionth mortgage in 2013.

The VA doesn't make home loans. Rather, it provides a financial guaranty, basically a form of insurance, to private VA-approved lenders. That insurance gives lenders confidence to extend financing along with some significant financial benefits, many of which can't be matched by any other lending option.

Here's a look at a few of those unbeatable benefits:

Benefit 1: No down payment

The ability to get into a home without having to make a down payment is the program's single biggest benefit. This saves veterans from having to stockpile money for years in order to come up with the necessary cash to close on their home loan. The average VA purchase loan is about $220,000. A 20 percent down payment would be more than $40,000 in cash. The average VA borrower has just under $7,000 in assets.

Benefit 2: No private mortgage insurance (PMI)

Private mortgage insurance (PMI) is a form of insurance that lenders typically require if you can't make a down payment of at least 20 percent. There is no PMI on a VA loan. PMI fees can vary based on your credit score, down payment and other factors, but they're typically 0.5 percent to 2 percent of the loan balance. That fee is added to your monthly mortgage payment by your lender.

Let's assume you have a $200,000 loan with a 0.5 percent PMI fee. In the first year, you'll pay an additional $83.33 in PMI fees each month. Perhaps $83 may not seem like much, but that adds up to roughly $1,000 over the course of a year. Imagine what you could do with that extra $1,000 as a new homeowner.

VA borrowers do pay a funding fee that varies based on service history and how many times they've used the program. We'll talk more about this in Chapter 5.

Benefit 3: Low interest rates

Interest rates on VA loans often fall 0.5 percent to 1 percent below conventional loan rates. This lower rate, combined with monthly PMI savings, can substantially lower your monthly payment.

Benefit 4: No prepayment penalties

These are disappearing because of new mortgage regulations, but some conventional loans can still carry a prepayment penalty, which is a fee for paying off your mortgage early. VA loans will never charge a prepayment penalty. In fact, it's actually illegal for a lender to charge you a prepayment penalty on a VA loan.

Benefit 5: Less stringent qualification guidelines

Conventional loans are typically a better fit for homebuyers with sterling credit and significant assets. VA loans, on the other hand, feature less stringent guidelines and are a great option for those with less-than-perfect credit. About 8 in 10 VA borrowers couldn't qualify for conventional financing.

Benefit 6: Low closing costs

The VA limits what lenders can charge in closing costs. There are also costs that VA borrowers are not allowed to pay themselves. The VA allows the seller to pay all loan-related closing costs and up to 4 percent of the home's appraised value in concessions, which can cover things like prepaid property taxes and homeowners insurance. Determining who will pay what in closing costs is part of the negotiation process with a home seller.

Federal Housing Administration (FHA) Loans

FHA loans share some similarities with VA loans. These loans are insured, but not issued, by the Federal Housing Administration. While an FHA loan offers some cost-saving benefits, it generally can't match the advantages of a VA loan. These can be a great fit for borrowers without great credit and assets who don't qualify for VA financing.

Here's a closer look at FHA loans:

Down payment
The minimum down payment for an FHA loan is typically 3.5 percent of the loan amount. This is lower than the 5 percent minimum for some conventional loans, but it still can't beat the VA's no-money down option.

Mortgage Insurance Premium (MIP) costs
FHA loans come with their own form of mortgage insurance, known as mortgage insurance premiums (MIP). Borrowers who can't put down at least 20 percent pay both an up-front funding fee and an annual mortgage insurance premium. These costs are typically financed into the loan and paid over the entire term of the mortgage.

United States Department of Agriculture (USDA) Loans
USDA loans are also known as Rural Development loans. These loans are tailored for those purchasing property in rural areas. The government-backed USDA program offers many of the same benefits of a VA loan, including 100 percent financing and less stringent credit qualifications. But they come with mortgage insurance premiums similar to the FHA program.

Your eligibility for a USDA loan is mainly based on location. You'll need to purchase a home in what the USDA deems a "qualified rural area." A surprising portion of the country meets this designation, but you'll want to consult your nearest Rural Development office for more details. USDA loans also have an income cap that excludes borrowers who make above a certain amount each year.

Conventional Loans

A conventional loan comes without government backing. Credit requirements and financial standards for conventional loans are often more restrictive. But borrowers with excellent credit and solid assets may find the best rates and terms on conventional loans.

Here's a closer look at conventional financing:

Down payment
Most conventional lenders require a minimum down payment of 5 percent. But to qualify for the best terms, borrowers may need to put down 20 percent of the loan amount. That's a big chunk of cash and a tall order for many potential borrowers.

Interest rates
Conventional loans often feature competitive interest rates, but you'll typically need great credit to get the lowest offerings.

PMI
Putting down less than 20 percent means you're likely paying private mortgage insurance. The PMI fee is added to your monthly payment and is typically required until you build up 20 percent equity in your home.

Qualification standards
Conventional loans usually feature stricter credit standards than government-backed loans. Each lender is different, but many require a credit score in the mid-to-upper 700s. That requirement alone snubs a huge portion of potential borrowers.

Loan Comparison Chart

Sometimes it helps to look at the four major loan options using hard, real-world numbers. For this example, let's say you're looking at a $200,000 mortgage with an interest rate of 4.75 percent. We'll estimate your property taxes and homeowners insurance costs at $260 per month.

Loan type	Minimum Down Payment	Funding Fee	Principal & Interest	Taxes & Insurance	Mortgage Insurance	Monthly Payment
FHA	$7,000	$3,500	$1,025	$260	$217	$1,502
USDA	$0	$4,000	$1,064	$260	$68	$1,392
Conventional	$10,000	$0	$991	$260	$114	$1,365
VA	$0	$6,600	$1,078	$260	$0	$1,338

At a glance, VA homebuyers have the lowest monthly mortgage payment given these parameters. But there are advantages and disadvantages to every loan option.

VA loans: Being able to purchase without a down payment is a tremendous advantage. The flip side is you won't have equity in the property to start. This example features the highest possible funding fee (3.3 percent). A first-time VA homebuyer would save even more each month, because they would pay a lower funding fee (2.15 percent). As with the other government-backed options, the fee in this example is financed into the loan.

Conventional loans: This loan requires the highest down payment, but you begin with the most equity. Borrowers who can't put down 20 percent (which in this example would be $40,000) will pay private mortgage insurance. For this example, we used a real-world PMI rate of 0.72 percent.

USDA loans: This is the only other no-down payment mortgage program. Mortgage insurance on USDA loans is less expensive than other types, but borrowers pay it for the life of the loan. These are also the most restrictive loans of the group. Home-buyers are required to purchase in a "qualified rural area" and have an income at or below 115 percent of the area median income.

FHA loans: These loans have more lax credit requirements and a lower minimum down payment than conventional loans, but they also feature the most expensive mortgage insurance, which borrowers now pay for the life of the loan.

Determining which loan product is the best fit for you is a conversation that should include a loan officer you trust. They can help you run the numbers and give you a clear sense of what makes the best financial sense. A VA loan isn't automatically the best fit for every veteran. Qualified borrowers who have excellent credit and the ability to put down at least 20 percent might find conventional financing a better option.

But that kind of sterling financial profile isn't the norm for many veterans, service members and military families.

That's what makes VA loans so powerful.

Borrower spotlight:
Todd and Karen Fontenot
Family of 11 Finds Their Dream Home With a VA Loan

Smyrna, Ga. — After nine years of proud service, Staff Sgt. Todd Fontenot was ready to leave the Air Force and return to civilian life.

The biggest draw: greater stability and certainty for his growing family, which can sometimes be hard to come by for service members.

Todd began his military career as a single 18-year-old at Tyndall Air Force Base in Florida. He left his final assignment — a two-year stretch in Turkey as part of Operation Provide Comfort — a married father of four.

Todd and his wife, Karen, returned to their hometown of Smyrna, Georgia, in 1994, and moved into a surprising rental: The parsonage belonging to Karen's long-time church.

Todd floated between jobs but landed steady side work doing lawn care for a local firm. He soon found himself in high demand and decided to open his own lawn-care business in 2003. A sole proprietor, Todd eventually picked up a second, part-time job at UPS to secure health benefits.

All the while, business wasn't the only thing growing. By the summer of 2005, Todd and Karen were anxiously awaiting the birth of their ninth child.

After 11 years, the family had all but outgrown the 2,000-square-foot parsonage. At the same time, a new incoming pastor wanted to live on the church grounds. That confluence of events prompted Todd and Karen to start looking for a home.

They worked with a local conventional mortgage broker and put offers on a couple homes, but problems with the properties — water leakage, termite damage — ultimately turned them off.

The real estate market was still booming, and the Fontenots struggled to find a home that could fit their space needs and price range. Their real estate agent dropped them as clients. They eventually found a sprawling rental through a friend from church.

Five years passed, and the family grew into the home.

In the spring of 2010, the owners of the rental contacted the Fontenots with some surprising news: They planned to hike the rent to $1,200 per month from $750 per month.

Stunned, Todd and Karen started to rethink a home purchase. The housing market had changed drastically in the last five years, certainly for the better for prospective homebuyers.

Karen went online to search for homes and found an advertisement for VA loans and Veterans United Home Loans. She thought about Todd's military service and decided to fill out a simple form on the Veterans United website.

Loan officer Brandon Severino called her within minutes.

"She couldn't believe how fast he responded," Todd said.

Brandon explained the benefits of VA loans and the loan approval process.

The VA Loan Guaranty program allows qualified service members to purchase a home worth up to $417,000 (and more in high-cost parts of the country) without a down payment. VA loans typically feature lower rates and more buyer-friendly terms than conventional financing.

Brandon also connected the family to a local Realtor through Veterans United's unique partnership with Veterans United Realty, a network of more than 5,000 real estate agents nationwide who specialize in helping veterans and military members purchase homes. Borrowers who use a VUR Realtor can receive up to $5,000 upon closing.

Still, both Karen and Todd were filled with anxiety as first-time buyers. They would sometimes call Brandon two or three times a day with questions or concerns.

"Just talking with Brandon made the whole process easier," Todd said. "I was wound up tighter than a jackrabbit on caffeine, and he was always cool and calm."

Brandon preapproved the couple for a $140,000 loan but told them he would need tax returns and other information to fully verify Todd's self-employment and part-time income.

While Veterans United Home Loan specialists worked to gather Todd's financial documentation, the couple found the house they had been waiting for, a massive two-story on four acres.

There was just one problem. The home was priced at $160,000, which was well above their prequalification amount. Todd and Karen put in an offer at their maximum. The seller countered at $150,000.

All that separated the Fontenots from their dream home was $10,000. Karen called Brandon in tears, afraid they would lose their only shot.

Brandon told the couple to rush them Todd's tax information so he could get it reviewed by the company's underwriters. An underwriter took a look at the file and alerted Brandon that based on Todd's verifiable income the pre-approval amount could be increased to $150,000.

The Fontenots were suddenly able to meet the seller's counteroffer.

Todd and Karen closed in early October 2010. Their monthly mortgage payment is less than the $1,200 they would have been paying in rent.

Best of all, they didn't wind up spending a dime out of pocket to buy their first home. They utilized the VA's no-down payment benefit and were able to recoup expenses because they used a Veterans United Realty agent.

"During these economic times, you guys were why we were able to buy a house," Todd said. "It's nice to know I won't get a phone call and someone's going to tell me I have to pay more in rent. It's nice to know that we're in control."

CHAPTER 2:
ELIGIBILITY AND REQUIREMENTS

The heart of the VA loan is a promise.

As a way to honor and thank those who served, the government pledges to stand behind VA borrowers. That promise comes in the form of a financial guaranty, an obligation to repay a portion of a borrower's mortgage in the event of default.

We'll talk later in this chapter about how the VA Loan Guaranty works and what it means for service members and their families. Before we get there, it's important for prospective borrowers to make sure they're a good match for a VA loan. Despite the program's flexibility, there are some things a VA loan cannot be used for at the present time.

VA Loan Uses

The vast majority of military buyers use their VA loan to purchase or refinance an existing single-family home. But veterans interested in purchasing a condo or building a home from the ground up can also utilize a VA loan.

Here's a look at the VA loan's primary eligible purposes:

- To purchase a residence that's owned and occupied by the veteran
- To refinance an existing VA-guaranteed or direct loan in order to lower the current interest rate

- To refinance in order to take out cash
- To make energy-efficiency improvements in conjunction with a VA purchase or refinance loan
- To purchase up to four one-family residential units in a condo development approved by the VA. One of those four units must be used as the borrower's primary residence

Now, let's take a look at a couple of these eligible uses more closely.

First, the phrase "owned and occupied" is a key one to remember. Military buyers utilizing their VA benefit have to live in their purchase as a primary residence. There are some timeframe issues and exceptions that we'll talk about later. But, as a general rule, you can't use a VA loan unless you're planning to live in the home full time.

That bleeds into one of the major ineligible uses for VA loans: investment properties. Veterans looking to flip houses or to get into the rental game have to secure financing through a different channel.

The same holds true for veterans and service members looking to purchase land, even if they plan to build a home on the parcel at some point in the future. Borrowers can't use a VA loan to buy acreage unless there's already a home in the immediate mix.

Veterans who hope to purchase a condo unit with their VA loan have to receive agency approval before moving forward. VA officials will review the condo's organizational documents to make sure they comply with department regulations.

Condo units approved by the Department of Housing and Urban Development (HUD) prior to Dec. 7, 2009, will typically get automatic approval from the VA. Otherwise, prospective borrowers should expect a full VA review.

Veterans can search an online database of HUD-approved condominium developments on the agency's website at https://entp.hud.gov/idapp/html/condlook.cfm.

Ineligible Uses

We've already touched on the most prominent "no-no" on the list, and that's investment properties. The VA is all about homeownership, which makes rental properties and real estate speculation such a tough sell.

Here's a look at other ineligible loan purposes as defined by the VA:

- Purchase of unimproved land with the intent to improve it at some point in the future
- Purchase or construction of a combined residential and business property, unless:
    - The property is mainly for residential purposes,
    - There's no more than one business unit, and
    - The business area accounts for less than 25 percent of the total floor space
- Purchase of more than one separate residential unit or lot unless the veteran will occupy one unit and there is evidence that:
    - The units are unavailable separately
    - They have a common owner
    - They have been treated as one unit in the past
    - They are assessed as one unit, or
    - Partition is simply not practical

Those last two provisions about assessment and partition can sound a bit confusing. In essence, you need to be careful if you're looking to run a home business or live where you work. There are also some unique properties and situations that result in veterans having to buy more than one home, but these are far from the norm.

Borrowers can also run into problems if a home is dissimilar to any closely located properties. For example, if you're buying a log home in New Jersey, it might be tough to find recent comparable home sales (or "**comps**," as they're called) for the appraisal. The same goes for earth contact homes, dome homes and even octagonal homes.

All-But-Impossible Uses

We could also call this the "Manufactured Homes and Construction Loans" section.

There are a couple of additional acceptable VA loan uses that aren't mentioned above. The reason is because they're becoming increasingly difficult, if not downright impossible, to bring to fruition in the current lending climate.

Manufactured homes are one of those eligible purposes that work on paper but rarely translate to the real world. The VA allows qualified borrowers to get a government-backed loan as long as the manufactured home has a permanent foundation. But lenders as a whole have all but stopped funding mobile home purchases. Military buyers need to know going in that they're probably not going to find a VA lender willing to finance this kind of purchase.

Service members seeking this type of housing solution typically obtain financing through a manufactured home distributor.

Construction loans are a bit more complicated. As with most manufactured homes, VA lenders have all but stopped financing loans to build new homes. There's simply too much risk and lenders aren't willing to outlay the capital it takes to finance new construction. In the same breath, this doesn't mean that service members interested in building their dream home can't somehow utilize their VA benefits.

There is a way to reconcile the two by using what's called a **Construction-to-Permanent Refinance Loan**. That's a mouthful, and we'll explain it fully when we start examining refinance loans in Chapter 6. For now, just note that getting a VA lender to finance your home construction is probably a no-go, which means you'll have to go through a builder. As we'll explain later, there is a way to tie it all back to your VA benefits.

VA Loan Eligibility

Prospective borrowers don't need to have a home picked out before starting the loan approval process. In fact, we typically advise borrowers to wait until they have a better handle on what type of loan they might be able to secure. There's little sense in getting your heart set on a $300,000 home when your real price ceiling is $250,000.

But it's a good idea to at least make sure your plans likely fit into the agency's acceptable uses. The next step is then determining your eligibility for participation in the program. Not every veteran or service member will ultimately qualify for a VA loan.

But a great deal do meet the requirements. Millions, in fact.

Service members should look at these eligibility guidelines closely, but remember that it's ultimately up to the VA to determine an applicant's status. To be eligible means to have an **entitlement** to VA home loan benefits.

It's not a word to be taken lightly. In light of their service, qualified veterans find themselves entitled to a VA guaranty. The agency also uses the word "entitlement" to mean the amount of money the VA will guaranty on a given loan. We'll explain that in greater detail shortly.

Borrowers still have to meet the program's other credit and income requirements, but this first step of determining eligibility is the starting block. A veteran who isn't deemed eligible by the VA cannot receive a VA-backed loan under any circumstances.

Eligibility: Armed Forces Veterans

The VA has separate requirements for those who served during wartime and during peacetime. The agency defines the two as:

Wartime	Peacetime
World War II 9/16/1940-7/25/1947	Post-World War II period 7/26/1947-6/26/1950
Korean conflict 6/27/1950-1/31/1955	Post-Korean period 2/1/1955-8/4/1964
Vietnam Era 8/5/1964-5/7/1975(The Vietnam Era begins 2/28/1961 for those individuals who served in the Republic of Vietnam.)	Post-Vietnam period 5/8/1975-8/1/1990
Persian Gulf War 8/2/1990-date to be determined	

Veterans are eligible if they served on active duty in the Army, Navy, Air Force, Marine Corps or Coast Guard after Sept. 15, 1940, and were discharged under conditions other than dishonorable after either:

- 90 days or more during wartime, or
- 181 consecutive days or more during peacetime

Veterans whose service began after Sept. 7, 1980, or who entered service as an officer after Oct. 16, 1981, must have completed:

- 24 consecutive months of active duty, or
- The full period they were called or ordered to active duty, as long as it's not less than 90 days during wartime or 181 days during peacetime

Eligibility: Reserves or National Guard

Those who served at least six years in the Reserves or National Guard are eligible, provided they're not already able to take advantage of loan guaranty benefits elsewhere. Prospective borrowers must have received an honorable discharge, unless they're still active or they're inactive and awaiting final discharge.

Eligibility: Surviving Spouses

An unmarried spouse whose veteran died on active duty or because of a disability connected to his or her service is eligible for VA home loan benefits. Surviving spouses who got a VA loan with the veteran before his or her death can also obtain a **VA Interest Rate Reduction Refinance Loan** (see Chapter 6 for more on refinancing).

There are also provisions for surviving spouses who remarried. Those who remarried upon or after turning age 57 and on or after Dec. 16, 2003, may be eligible for a VA home loan. Surviving spouses who remarried before that date are no longer eligible to participate.

The spouse of an active duty member who is listed as missing in action (MIA) or a prisoner of war (POW) for at least 90 days is eligible for one-time use of the VA home loan benefit.

Legislation passed in late 2012 broadened the eligibility requirements for surviving spouses. VA loan eligibility now extends to surviving spouses of veterans whose deaths were not service-connected, but who had permanent service-connected disabilities for at least a decade before their death.

Eligibility: Others

There's a whole class of people who have received veteran status over the years, making them eligible for the VA Loan Guaranty. This broad category often includes:

- Public Health Service officials
- Military service academy cadets
- Some merchant seamen
- National Oceanic and Atmospheric Administration officials
- Scores of others

For folks who might be on the fringes, it's best to inquire with a trusted VA lender or your VA Regional Loan Center.

Exceptions

The VA will usually look further into applications from prospective borrowers whose discharges were under conditions other than honorable. It's also important to note that there are a host of exceptions to the length of service requirements for both Armed Forces members and Guardsmen and Reservists. For example, a service-connected disability can shorten the required service time to just a single day.

Because of the sheer number of exceptions, it's always in the veteran's best interest to talk with a VA loan specialist.

The Certificate of Eligibility (COE)

If you believe you meet the eligibility requirements, the next step is to obtain a **Certificate of Eligibility**, or COE, from Veterans Affairs. This is where the VA will separate belief from reality.

The Certificate of Eligibility is an official document that basically attests to your right to participate in the VA Loan Guaranty program. Veterans and other prospective borrowers have to fill out a Request for a Certificate of Eligibility, which in military parlance is known as Form 26-1880 (see Appendix A).

It's a straightforward, single-page document. The only wrinkle is that applicants must have proof of their military service. For those who served in the Armed Forces, that's a DD Form 214, also known as a Certificate of Release or Discharge From Active Duty. You can submit a copy as long as it's clearly legible.

Those still serving on active duty have to submit a current statement of service that denotes:

- Veteran's full name
- Social Security number
- Date of birth
- Active duty entry date
- Duration of lost time, if any, and
- Name of the command providing the information

Reservists and National Guard members don't have a single discharge certificate like the DD-214. Instead, they should submit their latest annual retirement points summary along with evidence of their honorable service.

Army or Air National Guard members can submit NGB Form 22, a Report of Separation and Record of Service, or a points statement.

Like their Armed Forces counterparts, active members of the Reserves or National Guard must provide a signed statement of service that shows their key personal information. The statement also needs to clearly state that the applicant is an active Reservist or Guard member.

There's no need to panic if you're unable to find your proof of service. Documents get lost to time.

Veterans discharged from regular active duty should go ahead and submit their Request for a Certificate of Eligibility without the proof of service. It's important to keep the process moving, plus the VA can often issue a decision regarding your request based on its own internal records about your service.

But the VA doesn't have internal records on Reservists or National Guard members. In those cases, applicants need to submit a Request Pertaining to Military Records (Form SF-180) in order to obtain the necessary documents.

Automated Certificate of Eligibility (ACE)

Veterans and service members can get all these forms online; via fax, email and regular mail; and even in person if you're close to a VA center.

You can also let someone else do the work.

Veterans who have found a trusted VA lender can ask their loan officer to request their Certificate of Eligibility electronically. The veteran simply provides the lender with his or her proof of service. The lender then uses the VA's online COE portal, better known as the **Automated Certificate of Eligibility**, or ACE.

The creation of the ACE system in 2002 was more than a form processing upgrade. In many ways, it's a symbol of how far the VA has come in the last three decades. For years, real estate agents, mortgage brokers and borrowers steered clear of the agency because of its reputation as a bloated, bureaucratic mess.

Paperwork was done by hand and through the mail. The appraisal process (which we'll cover in Chapter 4) gave people nightmares. Loans could take months to close, leaving both buyers and sellers in the lurch.

Some of those vestiges still linger, but the VA loan process of today is a much more user-friendly and efficient experience compared to years past. The ACE system is an important cog in that more streamlined machine.

The ACE portal allows lenders to get an eligibility determination on a veteran in seconds.

Until recently, the VA restricted access to the ACE system to certain recognized lenders. Recent changes have opened the portal to all veterans, who can log in and obtain a Certificate of Eligibility themselves. The VA has an informative, 13-page downloadable guide with step-by-step directions for using the system at www.benefits.va.gov/homeloans/docs/veteran_registration_coe.pdf.

Veterans should know there are a handful of cases where ACE cannot make a determination about eligibility. Some of those cases include:

- Reservists and National Guard members
- Veterans who had a previous VA loan go into foreclosure
- Those who didn't serve the minimum required length of service and were not discharged for an authorized exception

- Veterans discharged under conditions other than honorable
- Veterans wanting to restore a previously used entitlement
- Unmarried surviving spouses

It's also important to note that veterans can't transfer an ACE-generated Certificate of Eligibility from one lender to another. That means you'll have to get a new COE if you decide to hop to a different lender at some point during the homebuying process.

Otherwise, there's rarely a need for eligible veterans to update their COE before closing on their VA loan. The only time that's an issue is if a service member is discharged or released once the process has started but prior to the loan closing. At that point, the lender is going to request a new determination of the veteran's eligibility.

The Certificate of Eligibility doesn't expire, but a borrower's circumstances can change. If closing delays or other problems push beyond three or four months, then the veteran will need to obtain a fresh Certificate of Eligibility to satisfy the lender. This is a relatively rare occurrence but does happen.

The VA tells mortgage lenders flat out: The COE is the only reliable way to prove a veteran is eligible for a loan. But this doesn't have to be your first step. We can and often do issue **loan preapproval** without a Certificate of Eligibility. But obtaining eligibility determination is important early in the process. Any delays or questions about the veteran's status down the road could delay closing or even upend the entire process.

VA Loan Limits

Getting preapproved for a VA loan involves filling out a loan application (your loan officer will do most of the heavy lifting on that) and providing some financial information to your lender. First, though, it's important to consider one of those early nagging questions: How much house can I buy?

It's not always an easy question to answer, especially when it comes to VA loans. If we go by the book, the response is that there technically isn't a ceiling for a VA-backed home loan. The reality is a different story.

Remember that each veteran has an entitlement, an amount that the VA pledges to guaranty to the lender in case the borrower defaults. Today, the basic entitlement amount is $36,000.

Since the VA covers up to a quarter of a borrower's mortgage, some simple math dictates that the maximum loan amount for most veterans would be $144,000 ($36,000 x 4).

While that figure is nothing to sneeze at, VA guaranties have historically handicapped military buyers in some of the country's costlier areas. To stay competitive with other loan products, the agency began to link its guaranty amounts to the **conforming loan limits** for conventional loans.

At present, the conforming loan limit in most parts of the country is $417,000. Since the VA guaranties a quarter of a borrower's mortgage, the agency basically had to create a new, secondary entitlement to cover the gap. That secondary entitlement of $68,250 automatically kicks in for any loan greater than $144,000.

That's a lot of numbers, and it can start to get confusing. This might be an easier way to think about it:

A. $417,000 is the conforming loan limit
B. One quarter of $417,000 = $104,250
C. The VA primary entitlement is $36,000

The difference between B and C is $68,250, or the secondary entitlement.

All of that said, and perhaps contrary to what you've read or heard, the VA doesn't have a maximum loan amount for qualified borrowers. Rather, the agency has loan limits in place that govern how much a veteran can borrow without making a down payment. In most of the country, the VA loan limit is $417,000. But veterans in high-cost parts of the country can have loan limits above $729,000.

In those cases, the VA guaranty is the lesser of two things:

- 25 percent of the VA county loan limit, or
- 25 percent of the loan amount

You can view the VA's current county loan limits at the VA's online home loan hub, homeloans.va.gov. These limits are subject to change each year.

While it's important to know the loan and guaranty limits, the reality is lenders are going to approve each applicant for a specific loan amount based on their unique financial situation, the potential property and other key factors. Veterans don't get to simply name their price.

Eligibility Isn't a Guarantee

It's also important to remember that being eligible for a VA loan and actually getting one are two very different concepts.

To be eligible means the VA has determined you meet the initial requirements and have earned some degree of home loan entitlement. But your Certificate of Eligibility isn't a coupon you can just redeem for a VA loan or refinance of your choice.

It just doesn't work that way. And, for that matter, it couldn't work that way. The reason is that veterans aren't getting a loan directly from the VA. Instead, the agency basically insures a portion of a loan that's being issued by an approved lending institution.

And mortgage lenders aren't in the business of doling out housing loans to folks who meet some basic requirements, even if those requirements are rooted in service to our country. Lenders simply have too much to lose.

That's why the process can't just stop once a veteran obtains the COE. If anything, that's the point of acceleration. It's also, to borrow a tired cliché, where the rubber begins to meet the road. The reality is that not every veteran and service member who qualifies for a VA loan will ultimately receive one.

A housing loan, even one backed with a VA guaranty, represents a major vote of confidence on behalf of a lender. And what they've become confident in is your ability to repay the hundreds of thousands of dollars they're loaning you, with interest, of course.

Veterans and service members with a shaky financial profile can find themselves on the outside looking in.

The VA does not have strict, chiseled-into-stone criteria when it comes to obtaining a loan. There are some broad requirements — we've already discussed a couple — that are generally much more forgiving than consumers typically find with conventional loans.

But satisfying the VA is only part of the battle. You also have to convince the lender that you're worth the investment. And what that really means is convincing the **underwriters**.

Underwriters are basically folks who evaluate a mortgage company's loan files to determine whether the loan applicant meets necessary guidelines and criteria and represents a safe investment. Some mortgage companies have their own in-house underwriters, while others outsource the work to larger or more specialized firms.

Veterans and service members will become increasingly familiar with underwriters as the process rolls on. They will be the source of requests for additional paperwork and old documents down the line.

We'll talk more about underwriters and the other major players in the loan process later in this chapter.

Now, though, let's step back and look at the two major pillars of VA loan qualification: credit and income. These are the key areas that both the agency and its approved lenders are going to focus on when evaluating an applicant.

Understanding Credit

Far and away, credit is the most misunderstood and needlessly mysterious aspect of the homebuying process, not just for military buyers but for consumers at large, too. It's amazing how many applicants don't know their credit score, let alone understand how credit works and why it's important.

Your credit profile is what governs your ability to get a car loan, auto insurance, credit cards and, of course, a mortgage. Poor or tattered credit can put these items out of reach. But consumers with more sterling credit profiles tend to get better interest rates when they need to borrow money.

To get credit means that someone is willing to lend you money with the expectation that you will repay the debt in a timely fashion. A simple example might be when a department store or a gas station issues you a credit card. In fact, those are great places for consumers to start establishing credit.

You build up your credit profile by repaying your charges each month, keeping balances in proportion and a few other ways we'll cover shortly. The entities that extend you credit also report your monthly transactions to one or more of the nation's three credit bureaus: Equifax, Experian and TransUnion.

The key is to lather, rinse and repeat, so to speak.

Credit tends to snowball after you've proven adept at repaying your debt on time. One credit card becomes three. Those help convince your local bank or auto dealership to finance a car loan. After months and years of dutiful repayment and keeping your balances in check, you've built a solid credit profile that gives lenders confidence.

Your credit profile and credit score is as good a tool as there is to indicate your willingness and ability to repay debt. And that's why it's vital to understand how it works and what it means in the context of your VA home loan application.

The VA doesn't have hard and fast rules when it comes to credit scores. In order to secure a VA guaranty, lenders have to determine that the veteran is a "satisfactory credit risk" who has shown a willingness to repay future obligations. That's the VA requirement.

Lenders tend to want something a little more concrete.

That's why they're going to seize on a three-digit number that follows you everywhere — your credit score. While the VA might not have a number in mind, you better believe that lenders do. They're not going to extend a loan to any applicant whose score falls below their standard, no matter how otherwise deserving.

Accessing Your Credit Report and Credit Score

Once a year, you're entitled to a free copy of your credit report from each of the three reporting agencies. To start, visit www.

annualcreditreport.com. Unlike some of the other, heavily advertised credit sites, this doesn't require you to purchase a report or any type of credit monitoring service. Forget all the ads and jingles. This one is actually free.

Be sure to download and print copies from all three credit bureaus. You should also make a note of the username and password you create for the site. Remember, you get only one free peek per year, so that log-in will be important if you want to go back and check something in the narrow window they allow you to access your reports.

Now, you'll eventually come to find there's one key ingredient missing from your free annual credit report: your credit score. The report details your accounts, balances, late payments and a host of other things. But you'll have to spend money to actually get your credit score for each bureau. The same goes for learning your **FICO score**.

Know the Score

So what do borrowers mean when they refer to their "credit score?"

It's not always a simple question to answer. There are actually five different types.

Fair Isaac Corporation, or FICO, created the first credit score in the 1950s. Today, the FICO score is perhaps the best known and most widely used credit metric. Over time, the three credit bureaus (Equifax, Experian and TransUnion) adopted and adapted FICO's general scoring formula to suit their own needs.

Each of the three now generate their own credit score, based in part if not entirely on FICO's risk assessment formula. The bureaus also banded together to compute a fifth, known as the VantageScore.

For consumers, that's a lot of credit scores to worry about. Scoring ranges for the different methodologies vary. Here's the essential takeaway: Lenders look at all of them but typically focus on the middle of the three credit bureau scores.

Prospective borrowers should consider shelling out money to see their Equifax, Experian and TransUnion scores. Some opt to purchase only their FICO score, which can serve as a pretty good indicator of that middle ground lenders are looking for.

In general, credit scores are calculated using a complex web of factors, some 20 in all, broken down into five broad categories that are surprisingly simple and easy to understand. Let's take a look at the categories and explain how each contributes to your overall score:

- **Payment History (35 percent of your score)**
  Paying your bills on time is the most important element of your credit score, hands down. The credit agencies have three classes of late payments: 30 days, 60 days and 90 days. On average, a 30-day late payment will knock 40 to 110 points off your score; a 90-day late payment will shave 70 to 135 points. Whatever it takes, make sure you hit your payment deadline each month, even if it's the minimum.

- **Credit Card Balances (30 percent of your score)**
  This is another reason why maxing out your cards is never a good idea. The scoring system looks at how much you owe and the total amount of credit available to you. Generally, it's best to keep balances at no more than 30 percent of the credit limit. So, if you have Visa with a $1,000 limit, make sure the balance doesn't exceed $300. The same holds true at a macro level. If

you have six credit cards with a cumulative credit limit of $10,000, strive to keep the total balance below $3,000. Even if you make payments on time, your score will still dip because of oversized balances.

- **Credit History (15 percent of your score)**
  This can be a painful lesson for some first-time buyers. Sometimes borrowers have a slightly lower score just because they aren't old enough to have built an established credit history. This is also why it's important to keep old credit cards open whenever you've paid the balance.

- **New Credit (10 percent of your score)**
  This involves opening new accounts and having credit card companies and other entities check your credit, which can damage your score depending upon the frequency. Checking your own credit will not harm your score, and in some cases opening new lines of credit can prove beneficial. But credit checks by credit card companies and others often take a negative toll on your overall credit profile. Applying for five new credit cards isn't going to boost your score. In fact, it will probably do the opposite.

- **Types of Credit Used (10 percent of your score)**
  The scoring system rewards consumers with multiple forms of credit, from several credit cards to mortgages, car loans and other consumer finance accounts. That diversity represents strength and stability in terms of handling debt and making good on repayment.

There's no uniform impact for one or more of those categories. Some factors wind up being more important for a given borrower than others, depending on his or her credit history. The scores reflect only what's in your credit report. There's nothing in there about income, work history, geography, demographics or any other personal identifier other than your name.

Believe it or not, most Americans have pretty decent credit. FICO slices its score range into eight categories:

Credit score	Percentage of consumers
499 and below	I percent
500-549	5 percent
550-599	7 percent
600-649	I I percent
650-699	I6 percent
700-749	20 percent
749-799	29 percent
800 and above	I I percent

Remember that there are scoring models and ranges unique to each of the three credit reporting agencies. It's a good idea to see where you stand with each of them, as well as to determine your FICO score, at the start of this journey. Your loan officer certainly will.

It's also important to remember that if you're planning to have someone else sign on your mortgage, the lender is going to consider his or her credit profile, too. You can access your FICO score by visiting myfico.com. Remember that you'll pay for the privilege.

Generally, the only acceptable co-borrower on a VA loan is either your spouse or another veteran. Some lenders do make joint loans to VA-eligible borrowers who want a non-spouse or non-veteran on the mortgage. In those cases, the borrower without VA loan eligibility would typically need to make a 12.5 percent down payment.

Credit Scores, Interest Rates and Loan Qualification

The FICO algorithm pools information from those five categories and churns out a score. And that's what your loan officer is going to gravitate toward in the early going.

At the outset, your credit score might all but disqualify you from obtaining a VA loan for the time being. Again, there's no by-the-numbers standard for veterans to participate in the VA Loan Guaranty program. The agency is looking for folks who represent a "satisfactory credit risk" and typically pay their bills on time.

But most lenders in today's marketplace aren't going to touch a borrower with a credit score below 620. Veterans who fall beneath that line have entered the **"subprime"** category, the riskiest and costliest lending bracket there is. Traditionally, subprime home loans have come with significantly higher interest rates and fees. They've also been marked by significantly higher default rates.

The subprime mortgage meltdown of 2007-08 and ensuing collapse of the housing market have made subprime lending an even less appealing endeavor for legitimate financial institutions. Veterans with sub-620 credit may still be able to obtain financing, but it's an increasingly risky proposition that fewer banks are willing to embrace.

One of the good things about credit scores is that they're fluid. Committed veterans can boost their credit score and chances of getting approved for a loan by taking a few serious steps. We'll cover those shortly. Even **prime** borrowers, or those with credit at or above 620, can save themselves money and headaches by working to improve their credit profile. And that's because your credit score will also play a major role in your loan's interest rate.

As you probably guessed, a higher credit score can result in a much lower rate. But VA borrowers with so-so credit can secure better rates than on conventional loans. That might not mean much until you start to look at some numbers. These figures are for a 30-year fixed-rate mortgage on a home purchased for $300,000. It's also important to remember that rates have been historically low the last few years:

Credit Score	APR	Monthly Payment
760-850	4.75%	$1,564
700-759	4.97%	$1,604
680-699	5.14%	$1,637
660-679	5.36%	$1,677
640-659	5.79%	$1,758
620-639	6.33%	$1,864

Compared to their brethren in the bottom category, borrowers in that top tier would save $300 a month in mortgage payments. That's a healthy chunk of change for any homebuyer. It's even more impressive when you consider the savings over the course of a 30-year mortgage would tally an additional $108,000 for the borrower with excellent credit.

That last bit of math only holds true if you're stuck in the same credit range for the next three decades. You certainly don't have to be. One of the cornerstones of credit scores is that they're dynamic. Your score can change in a matter of months.

Borrowers have a great degree of control over whether those changes are positive or negative. There are some tried-and-true methods veterans can employ to boost their credit score, either to land a better interest rate or, more importantly, to qualify for a loan. We'll list and develop those in a moment.

The fact is that lenders handle prospective subprime borrowers in different ways. Some try to sell those customer leads to other lenders. Others just forget the veteran's application entirely.

We wanted to do something a little more proactive, because credit problems can prove especially disastrous for military borrowers. It's almost a job hazard, at least in some respects. Service members are hopping across the country and sometimes the globe, either on short-term assignments, permanent changes of station or overseas deployments. Bills and payments can easily get lost in the shuffle.

Spouses wholly unfamiliar with household finances sometimes find themselves faced with juggling a host of new responsibilities and financial obligations. Military marriages can even dissolve under the strain, which adds a whole new layer of financial difficulty.

In general, the military does a great job of preparing service members and their families for the financial hurdles associated with deployment. There are classes, community support meetings and scores of pamphlets and information products to help ease the transition.

But folks do fall through the cracks.

It's tough to tell someone who has proudly served our country that their credit profile will keep them from purchasing a home.

To try and minimize those difficult conversations, we created an entirely new division within our company — the

Veterans United Lighthouse Program. Credit consultants educate veterans and service members about credit and what it takes to improve their scores. Prospective borrowers can track and monitor their progress through a free, online check-up system. A Lighthouse Program consultant alerts the veteran when it's time to pull credit scores again in anticipation of loan prequalification.

Hundreds of veterans have used the program to rebuild their credit and ultimately obtain a VA home loan. What they preach and teach in the Lighthouse Program isn't an industry secret. In fact, we'll soon go over the most important steps toward boosting your credit score.

First, here's a word of caution. Organizations like the Lighthouse Program are great for helping veterans learn how to boost their credit scores. There are others out there you can turn to for input and advice. But you should run away from any company that wants to charge you money in return for improving your credit.

Run.

Fast.

Plain and simple.

These shady companies don't wield any inside power or possess any unique credit-boosting abilities. In fact, all they're likely to do is charge you to take the same basic steps you could have taken on your own.

We don't recommend credit counseling services, either. There are some reputable agencies out there that will work with your creditors to arrange more manageable payments. But there aren't a lot of guarantees with these kinds of firms, and veterans can wind up doing more harm than good.

After a rash of scams in recent years, the Federal Trade Commission started issuing warnings to consumers on how to spot what officials call "credit clinics." Some of the warning signs include:

- An organization that guarantees to remove late payments, bankruptcies or similar information from a credit report
- An organization that charges a lot of money to repair credit
- A company that asks the consumer to write to the credit reporting company and repeatedly seek verification of the same credit account information in the file, month after month, even though the information has been determined to be correct
- An organization that is reluctant to give out its address or one that pushes you to make a decision immediately

The reality is you can do most of this yourself. Organizations like the Lighthouse Program are there to shepherd and offer support and guidance along the way, without dipping into a veteran's pocket.

Improving Your Credit Score

Boosting your credit score isn't an instant gratification kind of trick. It takes time, dedication and patience to bump your standing, although a lot can happen in a relatively short period. Military borrowers staring down a less-than-sterling credit score have to make a commitment to righting the ship, so to speak.

It's easy for bad habits to form when it comes to finances. They become ingrained over time, and these routines turn into immutable truths. In some respects, improving your credit score is about breaking a cycle.

Let's take a look at the most effective tools for turning around your credit.

Disputing Errors

Credit reports are often littered with errors. A survey conducted in 2004 by the U.S. Public Interest Research Group found that about 1 in 4 credit reports contains errors serious enough to keep people from obtaining big-ticket items like home loans. This survey, which looked at responses from 200 adults in 30 states, also found that:

- Seventy-nine percent (79%) of the credit reports contained mistakes of some kind
- Fifty-four percent (54%) of the credit reports contained personal demographic identifying information that was misspelled, long outdated, belonged to a stranger, or was otherwise incorrect
- Thirty percent (30%) of the credit reports contained credit accounts that had been closed by the consumer but incorrectly remained listed as open

This is why it's so important to check your report regularly.

Scour your credit reports line by line. Look for any credit cards, installment loans or anything else that shouldn't be there. If you're 30 years old and there's a 17-year-old credit card account on your profile, it's probably safe to say it isn't yours. It's not uncommon to find a foreign account on your report, especially if you have a common name.

That can spell serious trouble for your credit score if someone else's account is delinquent, littered with late payments or swollen with a huge balance.

When viewing your credit report online, you can easily dispute incorrect items by following the directions on screen. You can also dispute inaccuracies in writing. The FTC has an excellent sample dispute letter at http://www.ftc.gov/bcp/edu/pubs/consumer/credit/cre21.shtm.

Either way, make sure to dispute an incorrect item with every credit agency reporting it and not just to one. Each is legally required to alert the others if an investigation determines there's something wrong on your credit report, but it's always a good idea to hit all three.

In some cases, it's better to take your dispute directly to the source instead of the reporting bureaus. Fixing mistakes and clearing up inaccuracies with the original creditor can prove equally effective, if not more so. They can easily contact the credit monitoring agencies and update them with more accurate information.

You should also be prepared to back up your claims with documentation. Disputing items online is a simple, click-happy process. But if you're disputing late payments or other major inaccuracies, you're probably going to need canceled checks, bank statements or other verifiable documents that support your contention.

It's not just a matter of submit and forget.

The agencies usually have 30 days to investigate your disputes. They will respond via the same channel you sent your request, either email or regular mail. In most cases, it takes another 45 days for the updated information and newly calculated credit score to hit your report.

Clearing your report of inaccuracies and errors can make a huge difference in your credit score. It takes nothing but time and a little patience.

We also recommend that military buyers lean on their loan officers when the time comes to dispute credit report inaccuracies. The credit agencies actually service the lending industry, which means loan officers can usually get things done a lot faster and with considerably less headache. It's a competitive space, and credit companies that respond quickly and work seamlessly with loan officers tend to get their contracts renewed.

If for some reason you're not satisfied with the results of the investigation, you have the right to ask the credit agencies to include in your report a statement addressing the dispute. You can also ask the agencies to give that statement to anyone who got a copy of your credit report in the few months prior. But the hard truth is that these statements of explanation don't mean much to mortgage lenders. They're looking at the bottom line, which in this case is your score.

Making Payments

This is another crucial step. You simply cannot make late payments on your obligations without paying a penalty when it comes to your credit score. This is the first thing the credit bureaus will look for when calculating your score. Establishing a history of timely payments will do wonders for your score.

Tackle Your Debt

Don't open a bunch of new credit cards and shift your balances from one to another. That can actually hurt your score. Keeping your balances low — ideally no more than 30 percent of the limit — is key. Commit to paying off the debt instead of shuffling it around. It's also unwise to close unused credit cards to try and bump up your score. Credit history and the length of credit also play a role in determining your score. Closing older cards shortens your history and can negatively impact your score.

Take It Easy

Military borrowers with a minimal credit history should tread carefully at the outset. This is another area where our Lighthouse Program can help tremendously. Generally, borrowers in this situation should refrain from opening a bunch of new accounts in a short time because it might actually hurt their credit profile. But there are times when borrowers simply have to do this in order to qualify. Lighthouse Program experts will carefully assess an individual borrower's needs.

Keep Credit in Check

Overall, credit cards and loans are good for your credit score. That is, so long as you're using them responsibly. Keeping a mix of revolving credit and installments is important, but so is striking the right balance. One thing you shouldn't do is open a spate of new credit accounts in the spirit of having a good mix. There's little indication it will help, and it might actually hurt your score if, as we mentioned earlier, you have a substantial limit spread among many cards. People with a lot of credit tend to use it, and that's not always a good thing.

To sum up, the steps are relatively straightforward: Keep credit accounts open, use them responsibly, pay your bills on time and keep balances low. That's the basic formula right there. There's no special program or online tool you can purchase to magically rehabilitate your credit. It's a process that takes time, commitment and recognition of the benefits that come with fiscal responsibility.

For some veterans, a better credit profile may mean significant savings through lower interest rates. Others face a starker prospect, mainly that without improved credit their dream of homeownership will remain unfulfilled.

ELIGIBILITY AND REQUIREMENTS

The one thing veterans on shaky financial ground should not do is give up hope. We've watched scores of military borrowers embark on the journey and ultimately rebuild their credit, many with help from our Lighthouse Program and others strictly on their own.

It can be done. Just ask James Sawyer.

James came to us looking to get prequalified for a VA loan. He found the company online, read through some customer testimonials and decided to make a call. After trading brief introductions, a loan officer soon got to the heart of the matter, asking James about his credit score.

James was embarrassed to answer.

The loan officer pulled James' credit and found his FICO score was 536. He would need at least a 620 to get qualified for a VA loan.

Committed to boosting his credit score, James decided to take advantage of our Lighthouse Program. He connected with personal credit consultant Jake Levy, who examined James' file and crafted a plan of attack. He gave James a list of accounts to immediately work toward paying off and told him to stop having people pull his credit.

James didn't waste a moment. He poured himself into paying off his debts. His hard work paid off just seven months later. We pulled his credit again and found his score had risen to 673, an incredible jump of almost 140 points in just 28 weeks. He was immediately prequalified for the VA loan he so badly wanted.

But James wasn't satisfied. He continued to pay down debt and work to improve his credit. He soon raised his score to 721 and continues to keep a close eye on his report. Shortly after prequalifying, James found a beautiful two-story home in Conyers, Ga. He bought it a few weeks later.

Bankruptcy and Foreclosure

These events can have devastating consequences for your credit profile. But as painful as they are, neither bankruptcy nor foreclosure will necessarily disqualify you from getting a VA loan.

Bankruptcy

There are entire books dedicated to filing for bankruptcy and changes to the process in recent years. The two major types of personal bankruptcy protection — Chapter 7 and Chapter 13 — come with their own hurdles, perils and benefits. We'll leave that for another time and try to focus on what they mean in the context of your credit report and your VA entitlement.

There's no getting around the fact that a bankruptcy is going to crush your credit. Veterans and civilian borrowers alike can expect to see their credit score dip anywhere from 130 to 240 points. That alone would make qualifying for a VA loan incredibly difficult for most military buyers.

Even veterans with sky-high credit will still struggle to qualify for a VA loan during the first two years after their bankruptcy is discharged. In most cases, borrowers won't be able to meet that somewhat nebulous definition of being a "satisfactory credit risk" until they're two years beyond their bankruptcy discharge. The VA has carved out some exceptions here, if:

- Veterans can prove the bankruptcy stems from circumstances beyond their control, such as unemployment, prolonged strikes at work or medical bills not covered by insurance, and
- The veteran or spouse with the bankruptcy has since purchased consumer goods on credit and showed an ability to make on-time payments, or
- The veteran was self-employed and a business failure caused the bankruptcy, so long as the veteran got a job

after the failure; has no other major credit problems before or after the bankruptcy; and didn't cause the failure by doing something illicit

Veterans who filed for Chapter 13 bankruptcy protection, which seeks to repay debts rather than erase them, may be able to qualify for a VA loan after showing 12 consecutive months of on-time payments. Keep in mind that requirements and exceptions can vary by lender.

It's also important to note that it's not as if that prior bankruptcy just disappears after two years. An underwriter will most certainly consider that prior bankruptcy as a **negative compensating factor** if there are any other risk factors present. For example, say you slip and have a couple of late payments at some point after your bankruptcy filing. Even if they're relatively small credit accounts, an underwriter is almost always going to deny the loan application unless there's a really good explanation for those delinquent payments.

Here's the bottom line: A bankruptcy adds risk. That's why it's so important for military borrowers to become diligent — almost zealous — when it comes to rebuilding and maintaining their credit. Borrowers with a history of bankruptcy will always carry that with them, no matter how many years have gone by.

Leroy Garcia knows what it's like to scale that mountain after bankruptcy.

He left the Air Force after years of proud service and settled in Nevada. Stability didn't last long. His marriage collapsed in 2007 and he found himself buried beneath a stack of bills after the divorce.

A two-income household was suddenly down to one, and Leroy found it difficult to keep his head above water. After weeks of fighting the current, he finally relented and filed for bankruptcy protection later that year. He lost the house and his credit score plummeted from 750 to about 590.

But he was bent on getting back into a house. He spent the next two years renting apartments and rooms and trying to regain his financial footing. He came to us shortly after his bankruptcy passed the two-year mark. His credit was still spotty, and he wound up seeking help from our Lighthouse Program.

"I had some stuff on my credit report that I didn't know about," Leroy said. "I still had banks showing I had a balance when that was all wiped out with the bankruptcy. They helped me get my credit score back up and guided me through the whole process."

Four months later, Leroy's Lighthouse credit expert re-pulled his reports and found his score had rebounded enough to qualify for a VA loan. He made an offer on a house the same day he started looking.

He moved in two months later.

Foreclosure

Foreclosure and its counterparts (a **short sale** or a **deed-in-lieu of foreclosure**) can prove more problematic for military buyers.

Foreclosure is when the bank takes back your house through formal proceedings because you can't make the payments. A short sale is when the lender allows an underwater homeowner to sell the home for less than what is owed in order to recover at least some of the cost. And a deed-in-lieu allows a home-owner to basically return the house to the lender without for-mal foreclosure proceedings. None are particularly beneficial outcomes for borrowers.

In terms of a credit crunch, foreclosure, a deed-in-lieu of foreclosure or a short sale will generally cause your score to drop somewhere from 85 to 160 points. More importantly, a foreclosure typically means you will not be eligible for a VA loan for at least two years. Borrowers who experience foreclosure will want to spend that time rebuilding their fractured credit.

But there are some misconceptions out there about what a foreclosure means for future borrowing, especially when it's a foreclosure on a previous VA loan. Let's be clear at the outset, because it's been misstated many places: A veteran who has a VA loan foreclosed upon *can* obtain another VA loan in the future.

Countless service members have been told otherwise by bank officials, mortgage brokers and others who either didn't understand the program or who were looking to make a buck with their own financing options.

Foreclosure on a previous VA loan does not preclude another VA loan down the road. Instead, the more important question involves how much of a loan the veteran will be able to obtain when the time comes.

The concept here is called **second-tier entitlement**, and it's a confusing one for scores of folks both in and outside of the industry. As a refresher, in Chapter 1 we talked about the two entitlements that account for the VA's one-quarter guaranty:

Primary entitlement: $36,000

Secondary entitlement: $68,250

When a veteran has a VA loan foreclosed upon, the lender needs to determine how much, if any, primary entitlement the borrower has left. If the VA lost money on the original deal, odds are the veteran will not have much, if any, primary entitlement remaining. It might be $15,000. But it could just as easily be zero.

That's where second-tier entitlement comes into play. Since veterans essentially have two separate VA entitlements, agency-approved lenders can secure a loan based solely on the borrower's secondary entitlement. Of course, there's a formula and some math involved to help make it extra confusing.

Let's say the veteran has used $48,000 of entitlement on a prior loan, which may not be restored, and wants to purchase a $320,000 home in a county where the loan limit is $625,000. At that point, here's the formula VA-approved lenders will follow:

$625,000 x 25% = $156,250 Maximum VA Guaranty
$156,250 - $48,000 = $108,250 Entitlement Available
$108,250 x 4 = $433,000 Maximum Loan Amount with 25 percent guaranty

In this example, the borrower's loan amount ($320,000) is well below the maximum amount that carries a full VA guaranty ($433,000). Given that, the hypothetical borrower won't need to come up with a down payment. Maximum loan amounts are subject to change, so it's important to make sure you're using the latest figures in your own calculations.

One of the quirks of the second-tier entitlement option is that there's also a minimum loan amount of $144,001. Veterans using their second-tier entitlement have to purchase a home for at least that amount in order to utilize the VA guaranty.

The concept is also what allows veterans to have two VA loans at the same time. A good example is when a service member relocates because of a PCS and wants to rent out his old home and purchase at the new duty station.

You can see why so many people get confused about entitlement. But this is actually an incredible opportunity for veterans who have gone through hard times.

Second-tier entitlement allowed Tom Lindgren and his family to become homeowners again.

A disabled Vietnam veteran, Tom struggled to keep a regular job upon his return from Cambodia in 1971. Credit and financial issues mounted over time, and he eventually filed for bankruptcy protection in 2001. The bank foreclosed on his home, which he had purchased with a VA loan.

Years later, with his bankruptcy in the rear view, Tom and his wife fell in love with a house near their northern Utah rental. They started working with a local mortgage company and were told the process would be simple, streamlined and on budget.

The results were anything but. The Lindgrens were approved for an FHA loan, provided they put down $25,000. Since they couldn't cover that sizable down payment, they would have to use a state program that would essentially loan them the down payment, creating a second mortgage.

All told, with two mortgages and other related costs, they were staring at an $1,800-per-month payment. Needless to say, that was far beyond what they could afford.

Devastated, the couple started looking online for a way to utilize Tom's VA benefit. They found Veterans United, talked with loan officer Neal Roeder and a new phrase entered the couple's vocabulary: second-tier entitlement.

Back home, the local mortgage company tried to discourage the Lindgrens from using a VA loan. Tom's old broker said he had never heard of the entitlement option. Company officials told the couple they would wind up homeless because of the VA's bureaucracy.

Undeterred, the Lindgrens plowed ahead and pursued a VA loan with us. Their second-tier entitlement came through, and they closed on their new home without the need for a down payment or private mortgage insurance. Their monthly payment would now be $1,300.

Tom was a homeowner once more.

"It was just an answer to a prayer," he said. "It's the most comforting, the most exciting thing that I can say has ever really happened to us. I felt there was empathy, compassion, even, and concern for our well being."

When You Have No Credit

Nobody's born with a credit history. It's something you earn and develop over time. But not everyone is an early adopter. Service members who join right out of a high school might not have a chance to open a credit card account or seek a loan until after their discharge.

Others simply choose to pay for things with cash or don't want the responsibility — and, at times, the temptation — that comes with purchasing on credit. The lack of a credit history doesn't mean you're unable to participate in the VA Loan Guaranty program.

To determine eligibility in these cases, lenders can base the decision on what they know about the veteran's payment record on other items, such as rent, car insurance or utilities. Most lenders require at least three active credit lines with balances. We've closed loans with as few as one line of credit, provided we could verify those other payments (typically things like rent or utilities), but frankly those cases are few and far between.

That's why building a credit history is so important, and it all starts with that first line of credit. No doubt it can seem daunting at first. That's why a great place to begin is with retailers and gas stations. They're frequent targets for credit rookies and are generally more willing to take a chance.

Apply for and open a charge card at a local department store or a nearby gas station. Make some small purchases and pay off the balance each month. As we've mentioned before, don't go wild and open a bunch of new cards at once. Focus on that one account. Over time, you'll start to see credit card applications arrive in your mailbox. Convinced of your credit worthiness, the department store or gas station will increase your credit limit.

You can also consider starting with a secured credit card, which requires a deposit to open. Unlike prepaid credit cards, these actually report to the credit bureaus.

Credit and Eligibility

In some respects, military borrowers have to serve two masters when it comes to credit and purchasing a home with a VA loan. And one is much less forgiving than the other.

VA officials want to see a sustained pattern of on-time payments and good credit management. In the grand scheme, one-time blips and isolated occurrences of unsatisfactory repayment probably won't derail a service member's ability to participate in the program. Again, the agency wants to ensure the veteran is a "satisfactory credit risk." That phrase doesn't include a particular credit score or even a range.

But the VA doesn't issue the loan. The approved lender that does is going to take a much harder and more black-and-white view of a veteran's credit profile. While the VA guaranty inspires confidence, lenders are still on the hook for 75 percent of that loan if the borrower defaults. Mortgage lenders that issue home loans to shaky borrowers don't stay in business long.

In the end, it all works out to some cold calculus for military borrowers: You can't have poor credit and expect to purchase a home, regardless of the loan program.

Understanding Income

Veterans who are considered a "satisfactory credit risk" have met one of the program's two basic requirements. But they also have to show that they can handle the financial burden of homeownership and repay their loan on time.

That means examining employment and income. Like everyone else, military borrowers have household expenses and obligations that go far beyond shelter. Underwriters want to make sure the veteran has enough steady, legitimate income to cover a new mortgage payment along with those other recurring expenses. That stream of verified income needs to be three things: stable, likely to continue and enough to cover the borrower's needs.

Lenders over the years developed a straightforward way of examining a prospective borrower's ability to handle mortgage payments by calculating a **debt-to-income ratio, or DTI ratio**. In essence, this is a ratio of a borrower's total monthly debt payments to his or her gross monthly income. The world of VA lending looks at DTI ratio a bit differently than the other major lending avenues (FHA, USDA, conventional), in that the agency only cares about one ratio, which factors in all of the borrower's monthly debt, from housing costs and revolving debts to anything else that's pertinent. The other major loan options tend to favor two separate DTI ratios, one solely for housing expenses and a second, holistic tally.

Unlike its counterparts, the VA also takes **residual income** into account. This is basically how much income is left over each month after shelter expenses and other family and household obligations are considered.

We'll take a deeper look at those issues shortly. For now, let's look more closely at income and the types of streams both lenders and the VA look for from prospective borrowers.

Employment and Effective Income

Both lenders and the VA like steady, stable employment. For veterans and others who are no longer serving on active duty, lenders are generally required to verify that you've worked continuously for at least the last two years. The most common and straightforward way to do this is through — you guessed it — another VA form. This time, it's the Request for Verification of Employment, VA Form 26-8497 (see Appendix B). You can find it online at www.vba.va.gov/pubs/forms/VBA-26-8497-ARE.pdf

This is one of the few VA loan documents not meant for the applicant. Lenders ship these out to the veteran's employer(s) of record for the previous two years. It's not meant to be a burden to busy employers, so much so that the VA notes at the top of the form that it should take only 10 minutes to complete.

The veteran's current employer is asked to provide specific information on a handful of key areas, including:

- Current position
- Probability of continued employment
- Base, overtime, bonus and commission earnings, and whether the latter three are likely to continue

Previous employers are simply asked to verify the veteran's last position, pay totals and reason for leaving the company. The VOE, as the **Verification of Employment** is usually called, and a paystub are the basic tools for checking a veteran's employment status.

Job-hopping can sometimes prove problematic, or at least worrisome to lenders. People do change careers. But underwriters are going to look for some kind of continuity between positions, and even then borrowers still might face some serious questions.

To count income from overtime work, part-time jobs, second jobs and bonuses, the veteran needs to show that same two-year period of stability.

Veterans who are self-employed or who make a living in the building trades, doing seasonal work or working mostly on commission have some additional paperwork hurdles to face. Tax returns for the previous two years will be essential in verifying income.

Lenders can only use self-employment income that the borrower pays taxes against. From time to time, entrepreneurs and business owners stumble on unique and creative ways to reduce their tax liability. For example, if your business earns $100,000 per year but you write off $50,000 before paying taxes, a lender can only consider the remaining $50,000.

For commission-based workers, the longer you've been employed the better. The VA will rarely guaranty a loan for veterans who've been generating that income for less than two years. Anything short of that is generally considered unstable income, given the nature of commissions and sales-based jobs. There are some rare exceptions when the veteran has either previous related employment or some type of specialized training. But today anything short of that two-year benchmark is a tough sell.

The same typically holds true for self-employed veterans. Fledgling entrepreneurs in business less than two years usually can't count that income as stable and reliable. As always, there are a few exceptions, but otherwise newly self-employed veterans will need additional sources of stable income in order to satisfy the VA and most lenders.

Self-employment is also an area where a VOE doesn't quite work. The lender needs some kind of third-party verification of your income and financial standing, along with that of the business. A veteran signing off on his or her own VOE isn't exactly independent.

Self-employed veterans generally have to supply:

- Individual tax returns for previous two years
- Business tax returns for previous two years
- Financial statements like balance sheets and profit-and-loss statements

Lenders may also choose to obtain a credit report on the business as well as on the applicant. There's some estimated guesswork involved when reviewing the income potential of a self-employed veteran. Lenders will look at trends and at comparable businesses to try and determine whether the business owner is likely to make enough money to pay a mortgage in the coming years.

Similar to a veteran who has taken a pay cut with each successive job, self-employed veterans whose businesses are in decline will receive extra scrutiny. The last thing lenders want is to float a mortgage to an entrepreneur whose business is on the cusp of crumbling.

What about veterans who've been employed less than 12 months?

In most cases, their income isn't going to be considered stable and reliable. But it's not a black-and-white call. Underwriters can look at the veteran's current job and any specialized training he or she has and, if gainful employment is likely to continue, include that income when considering the loan amount.

Recently discharged veterans may have held a job for just weeks or months before deciding to pursue a VA-guarantied home loan. It's often a case-by-case basis that tests the patience and flexibility of an underwriter. Will they keep their job and a steady stream of income flowing? Do they have any employment experience or expertise beyond their military training?

This is where a letter of explanation from either the veteran or an employer can make a huge difference for many borrowers.

John King and his wife, Becky, serve as a great example. John had recently completed his military service, and the couple was preparing to move from California to Oregon so John could start work with the Oregon State Police Department. They were hoping to close the loan based upon John's anticipated income from the new job, before he received a single paycheck. Our underwriter gave the go-ahead to close the loan, provided John could produce a signed offer, an acceptance letter detailing his salary and a letter from the state police explaining why he was qualified for the job (in this case, his military experience).

Underwriters and lenders often wrestle with these and other significant questions regarding newly discharged service members. Underwriters who approve shaky loans that ultimately default don't stay in their jobs for long. At the same time, veterans seeking a fresh start in the civilian world deserve a thorough look and a genuine shot at homeownership.

Active Duty Employment

Lenders will require a **Leave and Earnings Statement** instead of a VOE for active service members. It contains the same basic financial information. Service members can acquire their LES online by using the MyPay portal at https://mypay.dfas.mil/mypay.aspx.

Base pay counts as stable and reliable as long as the service member isn't within a year of release from active duty. Lenders can also include as effective income a service member's

Basic Allowance for Housing and occasionally other military allowances — clothing, flight pay, combat pay and others — provided they're verified and expected to continue.

Service members within a year of their release from active duty or the conclusion of their contract term can present a unique challenge. If their discharge date falls within 12 months of the anticipated date of their loan closing, the lender has to take a few extra steps to satisfy the VA. It makes sense, considering there may be uncertainty regarding the type of job and income that awaits the recently discharged veteran.

Given those potential question marks, lenders typically have to document at least one of the following five elements, if not more:

- That the service member has already re-upped or otherwise extended active duty service beyond that 12-month window, or
- The service member has a legitimate job offer in the civilian world (information about earnings and other standard data has to be included), or
- Significant underwriting factors that compensate for uncertainty, such as a down payment of at least 10 percent or noteworthy cash reserves, or
- A written statement from the service member declaring his or her intent to reenlist or extend service, along with
- A written statement from a commanding officer confirming the member's eligibility to reenlist or extend service and that it's likely to go through

Other Sources of Income

Married veterans can rely on the income of their spouse as long as he or she will be contractually obliged on the loan.

Otherwise, the income of significant others, roommates and other non-family members will not have an impact.

Veterans can also choose to include income from alimony and child support provided those sources are likely to continue. You will have to provide a copy of the divorce decree, which includes specifics on child support and the age of the children. Prospective borrowers might not be able to include this income if the child is within three years of turning 18.

There's a whole array of "other types of income" that the VA lumps together as potential sources, including:

- Pension or retirement benefits
- Disability income
- Stock dividends

Lenders can also take into account income from sources like public assistance programs and workers' compensation. These aren't things a veteran has to disclose to a potential lender, but they're certainly free to do so. Generally, veterans can't include unemployment compensation as effective income, unless they're seasonal workers or otherwise rely on unemployment as a regular part of their annual income.

Secondary sources of income need to be documented for at least two years through income verification and tax information. Consistency is key here.

DTI Ratio and Residual Income

Income figures are critical because they are used to generate a veteran's debt-to-income ratio. Again, this is a ratio of a borrower's total monthly debt payments to his or her gross monthly income. In general, the higher the ratio, the more likely your monthly expenses will outstrip your monthly income. That's a red flag for lenders who are constantly on the lookout for warning signs and potential indicators of mortgage default. That's not to say that folks with a high DTI ratio are automatically disqualified from a VA loan. They're not. But it's part of the overall calculus involved in evaluating a loan applicant.

As mentioned earlier, the VA is interested in the big-picture ratio, the back-end number. The VA uses a DTI benchmark of 41 percent, which is often higher than what you'll find with conventional and even FHA financing.

Here's how it typically works: Your loan officer will plug all of your debt and income numbers into an automated loan program and instantly see your DTI ratio. A veteran with a ratio of 41 percent or less will probably sail through with no problems. But prospective borrowers with a debt-to-income ratio above that threshold shouldn't immediately resign themselves to renting. A DTI ratio greater than 41 percent triggers additional layers of scrutiny on the part of the lender, both to satisfy the VA as well as its own concerns.

This is where residual income enters the picture.

Residual income is the other major income guide used by lenders and the VA to evaluate loan applications. This one is rooted in subtraction rather than division. The lender essentially adds up all of your monthly expenses, from housing and taxes to debt payments for cars, credit cards and other obligations. That total is subtracted from your monthly income. What's left over is your residual income, which is essentially money left over for things like groceries, health care, gas and all the other trappings of consumer and family life. The VA wants to ensure that a veteran has enough money left over to take care of regular household and family needs.

The VA has actually created tables on residual income for VA-approved lenders to consult. Here's what it looks like:

VA Pamphlet 26-7, Revised
Chapter 4: Credit Underwriting

9. How to Complete VA Form 26-6393, Loan Analysis,
Continued

e. Item 44, **Balance Available for Family Support (continued)**

Table of Residual Incomes by Region For loan amounts of $80,000 and above				
Family Size	**Northeast**	**Midwest**	**South**	**West**
1	$450	$441	$441	$491
2	$755	$738	$738	$823
3	$909	$889	$889	$990
4	$1,025	$1,003	$1,003	$1,117
5	$1062	$1,039	$1,039	$1,158
over 5	Add $80 for each additional member up to a family of seven			

Key to Geographic Regions Used in the Preceding Tables			
Northeast	Connecticut	New Hampshire	Pennsylvania
	Maine	New Jersey	Rhode Island
	Massachusetts	New York	Vermont
Midwest	Illinois	Michigan	North Dakota
	Indiana	Minnesota	Ohio
	Iowa	Missouri	South Dakota
	Kansas	Nebraska	Wisconsin
South	Alabama	Kentucky	Puerto Rico
	Arkansas	Louisiana	South Carolina
	Delaware	Maryland	Tennessee
	District of Columbia	Mississippi	Texas
	Florida	North Carolina	Virginia
	Georgia	Oklahoma	West Virginia
West	Alaska	Hawaii	New Mexico
	Arizona	Idaho	Oregon
	California	Montana	Utah
	Colorado	Nevada	Washington
			Wyoming

Continued on next page

For example, an Ohio family of four must have at least $1,003 left over each month after paying those major obligations. The income levels are a bit higher in the Northeast and the West, each of which has a higher cost of living.

Like a veteran's DTI ratio, residual income alone isn't supposed to automatically trigger approval or rejection of a loan.

But it can be the basis for disapproving a loan, especially if the residual income level is far below what would likely be considered adequate for the region.

All VA borrowers – including those with debt-to-income ratios below 41 percent – have to meet these residual income guidelines. Those whose DTI ratio is greater than 41 percent – have to clear an additional hurdle — their residual income must exceed the regional requirement by at least 20 percent.

Here's a quick example: Say you're an Ohio veteran with a DTI ratio of 48 percent. At the same time, you and your spouse have good jobs and the residual income for your family of four amounts to $1,350 each month, which is about 35 percent more than the $1,003 threshold. In this example, the veteran has exceeded the 20 percent benchmark and likely has enough money left over each month to take care of family obligations and everyday living expenses.

The reality is we've helped veterans with a DTI ratio of 60 percent ultimately secure a VA home loan. It's not an everyday occurrence, but it certainly happens. One number or rate doesn't always tell a borrower's story.

But what about borrowers whose DTI ratio *and* residual income are borderline?

When one or both of those key elements are toward the margins, lenders can turn to what are called **compensating factors**. These are strengths that help offset concerns and weaknesses in the buyer's loan application. There's a laundry list of things that can be considered, including:

- A sterling credit history
- Minimal debt
- Long-term employment
- Significant liquid assets
- Military benefits

- Conservative use of credit
- And many others

The VA explicitly notes that compensating factors have to go above and beyond what would be considered a normal program requirement. Most of our veterans and service members benefit from a combination of compensating factors. There are some who zoom through with excellent credit and plenty of disposable income. What's important is that you won't be judged by one number alone, unless that one number happens to be your credit score.

The VA is unmistakably clear that compensating factors cannot counteract the effects of bad credit. Shaky DTI ratio or residual income? Might not be a huge problem depending on any compensating factors. But an unsatisfactory credit score isn't something that borrowers can mitigate or that lenders can justify.

Now, in terms of DTI ratio and residual income, there is another way to proceed. When a loan officer calculates your DTI ratio and residual income, he or she is doing so based on the estimated loan amount you're seeking. So, if you're looking at a 30-year fixed-rate mortgage at 5.25 percent and $250,000, the loan officer is crunching numbers based on a monthly mortgage payment (without taxes and insurance) of $1,380.

Let's say she runs the numbers and determines your DTI ratio at that loan amount is an unsavory 50 percent, and your residual income is also less than stellar. Well, here's an easy way to curb those monthly debts: Try a lower loan amount. That's exactly what the loan officer will do. If a $250,000 loan looks to be too much for the veteran, the LO can essentially just play with the numbers until they become workable. Instead of

$250,000, maybe try $225,000 or $215,000. This kind of plug-and-play with loan amounts is standard fare for lenders nationwide. It's also one more reason why seeking loan preapproval before shopping for a home is critical. We'll get to that in the next chapter.

Sure, it's disappointing when veterans discover the $250,000 house they've been eyeing for months isn't really in their price range. But a $215,000 house is better than none at all. And, of course, the other option is for prospective borrowers to tackle their credit and financial issues first and hold off on purchasing a home.

Borrower spotlight: Mario Batiste

Hospital Corpsman-turned-Naval Instructor Uses VA Benefits to Become a First-Time Homebuyer

Grayslake, Ill. — Mario Batiste joined the Navy for one reason: College tuition.

Bent on becoming a radio disc jockey, the Chicago native expected to serve four years and then use his GI Bill benefits to study broadcasting. But that plan began to fade when Mario was sent to Naval Hospital Corps School after boot camp.

He was immediately enthralled with medical training and the life of a hospital corpsman. Mario spent the next decade at Naval hospitals and clinics in Washington, Hawaii and California.

He left the Navy at age 30 and decided to pursue that dream of a college education — only this time to earn a degree in biological science. But college life proved more humdrum than he expected, and Mario began to miss his old life. About a year after his separation he joined the Naval Reserves.

His second attempt at college stalled in 2004 when he deployed to Kuwait with an expeditionary medical force. After a year in the Mideast, he was sent back to Washington state to help beef up the Navy's depleted stateside medical staff.

He left Washington for good in 2007, married his long-time girlfriend, Sherri, and returned to southern Illinois to take one more crack at college.

It didn't last long this time, either.

Soon after arriving Mario spotted a job opening he couldn't pass up: Health technician at Naval Station Great Lakes, which is the Navy's largest training station. It's also on the north side of Chicago, about an hour from where Mario grew up.

The Navy offered him the job. Mario accepted immediately and is still teaching future generations of hospital corpsmen.

"Learning how to treat people, that compassion for the sick and injured, that's what I loved being close to," he said. "To teach these younger kids how to do that, it's amazing."

Lifelong renters, Mario and Sherri decided their move to Chicago marked the perfect time to become homeowners. Mario had heard military friends talk about VA loans but knew next to nothing about the program.

He went online to do some research and found the website for Veterans United Home Loans, the nation's leading dedicated VA lender. Mario filled out a form on the site and soon received a call from loan officer Aimee Hall.

Aimee explained the requirements and the loan process to Mario, who was prequalified for a loan within minutes. She also helped Mario connect with a real estate agent from Veterans United Realty, a national network of more than 5,000 agents who work routinely with military borrowers and understand the power of VA loans.

Mario and Sherri looked at properties for months before finding one they truly felt could be home: a 50-year-old, four-bedroom one-story with a lake on the property. The couple made an offer, received a favorable counteroffer and came to an agreement with the seller. They were ecstatic when the home appraised for more than the purchase price, another signal that they got a great deal.

The sellers agreed to cover all closing costs, which is a key benefit of VA loans. The agency limits what veterans can pay out of pocket and allows sellers to pay closing costs and concessions.

Mario became a first-time homeowner in September 2011. He did it without spending a dime up front on a down payment, closing costs or any kind of mortgage insurance.

"To military friends, I always stress the VA loan now," Mario said. "I tell them to call Aimee Hall. She will get you where you want to go, plain and simple. Aimee held my hand all the way through."

C H A P T E R 3 :
Loan Prequalification
and Preapproval

We've given you a rather quick, high-level snapshot of the basic eligibility and usage requirements for a VA loan. These loans are an incredibly dynamic tool that offers significant flexibility and savings to those who have served. But they're not for everybody.

For example, a veteran interested in acquiring a rental property will have to look elsewhere. There are other circumstances and economic situations that might also make a VA loan untenable for some military borrowers. We'll get to those in due time.

Now it's time to talk about where we are in the grand scheme of the homebuying process. Maybe you've been thinking about purchasing a home for months or years, like Tom Lindgren and his wife. Or perhaps you're just now considering the possibility and trying to decide if homeownership represents a good fit. Everyone comes to the process with a different perspective and singular desires and needs.

Here's a little secret that might relieve some pressure: You don't need to know right away. Some prospective borrowers start the process without a clue as to whether they can actually afford a home. Others come to the table unable to tell the difference between PMI and the PTA. And there are a relative few who steamroll from start to finish, certain of their ability to qualify for, obtain and pay off that mortgage.

Once a veteran decides to move forward, the first question is usually: Where do I start?

The answer often depends on whether you're asking a real estate agent or someone on the mortgage side of the equation. Some military borrowers prefer to start by finding a real estate agent to work on their behalf. Others may decide to hunt for a qualified mortgage company that can give them an idea of how much they can actually afford to spend.

Granted, we're a bit biased on the subject. But if you begin by finding a real estate agent, one of their first questions will be: Have you been preapproved for a loan? So, you're going to circle back to the mortgage company sooner rather than later. We figure you might as well start there. Movement will be glacial at best until you've been preapproved for a loan.

If you start with the real estate agent, they'll quickly point you to a mortgage company. If you start with the mortgage company, they'll look to connect you with real estate agents they've worked with in the past. That's the way it works in general, no matter the type of home loan you're pursuing.

We tend to believe VA loans represent a unique wrinkle that tilts the balance.

The fact is VA loans aren't run-of-the-mill for a vast majority of real estate agents and mortgage companies. It's important for borrowers to understand that a lot of mortgage lenders and real estate agents are unfamiliar with VA loans or rarely work with military borrowers.

There are also some longstanding misconceptions and institutional stereotypes about VA loans and the process at large.

Some of those are grounded in a bit of truth. But the process today is much more streamlined and efficient than in decades past. Despite updates and changes, VA loans can still conjure a negative image or a bad taste for some agents and mortgage brokers. The mistaken impression can wind up pushing veterans away from a program designed explicitly to help them become homeowners with relative ease.

Veterans should find someone they're comfortable with and trust. It doesn't have to be us, but we know this program better than just about anyone out there. We've been helping military members and their families secure home financing for more than a decade, and we made available more than $4 billion in financing in 2013 alone. We also have a national network of real estate agents who have worked extensively with military families. But enough of the commercial.

There are certainly other qualified mortgage companies out there. Finding folks who truly understand this unique home loan program and work with it routinely is paramount.

Getting the Green Light

No matter which route you've chosen, you're going to wind up in search of loan preapproval.

It's important for veterans and military buyers, especially first-timers, to recognize that getting preapproved for a loan is different from getting prequalified for one.

A ham sandwich can get prequalified. OK, maybe it's not that easy, but **loan prequalification** involves a cursory, barebones look at a borrower's finances. You can call a lender, dish out some basic financial information and typically get prequalified for a loan in minutes. Heck, you don't even have to call anymore. Lenders will issue prequalification online.

You will get a broad, ballpark estimate of your loan amount generated without a look at your holistic financial profile or your ability to afford a home purchase.

You will get a tool, albeit a rather dull and blunted one.

Prequalification can help veterans get a feel for some of the general questions and issues they might need to address. But just know that the word "prequalified" does little to light the eyes of real estate agents and prospective sellers.

Preapproved is another story.

By comparison, getting preapproved for a loan is a much more arduous and involved process. It also carries much more weight with sellers and means you're really ready to shop for a home under realistic conditions and budgetary constraints.

In most cases, veterans and other military borrowers need to get preapproved for a VA loan before they go house hunting in earnest.

Your loan officer understands all of this perfectly. So why is he or she talking to you about getting prequalified for a loan? Mainly because we have to start somewhere.

Why Prequalification is Important

In essence, prequalification is a process of conversation and faith, at least of the financial sort. The process does three basic things:

- Gives the prospective borrower a broad estimate of purchasing power
- Tells the lender immediately if the veteran cannot obtain a VA loan at that time
- Lays a foundation for the underwriting process to begin once a contract is in place

LOAN PREQUALIFICATION AND PREAPPROVAL

Let's just say that, for the sake of a simple example, you're tooling around online for VA home loan information and you come across our company. You fill out a form with some basic, best-guess information, such as an estimate of your credit rating, the prospective loan amount, when and where you plan to purchase and a couple others. Veterans who call us or any other lender will give the same basic information over the phone.

You don't need exact figures and precise data, at least at this stage. The loan officer is taking you at your word in regard to your job status, income and other pertinent information.

But there's one part of the equation that requires more than just a good faith guess: the borrower's credit score. And that's because bad credit can kill your chances of getting a VA loan right out of the starting gate.

At the present time, prospective borrowers with a credit score below 620 may have trouble securing a VA loan. It's just that simple. Chalk it up to the subprime mortgage collapse and the slew of foreclosures that followed. The cutoff varies among lenders, but that's a pretty representative baseline.

So, you can ballpark your annual income. Heck, you can pretty much fudge most of the information you provide, although it really doesn't do you much good. But the loan officer is going to ask for your Social Security number and pull your credit profile and your credit score before a prequalification can be issued.

That you can't fake or fudge. At our company, prospective borrowers with a score below 620 immediately head to a different track — the Lighthouse Program, which we talked about earlier. Most lenders will not issue any kind of prequalification or preapproval to subprime borrowers.

Even if your credit score checks out, a good loan officer will work to develop the conversation and look for major red flags that signal potential trouble ahead. Employment status, which we covered last chapter, is a good example.

There's no way for a recently discharged veteran to have two years of steady employment, which is the agency's broad requirement. But if the veteran specialized in electrical systems in the military and has spent the past five months working as an electrician, that's likely going to be fine.

What likely won't fly is if that same veteran is instead working as a used car salesman.

Fudging the Facts

Now, a word here about honesty: There's absolutely no point in inflating your income level, your monthly debts or any other financial figures when you first start talking to mortgage folks. The bold, bare facts are going to become plainly evident if you continue down the path to purchasing. So gross exaggerations or patently false information only serves to waste time and resources, both on the lender's end and on the borrower's.

It's also illegal to falsify loan documents.

Lenders and loan officers have heard it all before. They've worked with multimillionaires and folks struggling paycheck to paycheck. The fastest way to make your homebuying process a tough and miserable one is to start with dishonesty. Don't ever be afraid to utter the phrase "I don't know." That's perfectly acceptable. But outright falsehood is something entirely different.

Loan Approval Paperwork

If there are no immediate, wildly apparent hurdles, the loan officer will take your credit score and unverified financial information and feed it into a what's called an AUS, or **Automated Underwriting System**. This is a high-tech computer program that instantly analyzes an applicant's key financial information and spits out a loan approval or a loan rejection. We'll talk more about these systems when we get to preapproval.

At this stage, running the numbers and cranking out an estimated loan amount is mostly academic. Loan prequalification is free and completely nonbinding for the veteran. It allows the lender to get a borrower profile and some basic information set up in the AUS. It allows the veteran to get a broad measuring stick weighed down with caveats and conditions.

It's worth noting that not every application is suitable for an AUS evaluation. There are a few adverse situations — almost always involving the veteran's credit history — when the loan will require a **manual underwrite**. We'll cover that shortly.

For now, prequalification is where the loan approval process starts. It also kicks off the paperwork.

By law, lenders have three business days to send you the official loan approval paperwork after pulling your credit score. Loan documents can be intimidating to prospective borrowers. Some have odd-sounding names and small-type legalese.

That's why we're going to go over some of the major documents in detail.

Most lenders will also have their own in-house forms in addition to the standard, government-required documents. Since those can vary, we'll just stick with forms that every prospective military borrower will encounter. Depending on the lender, you might sign some of these documents electronically, while others you'll encounter immediately and sign by hand.

At the outset, it's also important to note that your loan officer will fill out most of these forms for you, using information you supply over the phone and figures he or she is able to verify from tax forms and other important documents. You'll fill in some of the blanks on the following pages, but most of your work involves signing your name. That said, it's still helpful for some borrowers to get an overview of what awaits.

Uniform Residential Loan Application

The first significant document is the loan application itself, the **Uniform Residential Loan Application**.

This is the epitome of the standardized form, littered with boxes and requests for personal and financial information. There's no escaping it, either. If you're hoping to buy a home, you're filling out this form. It's the standard for all residential loans, no matter whether it's VA, FHA or conventional. You might hear it called a 10-oh-3, as it's formally known as Fannie Mae Form 1003 (it's also Freddie Mac Form 65). Whatever you want to call it, it's a time suck that's absolutely crucial.

We're going to go over each of the form's 10 sections one at a time. We'll reproduce the sections individually here, but you can see the form in total as Appendix C. You can also download the application directly from the Fannie Mae website at www.fanniemae.com.

The reality is your loan officer should complete this application. Borrowers will obviously provide key information, but lenders have a duty to explain to consumers how to complete these forms accurately. Reproducing them here is meant to help give prospective borrowers a sense of what lies ahead.

Section I: Mortgage Type and Terms

Uniform Residential Loan Application

This application is designed to be completed by the applicant(s) with the Lender's assistance. Applicants should complete this form as "Borrower" or "Co-Borrower," as applicable. Co-Borrower information must also be provided (and the appropriate box checked) when ☐ the income or assets of a person other than the Borrower (including the Borrower's spouse) will be used as a basis for loan qualification or ☐ the income or assets of the Borrower's spouse or other person who has community property rights pursuant to state law will not be used as a basis for loan qualification, but his or her liabilities must be considered because the spouse or other person has community property rights pursuant to applicable law and Borrower resides in a community property state, the security property is located in a community property state, or the Borrower is relying on other property located in a community property state as a basis for repayment of the loan.

If this is an application for joint credit, Borrower and Co-Borrower each agree that we intend to apply for joint credit (sign below):

Borrower		Co-Borrower			
		I. TYPE OF MORTGAGE AND TERMS OF LOAN			
Mortgage Applied for:	☐ VA ☐ FHA	☐ Conventional ☐ USDA/Rural Housing Service	☐ Other (explain):	Agency Case Number	Lender Case Number

You're applying for a VA loan. That's probably self-explanatory. You can always go back and change your selection if the VA for some reason finds you ineligible or if you decide another loan program makes better sense.

That's true for any other part of the loan application. You can make changes as the process moves forward, so don't worry about being locked into early choices.

Your loan officer will fill in the agency and lender case numbers. There are also spaces for the loan amount you're seeking, the length of your requested loan term (30 years is the most common) and the amortization type.

There are three main amortization types: fixed rate, adjustable rate (ARM) and graduated payment (GPM). We'll talk a lot more about loan types and rates in Chapter 5. For now, check one (we recommend fixed rate in most cases) and move on to the next maze of boxes.

Section II: Property and Purpose

II. PROPERTY INFORMATION AND PURPOSE OF LOAN							
Subject Property Address (street, city, state & ZIP)							No. of Units
Legal Description of Subject Property (attach description if necessary)							Year Built
Purpose of Loan ☐ Purchase ☐ Construction ☐ Other (explain): ☐ Refinance ☐ Construction-Permanent				Property will be: ☐ Primary Residence ☐ Secondary Residence			☐ Investment
Complete this line if construction or construction-permanent loan.							
Year Lot Acquired	Original Cost $	Amount Existing Liens $	(a) Present Value of Lot $		(b) Cost of Improvements $	Total (a + b) $	
Complete this line if this is a refinance loan.							
Year Acquired	Original Cost $	Amount Existing Liens $	Purpose of Refinance		Describe Improvements ☐ made ☐ to be made Cost: $		
Title will be held in what Name(s)				Manner in which Title will be held		Estate will be held in: ☐ Fee Simple ☐ Leasehold (show expiration date)	
Source of Down Payment, Settlement Charges, and/or Subordinate Financing (explain)							

There usually isn't a property address at this stage. A legal description will come down the road once you have a property in mind.

The purpose and property lines are important. We'll talk about refinancing with a VA loan in Chapter 6. We've already discussed how lenders frown upon, to put it mildly, VA construction loans. So the odds are you're either checking the Purchase or Refinance boxes here.

We've also already talked about how veterans can't use a VA loan to buy investment or rental properties. And make no mistake: Trying to beat the system is a bad idea. Lenders in general aren't apt to take a borrower at his or her word.

In fact, they will automatically review the property, examining things like the distance from work, drop in cost from current residence and other signs that this property isn't intended as a primary residence. In short, lenders will check thoroughly to satisfy this requirement.

Now, as we touched on earlier, there are times when a qualified borrower can have two VA loans in play at the same time. But whether you're looking to refinance or purchase, you're likely checking the "primary residence" box here.

The areas for title and estate holding sound confusing but are relatively simple to navigate. Your loan officer can help answer specific questions, but in general the title will be in your name or in conjunction with your spouse's name. To hold the estate in "fee simple" means that you own both the residence and the property it rests upon, while "leasehold" means you own the home but lease the land.

Veterans and service members will check the "fee simple" box here.

Section III: Borrower Information

Borrower				III. BORROWER INFORMATION	Co-Borrower			
Borrower's Name (include Jr. or Sr. if applicable)					Co-Borrower's Name (include Jr. or Sr. if applicable)			
Social Security Number	Home Phone (incl. area code)	DOB (mm/dd/yyyy)	Yrs. School		Social Security Number	Home Phone (incl. area code)	DOB (mm/dd/yyyy)	Yrs. School
□ Married □ Unmarried (include □ Separated single, divorced, widowed)		Dependents (not listed by Co-Borrower) no. ages			□ Married □ Unmarried (include □ Separated single, divorced, widowed)		Dependents (not listed by Borrower) no. ages	
Present Address (street, city, state, ZIP) □ Own □ Rent ___ No. Yrs.					Present Address (street, city, state, ZIP) □ Own □ Rent ___ No. Yrs.			
Mailing Address, if different from Present Address					Mailing Address, if different from Present Address			
If residing at present address for less than two years, complete the following:								
Former Address (street, city, state, ZIP) □ Own □ Rent ___ No. Yrs.					Former Address (street, city, state, ZIP) □ Own □ Rent ___ No. Yrs.			

This one probably looks painfully familiar. It's a request for the basic personal information you've given out dozens of times. The "Yrs. School" box is a vestige of decades past, when the loan approval process included a type of calculation to ballpark how much money you might make in future years. Since it's against the law to lie on a loan application, it's probably a good idea to play it straight here. Your loan application won't wind up in limbo or get rejected because you didn't finish high school or college.

Section IV: Employment Information

Borrower			IV. EMPLOYMENT INFORMATION	Co-Borrower		
Name & Address of Employer	☐ Self Employed	Yrs. on this job	Name & Address of Employer	☐ Co-Borrower ☐ Self Employed	Yrs. on this job	
		Yrs. employed in this line of work/profession			Yrs. employed in this line of work/profession	
Position/Title/Type of Business	Business Phone (incl. area code)		Position/Title/Type of Business	Business Phone (incl. area code)		

If employed in current position for less than two years or if currently employed in more than one position, complete the following:

Uniform Residential Loan Application
Freddie Mac Form 65   7/05 (rev.6/09)   Page 1 of 5   Fannie Mae Form 1003   7/05 (rev.6/09)

Borrower			IV. EMPLOYMENT INFORMATION (cont'd)	Co-Borrower		
Name & Address of Employer	☐ Self Employed	Dates (from – to)	Name & Address of Employer	☐ Self Employed	Dates (from – to)	
		Monthly Income $			Monthly Income $	
Position/Title/Type of Business	Business Phone (incl. area code)		Position/Title/Type of Business	Business Phone (incl. area code)		
Name & Address of Employer	☐ Self Employed	Dates (from – to)	Name & Address of Employer	☐ Self Employed	Dates (from – to)	
		Monthly Income $			Monthly Income $	
Position/Title/Type of Business	Business Phone (incl. area code)		Position/Title/Type of Business	Business Phone (incl. area code)		

Lenders like stability and predictability.

Someone who's been in the same job and the same line of work for two years or more usually files an application that screams "stable." That isn't to say that layoffs and career changes don't occur, but every loan is a gamble, at least to a degree. Mortgage lenders lose money by betting on the wrong horse.

Having a track record of job stability certainly helps. Moving from job to job isn't necessarily a bad thing, especially if that movement comes with corresponding pay hikes. But applicants who have been in their current job or line of work for less than two years might be looked at a bit differently.

For now, focus on filling out these fields as accurately as possible. Lenders will follow up with your employers to verify information, especially as it relates to your experience and income.

If you've been out of work during the previous two years, make sure to note the time frame and list the reasons for it.

Section V: Monthly Income and Combined Housing Expense Information

V. MONTHLY INCOME AND COMBINED HOUSING EXPENSE INFORMATION						
Gross Monthly Income	Borrower	Co-Borrower	Total	Combined Monthly Housing Expense	Present	Proposed
Base Empl. Income*	$	$	$	Rent	$	
Overtime				First Mortgage (P&I)		$
Bonuses				Other Financing (P&I)		
Commissions				Hazard Insurance		
Dividends/Interest				Real Estate Taxes		
Net Rental Income				Mortgage Insurance		
Other (before completing, see the notice in "describe other income" below)				Homeowner Assn. Dues		
				Other:		
Total	$	$	$	Total	$	$

* Self Employed Borrower(s) may be required to provide additional documentation such as tax returns and financial statements.

Describe Other Income   *Notice:* Alimony, child support, or separate maintenance income need not be revealed if the Borrower (B) or Co-Borrower (C) does not choose to have it considered for repaying this loan.

B/C		Monthly Amount
		$

Accurate income information is critical to the loan approval process. So is determining what kind of monthly obligations and debts a prospective borrower might have. Later in this process, the lender will determine your debt-to-income ratio.

For now, this section focuses on income and expenses related only to housing and shelter. Under the "Other" income heading, veterans don't need to include sources like alimony or child support if they don't want that considered.

The housing expense side is especially breezy for renters. Current homeowners should be sure to include information on all mortgages along with their tax and insurance information.

Section VI: Assets and Liabilities:

VI. ASSETS AND LIABILITIES		
This Statement and any applicable supporting schedules may be completed jointly by both married and unmarried Co-Borrowers if their assets and liabilities are sufficiently joined so that the Statement can be meaningfully and fairly presented on a combined basis; otherwise, separate Statements and Schedules are required. If the Co-Borrower section was completed about a non-applicant spouse or other person, this Statement and supporting schedules must be completed about that spouse or other person also.		Completed ☐ Jointly ☐ Not Jointly

ASSETS	Cash or Market Value	Liabilities and Pledged Assets. List the creditor's name, address, and account number for all outstanding debts, including automobile loans, revolving charge accounts, real estate loans, alimony, child support, stock pledges, etc. Use continuation sheet, if necessary. Indicate by (*) those liabilities, which will be satisfied upon sale of real estate owned or upon refinancing of the subject property.		
Description				
Cash deposit toward purchase held by:	$			
List checking and savings accounts below		**LIABILITIES**	**Monthly Payment & Months Left to Pay**	**Unpaid Balance**
Name and address of Bank, S&L, or Credit Union		Name and address of Company	$ Payment/Months	$
Acct. no.	$	Acct. no.		
Name and address of Bank, S&L, or Credit Union		Name and address of Company	$ Payment/Months	$
Acct. no.	$	Acct. no.		
Name and address of Bank, S&L, or Credit Union		Name and address of Company	$ Payment/Months	$
Acct. no.	$	Acct. no.		

Uniform Residential Loan Application
Freddie Mac Form 65   7/05 (rev. 6/09)

Page 2 of 5

Fannie Mae Form 1003   7/05 (rev.6/09)

VI. ASSETS AND LIABILITIES (cont'd)			
Name and address of Bank, S&L, or Credit Union		Name and address of Company	$ Payment/Months	$
Acct. no.	$	Acct. no.		
Stocks & Bonds (Company name/ number & description)	$	Name and address of Company	$ Payment/Months	$
		Acct. no.		
Life insurance net cash value	$	Name and address of Company	$ Payment/Months	$
Face amount: $				
Subtotal Liquid Assets	$			
Real estate owned (enter market value from schedule of real estate owned)	$			
Vested interest in retirement fund	$			
Net worth of business(es) owned (attach financial statement)	$	Acct. no.		
Automobiles owned (make and year)	$	Alimony/Child Support/Separate Maintenance Payments Owed to:	$	
Other Assets (itemize)	$	Job-Related Expense (child care, union dues, etc.)	$	
		Total Monthly Payments	$	
Total Assets a.	$	Net Worth (a minus b) ► $	**Total Liabilities b.**	$

Schedule of Real Estate Owned (If additional properties are owned, use continuation sheet.)

Property Address (enter S if sold, PS if pending sale or R if rental being held for income) ▼	Type of Property	Present Market Value	Amount of Mortgages & Liens	Gross Rental Income	Mortgage Payments	Insurance, Maintenance, Taxes & Misc.	Net Rental Income
		$	$	$	$	$	$
Totals		$	$	$	$	$	$

List any additional names under which credit has previously been received and indicate appropriate creditor name(s) and account number(s):

Alternate Name	Creditor Name	Account Number

Just a quick glance at this one is enough to make the eyes glaze over. It isn't as bad as it might look. It's definitely a good idea to go over this part with your loan officer. And please — please — ask questions, not just about Assets & Liabilities, but also about any aspect of the loan process or the mortgage industry at large.

This is one of the biggest investments you'll ever make, and probably the largest single purchase. Asking questions makes for an informed consumer. You should always work with a lender that's genuinely concerned with your best interests, but that doesn't absolve you from being your own best advocate. The bottom line is if you don't understand something or feel out of the loop, start asking questions. And don't stop until you get a satisfactory answer that you truly understand.

A prospective borrower's standing as it relates to assets has become increasingly important to lenders. In some ways, assets are almost as important as a solid credit history. And like a negative credit profile, an unhealthy asset balance can kill a transaction. A history of overdrafts or a lack of **reserves**, which are basically additional monies that can help solidify a loan application if there's some doubt or concern, can be especially damaging.

Let's take a look at the form. The first space is for information on the earnest money you put forth. **Earnest money** is basically a financial showing of seriousness and good faith. You'll put up an agreed-upon amount to show the seller you're interested in purchasing. You can also just think of it as a deposit. The amount you must put forward depends on where you live, the property in question and a few other key factors, but it's generally not more than a few thousand dollars.

Your earnest money goes into an escrow account that, if all goes as planned, will eventually be put toward closing costs or refunded to the borrower. Earnest money and the amount you have in reserve can also serve as a compensating factor to potentially offset lower credit scores. For example, having six months worth of mortgage payments in reserve might help convince a lender to work with your slightly dented credit. Veterans interested in holding onto one property while purchasing a second might be required to have six months of reserves on hand.

The rest of the asset section is self-explanatory. You don't need to list every account you have, just the major ones that showcase your ability to handle the financial obligations that come with homeownership. There's also room for non-liquid assets, or more tangible things like real estate, business net worth and even your car. The "other" category can prove a bit nebulous with anything from art and automobile collections to antiques up for consideration. If you've got something along these lines, by all means include it, but leaving this space blank won't raise any eyebrows.

As for your liabilities, the lender is looking for the kind of big-ticket items that can help or harm your credit score. Credit cards, bank loans, student loans and liabilities in that vein need to be documented to the best of your ability. Borrowers won't usually complete this section. Instead, the lender will go directly from a credit report.

Section VII: Details of Transaction

VII. DETAILS OF TRANSACTION	
a.	Purchase price	$
b.	Alterations, improvements, repairs	
c.	Land (if acquired separately)	
d.	Refinance (incl. debts to be paid off)	
e.	Estimated prepaid items	
f.	Estimated closing costs	
g.	PMI, MIP, Funding Fee	
h.	Discount (if Borrower will pay)	
i.	Total costs (add items a through h)	

VII. DETAILS OF TRANSACTION	
j.	Subordinate financing	
k.	Borrower's closing costs paid by Seller	
l.	Other Credits (explain)	
m.	Loan amount (exclude PMI, MIP, Funding Fee financed)	
n.	PMI, MIP, Funding Fee financed	
o.	Loan amount (add m & n)	
p.	Cash from/to Borrower (subtract j, k, l & o from i)	

Veterans can just skip this section entirely. In the age of automation, most loan officers will use a mortgage program to crunch the numbers and spit out the results for this section.

Section VIII: Declarations

VIII. DECLARATIONS				
If you answer "Yes" to any questions a through i, please use continuation sheet for explanation.	Borrower		Co-Borrower	
	Yes	No	Yes	No
a. Are there any outstanding judgments against you?	☐	☐	☐	☐
b. Have you been declared bankrupt within the past 7 years?	☐	☐	☐	☐
c. Have you had property foreclosed upon or given title or deed in lieu thereof in the last 7 years?	☐	☐	☐	☐
d. Are you a party to a lawsuit?	☐	☐	☐	☐
e. Have you directly or indirectly been obligated on any loan which resulted in foreclosure, transfer of title in lieu of foreclosure, or judgment?	☐	☐	☐	☐
(This would include such loans as home mortgage loans, SBA loans, home improvement loans, educational loans, manufactured (mobile) home loans, any mortgage, financial obligation, bond, or loan guarantee. If "Yes," provide details, including date, name, and address of Lender, FHA or VA case number, if any, and reasons for the action.)				

VIII. DECLARATIONS				
If you answer "Yes" to any questions a through i, please use continuation sheet for explanation.	Borrower		Co-Borrower	
	Yes	No	Yes	No
f. Are you presently delinquent or in default on any Federal debt or any other loan, mortgage, financial obligation, bond, or loan guarantee?	☐	☐	☐	☐
g. Are you obligated to pay alimony, child support, or separate maintenance?	☐	☐	☐	☐
h. Is any part of the down payment borrowed?	☐	☐	☐	☐
i. Are you a co-maker or endorser on a note?	☐	☐	☐	☐
- -				
j. Are you a U.S. citizen?	☐	☐	☐	☐
k. Are you a permanent resident alien?	☐	☐	☐	☐
l. **Do you intend to occupy the property as your primary residence?**	☐	☐	☐	☐
If "Yes," complete question m below.				
m. Have you had an ownership interest in a property in the last three years?	☐	☐	☐	☐
(1) What type of property did you own—principal residence (PR), second home (SH), or investment property (IP)?	_____		_____	
(2) How did you hold title to the home— by yourself (S), jointly with your spouse (SP), or jointly with another person (O)?	_____		_____	

LOAN PREQUALIFICATION AND PREAPPROVAL

There's no real magic or mystery to this section. It's a list of 13 questions that require a Yes or No answer.

Section IX: Acknowledgment and Agreement

Read and sign.

Section X: Information for Government Monitoring Purposes

Housing discrimination is illegal. Lenders cannot make decisions about an applicant or in any way discriminate on the basis of race, color or religion. There are also mandates on lenders to make sure they're providing opportunities to communities in need.

Submitting this personal information is optional. But it helps the government track patterns and more fully evaluate lenders from this perspective. If you don't voluntarily provide this information, the loan officer is required to make a guess as to your sex, ethnicity and race, strange as it may sound. So it's usually just easier and more accurate to fill in the information yourself.

Next document: Borrowers Certification and Authorization

Borrowers' Certification and Authorization

CERTIFICATION

The Undersigned certify the following:

1. I/We have applied for a mortgage loan through _____. In applying for the loan, I/We completed a loan application containing various information on the purpose of the loan, the amount and source of the down payment, employment and income information, and the assets and liabilities. I/We certify that all of the information is true and complete. I/We made no misrepresentations in the loan application or other documents, nor did I/We omit any pertinent information.

2. I/We understand and agree that _____ reserves the right to change the mortgage loan review processes to a full documentation program. This may include verifying the information provided on the application with the employer and/or the financial institution.

3. I/We fully understand that it is a Federal crime punishable by fine or imprisonment, or both, to knowingly make any false statements when applying for this mortgage, as applicable under the provisions of Title 18, United States Code, Section 1014.

AUTHORIZATION TO RELEASE INFORMATION

To Whom It May Concern:

1. I/We have applied for a mortgage loan through _____. As part of the application process, _____ and the mortgage guaranty insurer (if any), may verify information contained in my/our loan application and in other documents required in connection with the loan, either before the loan is closed or as part of its quality control program.

2. I/We authorize you to provide to _____ and to any investor to whom _____ may sell my mortgage, any and all information and documentation that they request. Such information includes, but is not limited to, employment history and income; bank, money market and similar account balances; credit history; and copies of income tax returns.

3. _____ or any investor that purchases the mortgage may address this authorization to any party named in the loan application.

4. A copy of this authorization may be accepted as an original.

Borrower Signature _____   Co-Borrower Signature _____

SSN: _____ Date: _____   SSN: _____ Date: _____

Calyx Form - borcsca.frm (12/05)

96

LOAN PREQUALIFICATION AND PREAPPROVAL

This is a standard release form that gives the lender the right to verify and distribute personal and financial information. Lenders originate home loans in what's known as the primary market. After making money on fees and charges, some lenders turn around and sell their mortgages to investors in the **secondary mortgage market.**

All kinds of entities, from private firms to public investors like Fannie Mae and Freddie Mac, purchase these, with the proceeds helping to fund more home loans in the primary market. The sale of a mortgage can actually include two distinct elements: the loan itself and the loan servicing, which is the coordination of payments and processing associated with a mortgage.

This form basically says that you're OK with the lender and secondary investors checking out your key financials, such as credit history, income and tax returns.

Next document: Servicing Disclosure Statement

SERVICING DISCLOSURE STATEMENT

Originator: Date:

NOTICE TO FIRST LIEN MORTGAGE LOAN APPLICANTS: THE RIGHT TO COLLECT YOUR MORTGAGE LOAN PAYMENTS MAY BE TRANSFERRED.

You are applying for a mortgage loan covered by the Real Estate Settlement Procedures Act (RESPA) (12 U.S.C. 2601 et seq.). RESPA gives you certain rights under Federal law. This statement describes whether the servicing for this loan may be transferred to a different loan servicer.

"Servicing" refers to collecting your principal, interest, and escrow payments, if any, as well as sending any monthly or annual statements, tracking account balances, and handling other aspects of your loan. You will be given advance notice before a transfer occurs.

☑ We may assign, sell or transfer the servicing of your loan while the loan is outstanding.

☑ We do not service mortgage loans of the type for which you applied. We intend to assign, sell, or transfer the servicing of your mortgage loan before the first payment is due.

☐ The loan for which you have applied will be serviced at this financial institution and we do not intend to sell, transfer, or assign the servicing of the loan.

Acknowledgment of Mortgage Loan Applicant(s)

I/We have read and understood the disclosure, and understand that the disclosure is a required part of the mortgage application as evidenced by my/our signature(s) below;

Applicant _____ Date _____   Applicant _____ Date _____

Applicant _____ Date _____   Applicant _____ Date _____

Calyx Form - sds.frm (01/06)

It might seem odd, but you typically don't send your monthly mortgage payment to the lender that helped you get a VA loan. In many cases, the lender sells your loan to a financial institution that invests in home mortgages. Sometimes the loan servicing follows to that new institution, and other times it is sold separately. This document informs prospective borrowers of their potential servicing scenario.

Next document: Request for Transcript of Tax Returns

Like most government forms, this one often goes by its formal number: 4506-T. It's a basic form that allows the lender to pull income tax transcripts for the previous two years. Those play a critical role in determining the veteran's debt-to-income ratio and employment status. It's crucial that prospective borrowers fill out these forms correctly. Double check names, spellings, date of birth, Social Security number and every other field to ensure accuracy. Any errors can cause big delays when it comes time to process and underwrite the loan. And the IRS doesn't offer much in the way of help or explanation. It simply rejects inaccurate requests without a rationale.

Next document: Credit Score Information Disclosure

NOTICE TO THE HOME LOAN APPLICANT
CREDIT SCORE INFORMATION DISCLOSURE

APPLICANT(S) NAME AND ADDRESS	LENDER NAME AND ADDRESS (ORIGINATOR)

In connection with your application for a home loan, the lender must disclose to you the score that a consumer reporting agency distributed to users and the lender used in connection with your home loan, and the key factors affecting your credit scores.

The credit score is a computer-generated summary calculated at the time of the request and based on information a consumer reporting agency or lender has on file. The scores are based on data about your credit history and payment patterns. Credit scores are important because they are used to assist the lender in determining whether you will obtain a loan. They may also be used to determine what interest rate you may be offered on the mortgage. Credit scores can change over time, depending on your conduct, how your credit history and payment patterns change, and how credit-scoring technologies change.

Because the score is based on information in your credit history, it is very important that you review the credit related information that is being furnished to make sure it is accurate. Credit records may vary from one company to another.

If you have questions about your credit score or the credit information that is furnished to you, contact the consumer reporting agency at the address and telephone number provided with this notice, or contact the lender, if the lender developed or generated the credit score. The consumer reporting agency plays no part in the decision to take any action on the loan application and is unable to provide you with specific reasons for the decision on a loan application.

If you have questions concerning the terms of the loan, contact the lender.

The consumer reporting agencies listed below provided a credit score that was used in connection with your home loan application.

Consumer Reporting Agency	Borrower:		Co-Brw:	
Experian P.O. Box 9701 Allen, TX 75013 (P)888-397-3742	Score:	Created:	Score:	Created:
	Factors		Factors	
Model Used:				
Range of Possible Scores ____ to ____				

page 1 of 2

Calyx Form - csid1.frm (11/07)

At least government forms tend to sound straightforward, even if the devil eagerly waits in the details. This one pretty much delivers what it promises. Military borrowers will see their credit scores from all three credit reporting agencies along with the factors affecting each of those scores (even folks with scores in the 800s still have a few negative factors). The disclosure also tells you when your credit was pulled, which is typically part of the prequalification process. This is the first of a two-page document.

Next document: Patriot Act Information Disclosure

PATRIOT ACT
INFORMATION DISCLOSURE

Applicant Name _____

Co-Applicant Name _____

Present Address _____

Mailing Address _____

To help the government fight the funding of terrorism and money laundering activities, Federal law requires all financial institutions to obtain, verify, and record information that identifies each person who opens an account.

What this means for you: When you open an account, we will ask for your name, address, date of birth, and other information that will allow us to identify you. We may also ask to see your driver's license or other identifying documents.

I/we acknowledge that I/we received a copy of this disclosure.

_____   _____
Applicant   Date

_____   _____
Applicant   Date

Calyx Form patactinfo.frm 04/04

A sign-and-date form created post-9/11.

Next document: Good Faith Estimate Provider Relationship

GOOD FAITH ESTIMATE PROVIDER RELATIONSHIP

Applicants: Prepared By:

Property Address:

Application No: Date Prepared:

Lender requires use of the following provider(s) of settlement services (if none are listed, Lender does not require the use of specified providers):

Provider: __Equifax Mortgage Solutions__   Provider: __N/A__
Address: __6 E. Clementon Rd., Suite A-2__   Address: __N/A__
__Gibbsboro, NJ 08026__
Phone: __800-925-7461__   Phone: __N/A__

Services to be rendered by this provider are items number   Services to be rendered by this provider are items number

above and the amounts listed are based upon the charges of this provider. If checked, Lender has the following type of business relationship with this provider:

[ ] The provider is an associate of Lender.   [ ] The provider is an associate of Lender.

[ ] The provider is an affiliate of Lender.   [ ] The provider is an affiliate of Lender.

[ ] The provider is a relative of Lender.   [ ] The provider is a relative of Lender.

[ ] The provider has an employment, franchise or other business relationship with Lender.   [ ] The provider has an employment, franchise or other business relationship with Lender.

[ ] Within the last 12 months, the provider has maintained an account with Lender or had an outstanding loan or credit arrangement with Lender.   [ ] Within the last 12 months, the provider has maintained an account with Lender or had an outstanding loan or credit arrangement with Lender.

[✔] Within the last 12 months, Lender has repeatedly used or required borrowers to use the services of this provider.   [ ] Within the last 12 months, Lender has repeatedly used or required borrowers to use the services of this provider.

Applicant   Date   Applicant   Date

GFE Provider Relationship   Modified 08/10/2010   1 of 1

We'll talk more about the **Good Faith Estimate** in Chapter 5. The GFE is basically a clear, compartmentalized breakdown of the costs and fees associated with your home purchase. Lenders are required to provide a GFE to prospective borrowers once a contract on a home is in place. This particular document discloses whether the lender requires specific service providers to be used for loan settlement purposes.

Next document: Verification of VA Benefits

This document is only for military borrowers who are, were or should be receiving VA disability benefits. It might look nondescript, but it's actually an incredibly important form. One of the few up-front costs that military borrowers have to cover is the **VA Funding Fee**, which we'll look at more closely in Chapter 5. This fee is a percentage of the total loan amount and is usually rolled into the total cost of the loan. Veterans with a service-connected disability and surviving spouses of veterans who died on active duty or because of a service-connected disability are exempt from paying the funding fee.

Next document: Request for Certificate of Eligibility

We've already talked about this one. Lenders eligible to use the automated system will certainly do so, but they still need the veteran to supply a DD-214 and sign the request. Unmarried spouses of deceased eligible veterans don't have to fill out this form, but they are required to complete VA Form 26-1817, the Request for Determination of Loan Guaranty Eligibility — Unmarried Surviving Spouse (they can find the form at http://www.vba.va.gov/pubs/forms/VBA-26-1817-ARE.pdf).

Next document: HUD/VA Addendum to Uniform Residential Loan Application

HUD/VA Addendum to Uniform Residential Loan Application

OMB Approval No.   VA: 2900-0144
HUD: 2502-0059 (expires 11/30/2010)

Part I - Identifying Information (mark the type of application)

1. ☐ VA Application for Home Loan Guaranty   ☐ HUD/FHA Application for Insurance under the National Housing Act

2. Agency Case No: (include any suffix)
3. Lender's Case No.
4. Section of the Act (for HUD cases)

5. Borrower's Name & Present Address (include zip code)

7. Loan Amount (include the UFMIP if for HUD or Funding Fee if for VA) $ 1.00
8. Interest Rate   1.000 %
9. Proposed Maturity   30 yrs.   mos.

10. Discount Amount (only if borrower is permitted to pay)
11. Amount of Up Front Premium $
12a. Amount of Monthly Premium $ /mo.
12b. Term of Monthly Premium months

6. Property Address (including name of subdivision, lot & block no. & zip code)

13. Lender's I.D. Code
14. Sponsor/Agent I.D. Code

15. Lender's Name & Address (include zip code)
16. Name & Address of Sponsor/Agent
17. Lender's Telephone Number

Type or Print all entries clearly

VA: The veteran and the lender hereby apply to the Secretary of Veterans Affairs for Guaranty of the loan described here under Section 3710, Chapter 37, Title 38, United States Code, to the full extent permitted by the veteran's entitlement and severally agree that the Regulations promulgated pursuant to Chapter 37, and in effect on the date of the loan shall govern the rights, duties, and liabilities of the parties.

18. First Time Homebuyer?
   a. ☐ Yes
   b. ☐ No

19. VA Only: Title will be Vested in:
   ☐ Veteran
   ☐ Veteran & Spouse
   ☐ Other (Specify):

20. Purpose of Loan (blocks 9 - 12 are for VA loans only)
1) ☐ Purchase Existing Home Previously Occupied
2) ☐ Finance Improvements to Existing Property
3) ☐ Refinance (Refi.)
4) ☐ Purchase New Condo. Unit
5) ☐ Purchase Existing Condo. Unit
6) ☐ Purchase Existing Home Not Previously Occupied
7) ☐ Construct Home (proceeds to be paid out during construction)
8) ☐ Finance Co-op Purchase
9) ☐ Purchase Permanently Sited Manufactured Home
10) ☐ Purchase Permanently Sited Manufactured Home & Lot
11) ☐ Refi. Permanently Sited Manufactured Home to Buy Lot
12) ☐ Refi. Permanently Sited Manufactured Home/Lot Loan

Part II - Lender's Certification

21. The undersigned lender makes the following certifications to induce the Department of Veterans Affairs to issue a certificate of commitment to guarantee the subject loan or a Loan Guaranty Certificate under Title 38, U. S. Code, or to induce the Department of Housing and Urban Development - Federal Housing Commissioner to issue a firm commitment for mortgage insurance or a Mortgage Insurance Certificate under the National Housing Act.

A. The loan terms furnished in the Uniform Residential Loan Application and this Addendum are true, accurate and complete.

B. The information contained in the Uniform Residential Loan Application and this Addendum was obtained directly from the borrower by an employee of the undersigned lender or its duly authorized agent and is true to the best of the lender's knowledge and belief.

C. The credit report submitted on the subject borrower (and co-borrower, if any) was ordered by the undersigned lender or its duly authorized agent directly from the credit bureau which prepared the report and was received directly from said credit bureau.

D. The verification of employment and verification of deposits were [obtained by the lender or its duly authorized agent and are true] to the best of the lender's knowledge and belief.

Items "H" through "J" are to be completed as applicable for VA loans only.

H. The names and functions of any duly authorized agents who developed on behalf of the lender any of the information or supporting credit data submitted are as follows:

Name & Address

Function (e.g., obtained information on the Uniform Residential Loan Application, ordered credit report, verifications of employment, deposits, etc.)

E. The Uniform Residential Loan Application and this Addendum were signed by the borrower after all sections were completed.

F. This proposed loan to the named borrower meets the income and credit requirements of the governing law in the judgment of the undersigned.

G. To the best of my knowledge and belief, I and my firm and its principals: (1) are not presently debarred, suspended, proposed for debarment, declared ineligible, or voluntarily excluded from covered transactions by any Federal department or agency; (2) have not, within a three-year period preceding this proposal, been convicted of or had a civil judgment rendered against them for (a) commission of fraud or a criminal offense in connection with obtaining, attempting to obtain, or performing a public (Federal, State or local) transaction or contract under a public transaction; (b) violation of Federal or State antitrust statutes or commission of embezzlement, theft, forgery, bribery, falsification or destruction of records, making false statements, or receiving stolen property; (3) are not presently indicted for or otherwise criminally or civilly charged by a governmental entity (Federal, State or local) with commission of any of the offenses enumerated in paragraph G(2) of this certification; and (4) have not, within a three-year period [preceding this application], [had one or more public transactions] (Federal, State or local) terminated for cause or default.

If no agent is shown above, the undersigned lender affirmatively certifies that all information and supporting credit data were obtained directly by the lender.

I. The undersigned lender understands and agrees that it is responsible for the omissions, errors, or acts of agents identified in item H as to the functions with which they are identified.

J. The proposed loan conforms otherwise with the applicable provisions of Title 38, U.S. Code, and of the regulations concerning guaranty or insurance of loans to veterans.

Signature of Officer of Lender
Title of Officer of Lender
Date (mm/dd/yyyy)

Part III - Notices to Borrowers. Public reporting burden for this collection of information is estimated to average 6 minutes per response, including the time for reviewing instructions, searching existing data sources, gathering and maintaining the data needed, and completing and reviewing the collection of information. This agency may not conduct or sponsor, and a person is not required to respond to, a collection information unless that collection displays a valid OMB control number can be located on the OMB Internet page at http://www.whitehouse.gov/omb/library/OMBINV.LIST.OF.AGENCIES.html#LIST.OF.AGENCIES.

Privacy Act Information. The information requested on the Uniform Residential Loan Application and this Addendum is authorized by 38 U.S.C. 3710 (if for DVA) and 12 U.S.C. 1701 et seq. (if for HUD/FHA). The Debt Collection Act of 1982, Pub. Law 97-365, and HUD's Housing and Community Development Act of 1987, 42 U.S.C. 3543, require persons applying for a federally insured or guaranteed loan to furnish his/her social security number (SSN). You must provide all the requested information, including your SSN. HUD and/or VA may conduct a computer match to verify the information you provide. HUD and/or VA may disclose certain information to Federal, State, and local agencies when relevant to civil, criminal, or regulatory investigations and prosecutions. It will not otherwise be disclosed or released outside of HUD or VA, except as required and permitted by law. The information will be used to determine whether you qualify as a mortgagor. Any disclosure of information outside VA or HUD/FHA will be made only as permitted by law. Failure to provide any of the requested information, including SSN, may

page 1

form HUD-92900-A (09/2010)
VA Form 26-1802a

Calyx Form - fhavae1.frm (09/10)

This four-page form is required for any government-backed mortgage. It looks long and confusing, but it's really just the government wanting to learn more about the type of home you're hoping to purchase, if not the actual home in question. As with most of these other forms, your loan officer will likely mark the places that require your response. He or she will handle the rest.

This document also might be the first time you see an interest rate tied to your purchase. Relax, as it's just a placeholder. We'll talk more about interest rates in Chapter 5. For now, know that the loan amount, interest rate and other key figures related to the purchase are all subject to change at this point. We just need to have something on paper.

Next document: VA Amendment to Contract

VA - AMENDMENT TO CONTRACT

Property Address : _____   File No.: _____

It is expressly agreed that notwithstanding any other provisions of this contract, the purchaser shall not incur any penalty by forfeiture of earnest money or otherwise or be obligated to complete the purchase of the property herein, if the contract purchase or the cost exceeds the reasonable value of the property established by the Veterans Administration. The purchaser shall, however, have the privilege and option of proceeding with the consummation of this contract without regard to the amount of the reasonable value established by the Veterans Administration.

_____   _____
Purchaser   Date

_____   _____
Purchaser   Date

_____   _____
Seller   Date

_____   _____
Seller   Date

The purchase agreement must include, or is amended to include, the above statement if the purchase agreement was signed by the Veteran/Applicant prior to his receiving notice of the reasonable value of the subject property.

CALYX Form   Amecon frm 9/99

You might not be shopping for a home yet, but you'll want to sign and date this form. The lender will fill in the exact address once you have one. This is an important document that gives the veteran some flexibility and breathing room in case the home appraisal determines the house is worth less than the contract price. Should that occur, this form ensures the veteran can walk away from the deal with their earnest money.

Next document: Truth in Lending Disclosure Statement

This one is a heavy hitter and among the most significant in the stack. There's a host of laws and regulations governing the TIL, as it's often called. This statement, which is not to be confused with a Good Faith Estimate, provides the veteran with an explicit breakdown of costs, fees and rates associated with the home purchase. There are two pages, so let's briefly look at each in more detail:

Disclosure Statement

TRUTH-IN-LENDING DISCLOSURE STATEMENT
(THIS IS NEITHER A CONTRACT NOR A COMMITMENT TO LEND)

Applicants:
Property Address: Prepared By:

Application No: Date Prepared:

ANNUAL PERCENTAGE RATE The cost of your credit as a yearly rate	FINANCE CHARGE The dollar amount the credit will cost you	AMOUNT FINANCED The amount of credit provided to you or on your behalf	TOTAL OF PAYMENTS The amount you will have paid after making all payments as scheduled
%	$	$ 1.00	$ 1.00

☐ REQUIRED DEPOSIT: The annual percentage rate does not take into account your required deposit

There is no guarantee that you will be able to refinance to lower your rate and payments

INTEREST RATE AND PAYMENT SUMMARY

	Rate & Monthly Payment
Interest Rate	1.000 %
Principal + Interest Payment	
Est. Taxes + Insurance (Escrow)	
	$ 0.00
Total Est. Monthly Payment	**$ 0.00**

☐ DEMAND FEATURE: This obligation has a demand feature.

☐ VARIABLE RATE FEATURE: This loan contains a variable rate feature. A variable rate disclosure has been provided earlier.

SECURITY: You are giving a security interest in:
☐ The goods or property being purchased   ☐ Real property you already own.
FILING FEES: $
LATE CHARGE: If a payment is more than   days late, you will be charged   % of the payment.
PREPAYMENT: If you pay off early, you ☐ may ☐ will not have to pay a penalty.
                                     ☐ may ☐ will not be entitled to a refund of part of the finance charge.

Calyx Form - NEWTIL1.frm (01/11)

This gives prospective borrowers a clear look at what a mortgage loan will really cost them over the course of 15 or 30 years. While it's important to see the finance charge, the key figure on this page is actually the **annual percentage rate**, or APR. This is not the same thing as your loan interest rate (which you'll also hear called the "note rate"). In fact, the APR is a more accurate reflection of what the loan will actually cost you. This rate takes into account the other fees and charges that get tacked on to the cost of your loan over its life. If you're planning to shop around and compare loan offers, this is the figure to look at instead of relying solely on the interest rate.

In years past, this became a hot-button issue because mortgage lenders were essentially hoodwinking borrowers with a bait-and-switch. They would hide fees and charges behind an incredibly low interest rate. The Truth in Lending Act requires lenders to clearly show borrowers the APR, allowing them to make accurate comparisons among other lenders and offers. A loan with a slightly lower interest rate could wind up costing more in the long term because of fees and additional costs.

This is the first page of a two-page document.

Initial Fees Worksheet

FEES WORKSHEET
Fee Details and Summary

Applicants:	Application No:
Prepared By:	Date Prepared:
	Loan Program:

THIS IS NOT A GOOD FAITH ESTIMATE (GFE). This "Fees Worksheet" is provided for informational purposes ONLY, to assist you in determining an estimate of cash that may be required to close and an estimate of your proposed monthly mortgage payment. Actual charges may be more or less, and your transaction may not involve a fee for every item listed.

Total Loan Amount: $ 1   Interest Rate: 1.000 %   Term/Due In: 360 / 360 mths

Fee	Paid To	Paid By (Fee Split**)	Amount	PFC / F / POC
ORIGINATION CHARGES				
OTHER CHARGES				

TOTAL ESTIMATED FUNDS NEEDED TO CLOSE:

				TOTAL ESTIMATED MONTHLY PAYMENT:	
Purchase Price (+)	1.00	Loan Amount (-)	1.00	Principal & Interest	
Alterations (+)				Other Financing (P & I)	
Land (+)				Hazard Insurance	
Refi (incl. debits to be paid off) (+)				Real Estate Taxes	
Est. Prepaid Items/Reserves (+)				Mortgage Insurance	
Est. Closing Costs (+)				Homeowner Assn. Dues	
				Other	
Total Estimated Funds needed to close				Total Monthly Payment	

* PFC = Prepaid Finance Charge   F = FHA Allowable Closing Cost   POC = Paid Outside of Closing
** B = Borrower   S = Seller   Br = Broker   L = Lender   TP = Third Party   C = Correspondent

Calyx Form - feews.frm (09/2010)

This document offers a detailed, line-by-line breakdown of the costs and fees that contribute to that overall APR, including the origination, processing and underwriting charges generated by the lender. Items checked as PFC are prepaid finance charges. Other than the VA Funding Fee, these charges are not rolled into the loan and must be paid at closing. Those marked POC, or paid outside of closing, can also be paid for by the borrower or seller.

We'll cover closing costs in Chapter 5, but it's important to note that the VA allows sellers to cover all loan-related closing costs and pay up to 4 percent of the home's value in concessions, which can include things like the VA Funding Fee and prepaid taxes and insurance.

In many cases the veteran will pay little up front and out-of-pocket when buying a home. The bottom of the worksheet carries a disclaimer that it is for "informational purposes ONLY." That's because lenders don't want prospective borrowers to confuse this with a Good Faith Estimate. That's a formal and legally involved document that becomes more relevant once a borrower is actually under contract on a home. We'll look more closely at the GFE when we talk about closing costs.

Next document:
Report and Certification of Loan Disbursement

This form is filled out almost completely by the lender. Only the third section, which covers a veteran's certifications, requires the borrower's attention. This is the first of a two-page document.

Next document: VA Loan Summary Sheet

VA Department of Veterans Affairs

VA LOAN SUMMARY SHEET

1. VA'S 12-DIGIT LOAN NUMBER

2. VETERAN'S NAME *(First, middle, last)*

3. VETERAN'S SOCIAL SECURITY NUMBER	4. GENDER OF VETERAN *(Check one)* ☐ MALE ☐ FEMALE	5. VETERAN'S DATE OF BIRTH *(mm /dd/ yyyy)*

6A. ETHNICITY	6B. RACE *(May select more than one)*
☐ NOT HISPANIC OR LATINO ☐ HISPANIC OR LATINO	☐ AMERICAN INDIAN OR ALASKAN NATIVE ☐ ASIAN ☐ BLACK OR AFRICAN AMERICAN ☐ NATIVE HAWAIIAN OR PACIFIC ISLANDER ☐ WHITE ☐ UNKNOWN

7. ENTITLEMENT CODE *(01 to 11, from VA Certificate of Eligibility)*	8. AMOUNT OF ENTITLEMENT AVAILABLE *(From VA Certificate of Eligibility)*

9. BRANCH OF SERVICE *(Check one)*
☐ 1. ARMY   ☐ 2. NAVY   ☐ 3. AIR FORCE   ☐ 4. MARINE CORPS   ☐ 5. COAST GUARD   ☐ 6. OTHER

10. MILITARY STATUS *(Check one)*
☐ 1. SEPARATED FROM SERVICE   ☐ 2. IN SERVICE

11. FIRST TIME HOME BUYER *(Check one)*
☐ YES   ☑ NO | This means a veteran who has not previously purchased a home, either by cash, assumption, or new financing.

12. LOAN PROCEDURE *(Check one)*
☐ AUTOMATIC   ☐ AUTO-IRRRL   ☐ VA PRIOR APPROVAL

13. PURPOSE OF LOAN *(Check one)*
☐ 1. HOME (INCLUDES MH ON PERMANENT FOUNDATION)   ☐ 2. MANUFACTURED HOME   ☐ 3. CONDOMINIUM
☐ 4. ALTERATIONS/IMPROVEMENTS   ☐ 5. REFINANCE

14. LOAN CODE *(Check one)*
☐ 1. PURCHASE   ☐ 2. IRRRL (STREAMLINE REFINANCE)   ☐ 3. REGULAR ("Cash-out") REFINANCE
☐ 4. MANUFACTURED HOME REFINANCE   ☐ 5. REFINANCING OF CONSTRUCTION LOAN, LAND SALE CONTRACT OR LOAN ASSUMED AT HIGHER RATE OF INTEREST *(*Maximum guaranty on these loans is $36,000)*

15. PRIOR LOAN TYPE *(Note: Must be completed if Regular ("Cash-out") Refinance is selected in Item 14)*
☐ 1. FHA-FIXED   ☐ 2. FHA-ARM/HARM   ☐ 3. CONVENTIONAL-FIXED   ☐ 4. CONVENTIONAL ARM/HARM
☐ 5. CONVENTIONAL-INTEREST ONLY   ☐ 6. VA-FIXED   ☐ 7. VA-ARM/HARM   ☐ 8. OTHER

16. TYPE OF MORTGAGE *(Check one)*
☐ 0. REGULAR FIXED PAYMENT   ☐ 1. GPM-NEVER TO EXCEED NOV   ☐ 2. OTHER GPMs
☐ 3. GEM   ☐ 4. TEMPORARY BUYDOWN   ☐ 5. HYBRID ARM   ☐ 6. ARM

17. TYPE OF HYBRID-ARM *(NOTE: Must be completed if Hybrid Arm selected in Item 16)*
☐ 3/1   ☐ 5/1   ☐ 7/1   ☐ 10/1

18. TYPE OF OWNERSHIP *(Check one)* ☐ 1. SOLE OWNERSHIP *(VETERAN & SPOUSE OR VETERAN ONLY)* ☐ 2. JOINT - 2 OR MORE VETERANS ☐ 3. JOINT - VETERAN/NON-VETERAN	19. CLOSING DATE *(mm /dd/ yyyy)*

20. PURCHASE PRICE *(N/A for Refinance Loans)*	$	1

21. REASONABLE VALUE *(For IRRRLs - If appraisal has not been done, loan amount of prior VA loan)*	$	

22. ENERGY IMPROVEMENTS *(Check all applicable boxes)*
☐ NONE   ☐ INSTALLATION OF SOLAR HEATING/COOLING
☐ REPLACEMENT OF A MAJOR SYSTEM   ☐ ADDITION OF A NEW FEATURE
☐ INSULATION, CAULKING WEATHER-STRIPPING, ETC.   ☐ OTHER IMPROVEMENTS $

23. LOAN AMOUNT (Purchase - Purchase Price or RV (lesser) + Funding Fee) (Refi - Max 90% LTV + Funding Fee) (IRRRL - Old Loan Payoff + All Closing Costs)	$	1

24. PROPERTY TYPE *(Check one)*
☑ NEITHER   ☐ PUD   ☐ CONDOMINIUM

25. APPRAISAL TYPE *(Check one)*
☐ IND - SINGLE PROPERTY-IND APPRAISAL   ☐ ONE- MASTER CRV CASE (MCRV)   ☐ LAPP - LENDER APPRAISAL
☐ MBL- MANUFACTURED HOME   ☐ HUD - CONVERSION   ☐ PMC - PROP. MGMT. CASE

VA FORM NOV 2008   **26-0286**   SUPERSEDES VA FORM 26-0286, AUG 2006, WHICH WILL NOT BE USED.   Calyx Form - valsa1.frm (04/09)

This one also lives up to its billing. It's a detailed snapshot of your loan profile, covering everything from your military status and the type of mortgage to your loan amount and income information. There's no signature or other borrower action required. It's simply a summary of where things stand with your loan.

This is the first of a two-page document.

Next document: Loan Pricing Agreement Defining Interest Rates and Terms

terminated for any reason by one or more of the above listed agencies applicable to this loan, this commitment/Agreement is void on the announced date and may be renegotiated at (mortgage company's) option.

Borrower's Certification

Please place an X in the appropriate box below to select either Option A or Option B, and initial your choice. Subprime borrowers must select Option C.

OPTION A - LOCK ☐

[____] [____]   I choose to establish the interest rate, discount points and other loan terms which are stated below:
Borrower's Initials

    <u>ALL LOANS</u>

    Interest Rate 5.375%   Discount Points <u>0%</u>   Origination Fee $ 1,379.00
                                    Buyer
    Lock-In Expiration Date: Typically within 60 days of lock-in date; exceptions to notice for rate lock extensions.

    <u>ADJUSTABLE LOANS ONLY</u>

    Margin <u>N/A</u> %   Frequency of Change Period <u>N/A</u>

    Life of Loan Cap <u>N/A</u> %   Per Adjustment Cap <u>N/A</u> %

OPTION B - FLOAT ☒

[____] [____]   I choose to float. In other words, I will accept the interest rate, discount points and other terms/fees in existence at the time I
Borrower's Initials   set my rate. I understand that the interest rate, discount points and other terms stated above in Option A do not apply to this
                  option.

OPTION C - SUBPRIME LOCK (MANDATORY) ☐

[____] [____]   I understand that my loan is a subprime loan and therefore the rate, discount points, terms and fees will be set at some point in
Borrower's Initials   the future **after** a lender/investor has **approved** the loan. I also understand that this rate, discount points, fees and terms will
                  normally only be honored for a specified period of time. I will be informed of what these terms are at the time of loan
                  approval and understand that I may elect to proceed or not to proceed with this transaction at that time. Finally, I understand
                  that any application fees tendered may not be refundable if I elect not to proceed with the transaction.

When you receive a copy of this Agreement signed by an Authorized Representative, you have five (5) business days within which to sign this Agreement. However, once you have selected your option, no other option may be selected and you will have five (5) days to return this Agreement. This Agreement shall only be valid and binding if either Option A, B, or C above have been selected and initialed, your signature, as well as the signature of an Authorized Representative appear below and this Agreement is dated by all parties. If this Agreement is not returned within five (5) days, this Agreement will become null and void and shall have no further obligation under this agreement whatsoever. During that five (5) day period, (mortgage company) will not revoke this Agreement.

This is an enforceable Agreement. Any attempts to breach this Agreement, after it is fully executed, by you or any other person, company, corporation or entity, or attempt to influence you to breach this agreement by any other person or business entity will result in seeking all remedies available, including litigation.

By signing below, all parties acknowledge their understanding and acceptance of the terms and conditions of this Agreement. If you are unsure about any aspect of this Agreement, you should seek the advice of an attorney. THIS AGREEMENT DOES NOT CONSTITUTE A LOAN APPROVAL OR COMMITMENT.

Borrower	Date	Borrower	Date

Authorized Representative's Signature	Date

This three-page document explains what it means to lock your interest rate or float, two terms we'll cover in Chapter 5. We only mention this form now to underscore that, at this point in the process, your choice will be "Option B – Float" by default. The lender can't lock in an interest rate until there's a physical address, so the rate status will always float during loan prequalification, unless the borrower is pursuing a refinance loan.

This is the final page of a three-page document.

Next document: VA Loan Disclosures

VA LOAN DISCLOSURES

FEDERAL COLLECTION POLICY NOTICE

The Federal Government is authorized by law to take any or all of the following actions in the event your VA-guaranteed or VA-financed loan payments become delinquent or you default on your VA-guaranteed or VA-financed loan:

- Your name and account information may be reported to a credit bureau.
- Additional interest and penalty charges may be assessed for the period of time that payment is not made.
- Charges to cover additional administrative costs incurred by the Government to service your account may be assessed.
- Amounts owed to you under Federal programs may be offset.
- Your account may be referred to a private collection agency to collect the amount due.
- Your account may be referred to the Department of Justice for litigation in the courts.
- If you are a current or retired Federal employee, your salary or civil service retirement benefits may be offset.
- Your debt may be referred to the Internal Revenue Service for offset against any amount owed to you as an income tax refund.
- Any written-off debt may be reported to the Internal Revenue Service as taxable income.

All of these actions can and will be used to recover any debts owed the Department of Veterans Affairs when it is determined to be in the best interest of the Government to do so.

Certification

I have read and I understand the actions the Federal Government can take in the event that I fail to make scheduled payments in accordance with the terms and conditions of my agreement to purchase property with a VA-guaranteed or VA-financed loan.

COUNSELING CHECKLIST FOR MILITARY HOMEBUYERS

1. Failure on the part of a borrower on active duty to disclose that he/she expects to leave the area within 12 months due to transfer orders or completion of his/her enlistment period may constitute "bad faith". If your loan is foreclosed under circumstances which include such bad faith, you may be required to repay VA for any loss suffered by the Government under the guaranty. (In ANY case in which VA suffers a loss under guaranty, the loss must be repaid before your loan benefits can be restored to use in obtaining another VA loan.)
2. Although real estate values have historically risen in most areas, there is no assurance that the property for which you are seeking financing will increase in value or even retain its present value.
3. It is possible that you may encounter difficulty in selling your house, recovering your investment or making any profit, particularly if there is an active new home market in the area.
4. Receiving military orders for a permanent change of duty station or an unexpected early discharge due to a reduction in force will not relieve you of your obligation to make your mortgage payments on the first of each month.
5. "Letting the house go back" is NOT an acceptable option. A decision to do so may be considered "bad faith". A foreclosure will result in a bad credit record, a possible debt you will owe to the government and difficulty in getting more credit in the future.
6. If unexpected circumstances lead to difficulty in making your payments, contact your mortgage company promptly. It will be easier to resolve any problems if you act quickly and be open and honest with the mortgage company.
7. YOUR VA LOAN MAY NOT BE ASSUMED WITHOUT THE PRIOR APPROVAL OF VA OR YOUR LENDER.
8. DO NOT BE MISLED! VA does not guarantee the CONDITION of the house which you are buying, whether it is new or previously occupied. VA guarantees only the LOAN. You may talk to many people when you are in the process of buying a house. Particularly with a previously occupied house, you may pick up the impression along the way that you need not be overly concerned about any needed repairs or hidden defects since VA will be sure to find them and require to be repaired. This is NOT TRUE! In every case, ultimately, it is your responsibility to be an informed buyer and to assure yourself that what you are buying is satisfactory to you in all respects. Remember, VA guarantees on the loan – NOT the condition.
9. If you have any doubts about the condition of the house which you are buying, it is in your best interest to seek expert advice before you legally commit yourself in a purchase agreement. Particularly with a previously occupied house, most sellers and their real estate agents are willing to permit you, at your expense, to arrange for an inspection by a qualified residential inspection service. Also, most sellers and agents are willing to negotiate with you concerning what repairs are to be included in the purchase agreement. Steps of this kind can prevent many later problems, disagreements, and major disappointments.
10. Proper maintenance is the best way to protect your home and improve the chance that its value will increase.
11. If you are buying a previously owned house, you should look into making energy efficient improvements. You can add up to $6,000.00 to your VA loan to have energy efficient improvements installed. Consult your lender or the local VA office.

MILITARY ACTIVATION/DEPLOYMENT CERTIFICATION

	Veteran		Co-Borrower	
1. I am currently a member of a United States Military Reserve or National Guard Unit.	☐ Yes	☐ No	☐ Yes	☐ No
2. I am a member of a United States Military Reserve or National Guard Unit. As of this date, I have not been notified of the mobilization of my military unit.	☐ Yes	☐ No	☐ Yes	☐ No

This one is where it really starts to feel a bit repetitive. At least you're near the end. The disclosures form spells out what the government can do if your loan becomes delinquent or goes into default. The prospective borrower also has to answer questions about disability benefits, education loans and debt. This form also explains the VA's **Energy Efficient Mortgage** program, which we'll talk about in Chapter 5.

This is the first of a two-page document.

Last document: Mortgage Broker Fee Agreement and Disclosure

MORTGAGE BROKER FEE AGREEMENT AND DISCLOSURE
Do not pay any fees before entering into this agreement with your Broker.

BROKER SERVICES – A mortgage broker charges fees to arrange a loan from a lender who will fund the loan. You have engaged VAMortgageCenter.com ("Broker") to arrange a loan for you in the amount of $---- (Note: For a line of credit, the loan amount is the maximum credit limit on the line).

Broker will assist you in obtaining a loan, but Broker does not distribute the products of all lenders. Be sure that you understand and are satisfied with the product and terms Broker arranges for you.

BROKER FEES - You agree to directly pay Broker the following fees:

    Application Fee: $----
    Processing Fee: $----
    Other: $---- (Origination Fee, Underwriting Fee)
    Broker Fee (Points):$---- This fee will not exceed --% of your loan amount

These fees will be paid with cash you must bring to closing, or, depending on your loan approval, you may include some or all of these fees in your loan amount and pay your Broker at closing out of your loan proceeds.

You also agree that the lender may pay your Broker additional fees. Any additional fees paid by the lender to Broker will increase the interest rate on your loan beyond what the interest rate would be if some or all of these fees were paid directly by you. Based on current market rates and your current loan request, the lender may pay Broker $----, but it may go up to $---- based on your current loan amount of $----. In no event will the lender pay the Broker more than 3.50% of your loan amount.

Once your interest rate is locked and your loan amount and terms are finalized, your Broker will be able to tell you the exact amount of all fees.

BASED ON A LOAN AMOUNT OF $----, THE MAXIMUM AMOUNT OF FEES THE BROKER MAY RECEIVE AT CLOSING IS $----.

THE FEES IN THIS AGREEMENT ARE FOR BROKER SERVICES ONLY AND DO NOT INCLUDE OTHER CLOSING COSTS OR CREDITS FROM BROKER OR OTHER PARTIES. See your "Good Faith Estimate of Closing Costs". (Note: If your application is for a line of credit, you will not receive a Good Faith Estimate. Rather, at the time of application, you will receive an estimate of the closing fees. You may also request an itemization of those fees.)

DO NOT SIGN THIS DOCUMENT IF YOU DO NOT UNDERSTAND IT.

Borrower:_____   Co-Borrower:_____
Signature:_____   Signature:_____
Date:_____   Date:_____

by: Signature:_____   Address:_____
Printed Name:_____   _____
Title:_____ Date:_____   Phone:_____

MBFA Mortgage Broker Fee Agreement and Disclosure   1 of 1

Like most Americans, mortgage industry folks don't work for free. We'll look more closely at how they get paid in Chapter 4. This form shows what we will charge for our services. These fees are among those that can be paid for by the seller. And quite often that's exactly what happens.

Loan Preapproval

Except for a few lender-specific forms likely to be thrown in, that's the meat of the loan prequalification packet. There's no deadline to return the forms, although veterans interested in purchasing sooner rather than later should act with some expediency. We'll close the file on a prospective borrower who doesn't return the packet. It can be reopened at a later date, but loan files that are returned can be kept open indefinitely. That means we can spring into action whenever you're ready.

Plus, wait too long and you might tempt the credit gods. The lender will have to pull your credit again after 120 days.

Of course, a loan officer will be sure to remind you that interest rates fluctuate constantly and that the sooner you act the better. And there's definitely a lot of truth in there, especially as it relates to interest rates. We'll look much more closely at rates later on, but it's important to recognize that they really do change constantly, and, of course, not always in a downward, borrower-friendly direction.

Once everything is back in the lender's hands, the loan officer can re-input the verified information and get a more complete picture. Maybe the veteran who claimed to earn $50,000 a year actually makes $45,000, which causes his debt-to-income ratio to climb a couple percentage points.

These kinds of discrepancies usually fail to make a huge difference. The nature of the Automated Underwriting System gives lenders some room to play with the numbers, so to speak, and make things work for the veteran, provided there are no major problems involving income, DTI ratio or residual income.

For example, the Automated Underwriting System might bounce an application for a $325,000 loan now that it has a more complete picture of a veteran's finances. In that case, the loan officer simply re-inputs the same information with a lower loan amount, say $300,000, and tries again to get AUS approval.

As we mentioned earlier, this plug-and-play method can continue until the loan officer finds a workable loan amount. Part of a loan officer's job is to be a problem solver. And that's why they'll tweak the numbers and provide suggestions in order to find a solution. They might suggest paying off a debt, using a co-borrower or coming up with a down payment. In most cases, these folks know what will and what will not be approved at first glance.

Military borrowers should approach preapproval without fear. Veterans who sail through the preapproval process with our company receive a letter giving them the go-ahead to enter into a purchase contract up to a specific loan amount. Here's a sample of what the letter typically looks like:

John Smith
123 Main St.
Anywhere, USA

November 29, 2012

Dear John Smith,

Congratulations, your VA loan request has been pre-approved based on the current application. You are pre-approved for a purchase price of up to $380,000. The loan is contingent upon the following:

1. Acceptable appraisal to support the value on signed purchase agreement
2. Acceptable title policy
3. Acceptable flood certification
4. Clear termite inspection
5. Sellers assistance for closing costs
6. Verification of Rent
7. Final underwriting approval

This pre-approval is subject to expire should any of the credit information obtained from the initial application change. Any increase in assets or income will not adversely affect this pre approval.

Thank you for allowing Veterans United Home Loans to provide you with service. Please contact me with any questions you may have regarding this pre-approval.

Sincerely,

Jeff Magsamen
Sr. Loan Specialist
NMLS 50787

800-814-1103 ext. 3249
573-489-6967 mobile
201-215-9530 efax
Jeffm@veteransunited.com

Veterans United Home Loans - NMLS 1907
A VA Approved Lender; Not a Government Agency
2101 Chapel Plaza, Suite 107 Columbia, MO 65203
Office: 800-405-6682
veteransunited.com

EQUAL OPPORTUNITY LENDER

But borrowers should also recognize that just as prequalification and preapproval aren't the same thing, neither are preapproval and loan approval. Preapproval isn't a guarantee or any kind of binding contract. It's an expression of confidence that the borrower can handle the financial obligations that come with a particular loan amount.

There's a reason that "pre-" prefix is there.

Typically included with the preapproval letter is a list of conditions the borrower must meet in order to secure full loan approval. This gives the veteran a clear understanding of the documents and information that still need to be verified or obtained. For example, this sample preapproval letter lists seven outstanding areas, five of which are part of almost every preapproval:

- Acceptable appraisal to support the value on signed purchase agreement
- Acceptable title policy
- Acceptable flood certification
- Clear termite inspection
- Final underwriting approval

At minimum, these five issues will have to be addressed in order for VA borrowers to receive full loan approval. There certainly might be more paperwork and documentation necessary as the process rolls on. For now, though, a veteran with this preapproval letter in hand is ready to hit the streets and ink a purchase contract on a house.

Manual Underwriting

For some veterans, the process might work a little differently. There are times when an AUS approval isn't possible for a prospective borrower. Almost always, the reason why relates to the veteran's credit history. While bankruptcy and foreclosure aren't deal breakers for a VA loan, prospective borrowers with a history of one or both are not likely to get AUS approval.

In that case, the loan file must be underwritten manually. These borrowers are in line to face significantly more scrutiny because the lender wants to ensure the veteran represents a safe investment.

Loan officers will try to determine whether you need a manual underwrite during the prequalification process.

Today, the vast majority of VA loans are processed through an AUS. Part of it is efficiency and ease. But it's also because lenders like to ensure they're not exposed to financial harm if their loans go bad.

The VA guaranty only extends to qualified lenders who issue a loan that meets agency guidelines. If a lender goes beyond VA guidelines and issues a loan that ultimately defaults, the VA is under no obligation to cover its guaranty.

That means lenders will be extremely cautious — and routinely rigorous — when considering a manual underwrite. In most cases, the veteran will need to have a solid credit score and debt-to-income ratio in order to proceed. Most lenders have their own distinct guidelines for working with manual underwrites. For example, some will bounce an application automatically if the veteran's debt-to-income ratio is above the VA's 41 percent guideline.

Others are more lenient. Each case is different, except for one common thread: A human underwriter will ask for documents upon documents when examining the application of a veteran closer to the edge.

We do hundreds of manual underwrites each year. The Automated Underwriting System is safe, but a manual underwrite is still in many ways the most thorough method.

Either way, once borrowers have an approval in hand, it's time to look for a house.

Borrower Spotlight: Cameron Calhoon

Air Force Load Master Utilizes Basic Allowance for Housing (BAH)
to Nab His First Home

Destin, Fla. — Military service was always in the cards for Staff
Sgt. Cameron Calhoon.

Homeownership seemed a much less certain path.

Growing up in California, at the southern edges of Sequoia
National Forest, he heard stories of his great-grandfather, a
Navy sailor, and his grandfather, an Air Force fireman. By the
time he turned 21, Cameron was ready to continue the family
tradition.

He enlisted in the Air Force and settled at Pope Air Force
Base in North Carolina.

But he quickly learned that his stay at the sprawling base
would be a limited engagement. Days after his arrival in the
fall of 2005, Pope AFB landed on the Base Realignment and
Closure (BRAC) list of installations to be shuttered.

Cameron had planned to pursue a home purchase in North
Carolina, but word of the BRAC decision forced him to recon-
sider. He didn't see a lot of sense in moving forward, given that
he could get reassigned at a moment's notice.

Instead, Cameron spent the first two years living on base
before moving in with his sister, who lived in nearby Fayette-
ville. Three years passed.

Finally, Cameron, a C-130 load master, received his new
orders in December 2009. He would be moving in 12 months
to Hurlburt Field, in the shadow of Elgin Air Force Base in
northwestern Florida.

The shift would bring newfound certainty. The nature
of Cameron's job meant that Elgin was the only base in the

country where he could work. There was little doubt he would be there for years to come.

He started looking for homes online in February, but the process fizzled after just a couple months. Cameron had to leave in early spring for what was slated to be 60 days of specialized training. He planned to revisit his home search in earnest upon his return.

But delays and other problems stretched his training to 120 days. He finished in August, with just four months remaining until his departure day.

This time, he decided to dive into the homebuying process full bore.

He had heard of the VA home loan program but didn't know much about mortgages and buying a home. Most of what he found online only confused him.

So, it was with some relief that his online search led him to Veterans United Home Loans. He decided to call and talk with a VA loan specialist.

Cameron was connected with loan officer Mike Mange. With that, his confusion and questions came to rest.

Mike walked Cameron through the process of loan preapproval.

Cameron learned within minutes that he was eligible for a VA loan and had a solid sense of how much home he could afford. While he had saved a solid chunk of change over the last five years, Cameron would be able to purchase a home with no money down.

He would also be able to use his Basic Allowance for Housing to defray some or all of his mortgage expenses. BAH payments represent a verifiable and reliable income stream that can be used to calculate a prospective borrower's debt-to-income ratio, a key factor in loan underwriting.

Mike then connected Cameron to a Destin Realtor through Veterans United's unique partnership with Veterans United Realty. Cameron spent a week in Destin in the fall. He looked at more than two dozen houses in a two-day frenzy. One of the first houses he and his girlfriend looked at stuck in their minds during the visit. The original owners were an older couple who did a great job keeping the home up to date.

On his third day in Destin, Cameron decided to put down an offer on the home. He received and accepted a counteroffer that was a mere $600 off his asking price.

As the homebuying process moved forward, Cameron again found guidance and constant updates in Mike.

"He's the most helpful person I have ever encountered," Cameron said. "I would always be able to reach him, every time I needed to talk to him."

The home passed a couple inspections, including one for wind mitigation, a necessity in hurricane-prone regions. Cameron closed on the home just a few weeks after inking the contract.

Cameron's BAH completely covers his $871 monthly mortgage payment, leaving enough to pay his electric bill. His flight pay covers the rest of the utilities.

He has friends in nearby apartments who pay more per month in rent than his mortgage.

And he has one piece of advice for veterans and service members considering a home purchase: "I would send them to Mike," Cameron said. "They just need to call you guys. That's way easier."

CHAPTER 4:
PURCHASING A HOME WITH A VA LOAN

Once you're preapproved, the next step is to find a house that meets your needs and your budget. Buying a home is one of the biggest and most personal investments a veteran will ever make. It's also a process that comes with its own language, complexities and pitfalls.

That's one of the main reasons we recommend veterans relinquish any ideas they have about navigating the process alone.

Use a **Realtor** when purchasing a home. It's that simple.

Actually, it's almost that simple.

Use a Realtor who understands VA loans.

Finding a Realtor who's worked with military buyers in the past and has familiarity with the VA home loan program can make a huge difference for borrowers. Before we start parsing between Realtors, let's first look more closely at why they're important in general.

Why Bother with a Realtor?

How about this one: What's a Realtor? Maybe we should start there.

The term is actually trademarked. We're not just using the capital "R" for effect. A Realtor is a real estate agent who's a member of the National Association of Realtors, a professional organization with more than 995,000 members. Realtors pledge to abide by a strict code of ethics and uniform standards of practice. Every Realtor is a real estate agent, but not every real estate agent is a Realtor.

Does the capital "R" make a big difference? It really depends on the individual agent. There are other impressive real estate associations and organizations out there. There are also plenty of honest and effective independent agents who aren't affiliated with a trade group. Again, it often comes down to comfort, communication and trust. Since we work primarily with Realtors, we'll stick with the capital "R" moving forward.

So why bother? There's a litany of reasons, but we'll look at a few of the big ones:

- **Expertise**

  Realtors help people purchase homes every day. This is their business, their profession. In contrast, buying a home is something you'll probably do a couple times in your life at most. It's true the Internet has taken much of the mystery out of the process. But we still think it's better to have a trained, professional advocate to navigate the process, order inspections, help craft an offer and finalize the contract. Realtors have ready access to information on comparable home sales, school districts, zoning and land use regulations and all kinds of community-related data.

- **Hunting for Houses**

  Realtors will have access to the **Multiple Listing Service**, or MLS, in your area. This reaches into corners and crevices the everyday Internet cannot. Realtors can use the MLS's exhaustive categorizing to create custom searches for your dream home. They can get constant updates whenever a home that meets your parameters hits the listings. That doesn't mean you can't hunt for houses on your own. Just be sure to have your Realtor on speed dial.

- **You Have an Advocate**
  In most cases, the person selling the home will be using another Realtor, a listing agent, to showcase the property and find a buyer. His or her sole job is to get the best offer possible from a qualified buyer. It's a good idea to have an expert who can advocate for you and, if necessary, go toe-to-toe with the listing agent. Your Realtor, the **buyer's agent**, is there as a surrogate, charged with acting in your best interests.

- **It Costs Zero Dollars**
  It's not because Realtors work for free. They don't. But throughout most of the country, the person buying the house pays nothing to use a Realtor. Instead, the agent working on your behalf will split a sales commission with the agent who listed the property on behalf of the seller. Leveraging a Realtor's expertise and access costs a borrower nothing. If you have any doubt on that, simply ask the agent or call the office. Look elsewhere if you don't get a straight answer.

About 90 percent of homebuyers use a real estate agent or broker, according to the National Association of Realtors. Does that mean you have to?

No.

You can certainly spend time scouring real estate sites and home listings online. The Internet has a wealth of information that has helped to demystify the homebuying process. Being an educated buyer is key to getting the best deal possible. But it doesn't replace the expertise and familiarity that comes with having a Realtor.

If nothing else, consider the size and scope of this investment. You're getting ready to make a huge purchase — maybe it's $150,000, or $350,000, or even more. Why go it alone?

Now Dig a Bit Deeper

That said, all real estate agents aren't created equal. It might not matter too much if you're purchasing with a conventional, run-of-the-mill loan. But the VA loan is a unique tool that requires specialized knowledge.

The VA mandates that a home have proper maintenance and be in good repair. Condos and homes that are part of an association require VA approval. Private wells, septic systems, termite inspections and shared maintenance of roadways all have specific VA guidelines. A good buyer's agent will know this.

But many do not.

So, it's not enough to find a Realtor. We urge military borrowers — implore, really — to take the time to track down an agent who's worked with VA loans and understands their demands. It's not always an easy task.

Sometimes, it's because the veteran is pulled by forces closer to home: a cousin, a former coach or a friend from church happens to be a Realtor. Those bonds are hard to break, and it's understandable if you sacrifice VA expertise for the sake of the social contract.

But, more often than not, it's difficult because real estate agents have varying degrees of exposure to military borrowers and the intricacies of the VA Loan Guaranty program. In military-dense parts of the country, finding a Realtor who's recently closed VA loans shouldn't present much of a problem.

Veterans who live near military installations have a distinct advantage. Expertise with VA loans is a competitive advantage for Realtors in these areas, and military borrowers should have a much easier time finding a qualified agent. In these parts, good Realtors won't be shy when it comes to advertising their VA loan expertise.

It then becomes a matter of finding the right VA-savvy Realtor. There are myriad ways to evaluate them, but it's tough to provide prospective borrowers with a black-and-white diagram for how to do so.

"Don't just open the phone book and say, 'I'm going to choose this person,'" said Ruben Moya, who with his wife, Kerry, an Air Force veteran, purchased their Nevada home with a VA loan. "Do your homework on this person. Make sure they're looking out for your best interests. It's one of the biggest investments in your life."

In general, the more listings the agent has, the higher up the food chain he or she probably is. More listings mean more closings, which means more negotiation experience and closing expertise. But remember that you're in search of a buyer's agent. You can't call the Realtor who's listing a property you're smitten with and expect him or her to represent you.

Yes, there are factors and variables to consider. In the end, though, it's usually best to go with your gut. Spend time talking with a couple promising Realtors who clearly understand the rigors and incredible benefits of the VA loan. Let comfort, rapport and trust be your guides.

But what about everywhere else?

Veterans make up fewer than 13 percent of the population in almost a dozen states, from California and Texas to Illinois and New York.

It can be much more of a struggle to find Realtors who have experience closing VA loans in areas with minimal veteran populations. What's worse is that military borrowers in these communities often find flat-out resistance to VA loans from agents who don't really understand how the program works in today's marketplace.

Myths and Misconceptions

Some of that resistance is justified. Or, at least, it was.

For years, VA loans have been dogged by a reputation as bureaucratic, time-sucking black holes. A lot of it goes back to the VA of yesteryear, which certainly had some institutional problems.

Part of that was the nature of doing things by hand. Part of it, to be quite honest, was the nature of a giant governmental agency doing business.

At the same time, some major pillars of the VA's loan program have long been misunderstood or mischaracterized. The agency caps what a veteran can pay in closing costs and up-front fees, a significant benefit that helps extend housing opportunities to those who might not otherwise have the financial ability. It's another small way to thank those who have served.

But they're also costs that have to be covered. The lender can step in and take care of them, but it's usually the seller who winds up footing the bill for a decent chunk of those closing costs. In the past, that's been a big hurdle for some agents to scale. Many, understandably, were worried about losing commissions or getting tied up for weeks with a slow-moving bureaucracy.

The VA appraisal process is another big one. It's a fair but stringent process that puts a premium on a veteran's health and safety. A VA appraisal is more thorough than a typical appraisal and mandates repairs that need to be made in order to meet agency guidelines.

There are always exceptions, but most VA loans close within a standard 30- to 45-day window. The way appraisals are ordered has changed in recent years, and the agency's standards are posted online for all to see.

But Realtors who haven't closed a VA loan in years might be needlessly concerned about appraisals and timing. That's not only a shame but a huge disserve to military borrowers hoping to capitalize on the benefits earned by their service.

And now you can begin to see the hurdles possibly lurking.

Military borrowers in those low-density areas will find agents fluent in the language of conventional loans. You'll also find a good deal who speak FHA. But there might be a lot of silent shrugs when it comes to VA loans.

Or worse — the agent will try to talk you out of even considering your VA loan benefits.

Finding an Agent Who Speaks VA

If you can find local agents who tout their experience with VA loans online or in traditional advertisements, consider starting there. Another good place is within your own community of military colleagues. Check with people at the local VFW or American Legion post. Ask every home-owning veteran you come across: Did you use a VA loan and, if so, who helped you with it?

If those paths fail to turn up anything meaningful, your best bet might be to focus on *who* a Realtor knows instead of *what* a Realtor knows. In this case, look for Realtors who work with established lenders that possess a track record of helping military borrowers navigate the VA process. An experienced loan officer who understands VA loans can more than make up for an inexperienced agent.

Still, it's not the most ideal situation. Realtors are there on the ground, showing houses and shepherding veterans through the process in person. Those who work frequently with military borrowers can wind up making a huge difference on behalf of their clients. Agents who can maneuver through the agency's procedures and requirements can save borrowers from big-time hassles and headaches on things like appraisals and property requirements (we'll cover both in this chapter).

Army veteran Calvin Eley is a great example.

He and his fiancée, Lynnecia Johnson, came to us in 2010 hoping to purchase a home in northern Maryland. The couple had done some cursory home shopping and, given their budget, figured a townhome would be their only real option. They opted to take advantage of Veterans United Realty, our national network of more than 5,000 real estate agents who work routinely with military buyers. Borrowers who use a VUR agent can receive up to $5,000 upon closing.

Through their loan officer, the couple contacted a VUR agent who took them through dozens of homes, pointing out deficiencies and issues that would prove problematic for the VA. The agent ultimately found a single-family home that met the couple's needs and actually came in below their price point.

"The home we found, I believe we were the only ones who had a chance to walk through and see it," Lynnecia said. "It went on the market, [our agent] notified us the same day, we saw it and put in an offer. She was able to steer us in the right direction as far as finding a home that the VA would approve."

We want to underscore that any military borrower can utilize Veterans United Realty. It's not a service solely reserved for our customers, and it's completely free. Let this be another avenue to explore if your search for a local VA-savvy agent comes up dry.

Why Experience Matters

Calvin and Lynnecia's experience helps explain in part why it's so important to work with agents and loan officers who know VA loans. Who knows how much time and money they could have wasted if their Realtor hadn't steered them from properties that were likely to get bounced by the VA? That expertise saved the couple hundreds of dollars on needless appraisal fees alone.

Appraisals and inspections are key parts of the home-purchasing process regardless of how it's being funded. But these two take on a heightened degree of importance for military borrowers using a VA loan.

Of all the historical gripes against the VA Loan Guaranty program, the appraisal process is perhaps the most frequent target. It's also often the most misunderstood. We'll take a closer look shortly.

The VA has some firm requirements and standards when it comes to home appraisals. Agents and sellers burned by the process often see it as punitive and arbitrary. It's really anything but.

The entire focus is on ensuring the health and safety of veterans and their families. The VA isn't going to guaranty a loan on a home with major issues that could jeopardize the safety of its inhabitants.

Realtors who know the VA's method and process can help veterans avoid pitfalls and potential problems long before they arise. But sometimes there's simply no way to know there's a problem until appraisers and inspectors start digging around and looking at the innards of the pending home purchase.

Signing a Purchase Agreement

There are books, pamphlets and web pages galore dedicated to teaching borrowers how to negotiate with sellers for their dream home. They're all a bit beyond the scope here, but there is one thing — other than relying on the expertise of your Realtor — that we would stress: Don't be inflexible. Locking yourself into a single property or a hard-and-fast price might wind up limiting your options.

The fruits of negotiation and of investing in an experienced Realtor should pay off in a contract that benefits both parties. Some sellers have historically argued that the deck is stacked against them when it comes to VA loans. We'll look more closely at closing costs in the next chapter, but it's certainly true that VA borrowers reap a ton of benefits and save a good chunk of change compared to most conventional buyers.

The terms of a deal come together in a contract of sale, which is also known as a **purchase agreement**. It's exactly that: You're agreeing to purchase a home. You're not actually purchasing it quite yet. That's going to require a few more steps that, if all goes well, culminate in your lender transferring a huge pile of money to the seller.

Before we get there, let's take a closer look at purchase agreements.

This is a formal legal document that requires signatures from the buyer and the seller. In most cases, the buyer will put down earnest money when the time comes to ink a purchase agreement.

Otherwise, a purchase agreement typically includes information regarding:

- **Purchase Price**

  Veterans should make sure the contract explains that the price isn't subject to change. Those using a VA loan to build a home may find resistance from contractors, who will want some flexibility because the cost of materials can increase. In that case, it's best to check with a legal expert before signing your name. But, again, this isn't much of an issue at present, given the reluctance among VA lenders to issue construction loans.

- **A Timetable**

  This protective measure basically gives the seller a brief window of time to respond to the offer. Otherwise, you're inviting the seller to use your offer as a bargaining chip to stir up a better deal.

- **Closing Costs**

  Again, we'll cover this important topic in the next chapter. The purchase agreement should spell out how the closing costs will be covered. Sellers often wind up paying most if not all of a VA borrower's closing costs.

- **Down Payment**

  The agreement usually specifies the borrower's down payment and how he or she is financing the remainder. Nine out of 10 VA buyers don't have a down payment, but the agreement also should detail how and when the purchase will be financed.

- **Transfer Date**

  This is always subject to change but purchase agreements include a specific date that the seller must transfer the property to the purchaser. Closing dates in a purchase agreement are not set in stone.

- **Responsible Party**

  Make sure the contract explains who is responsible for the property from the time the contract is signed until it's transferred to the buyer. In most cases the seller will retain control, but it's always a good idea to make sure the language is correct.

- **Additional Items**

  Veterans and buyers in general often want to buy more than the house. They'll take the furniture, appliances and other items that aren't part of the home's permanent structure. Many first-time buyers are surprised to discover some items don't necessarily come with the home. Anything the buyer wants to purchase should be included in the purchase agreement. But anything of value will have to be included as part of the seller's 4 percent cap on concessions, which we'll discuss later in more detail.

- **Mortgage Protection**

  This is a common one that basically says the veteran isn't on the hook for buying the house if his or her loan doesn't come through as specified.

- **Home Inspections**

  Be sure to include a stipulation that gives you the right to pay for a home inspection. Clauses can also be inserted to provide the borrower with a way out if the home inspection uncovers problems with the property.

- **Existing Home Sale**

  This one can be especially important for military borrowers who face frequent relocation. Veterans who already own a home may want to see if they can make the new purchase contingent upon their ability to sell their current property.

The reality is there isn't a standard purchase agreement. They're subject to change based on the whims of individual buyers and sellers. As with any contract, there's no guarantee the seller will sign off on your proposed stipulations, but reasonable ones are always worth a shot.

The most important thing is to ensure you're protected financially as much as possible.

That's why having an attorney look over the purchase agreement can be an important step. In general, attorneys play varying roles in the homebuying process, often depending on where you're purchasing. Some states require that attorneys examine and OK all mortgage papers before a transaction can be official. Others have no mandate and allow buyers and sellers to navigate the process themselves.

This is typically a cost borne by the veteran and not something you can roll into the cost of the loan or expect the seller to cover. Military buyers may not need to spend the extra cash when it's a straightforward, relatively no-nonsense purchase agreement. But if things start to get confusing or loaded with contingencies and clauses, it's certainly something to consider.

Once the purchase agreement is hammered out, agreed upon and signed, it's time to celebrate, albeit cautiously. You can't buy a house without a contract, but having a contract doesn't mean you've bought yourself a house.

VA Appraisals

Let's deal with the semantics first: Appraisals and inspections are not the same thing.

Once you've entered into a purchase agreement, the lender is going to order an appraisal. Today, VA **appraisals** are ordered automatically and electronically through the **Lender Appraisal Processing Program**, also known as LAPP.

This computerized system was created to modernize the appraisal process by allowing authorized lenders to directly order, receive and handle appraisals. LAPP isn't a perfect program, but it's another major signpost of the VA's commitment to streamlining and efficiency.

For military borrowers, the appraisal has two primary and essential functions: determining the value of the property you intend to purchase or refinance, and ensuring it meets the agency's **Minimum Property Requirements**.

The Minimum Property Requirements, or MPRs, are the basic health and safety conditions the property must meet in order to secure a VA guaranty. They're also the conditions that make the home sellable. A home purchase can go off the rails in a hurry if the property doesn't live up to these conditions, which we'll look at shortly in greater detail.

First, though, let's look more closely at the valuation aspect of the process.

Appraisers are charged with determining the market value of the property in question. Defining "market value" can be a nebulous task, but it's generally considered the price two people are willing to settle on when neither is under any pressure to purchase or sell the property. You might also hear VA loan experts refer to it as "appraised value" or sometimes "reasonable value."

There's a host of things that can change or play with a home's market value. The house's condition and architectural style can play a role. So do the number of bedrooms and the type of water and sewer system. What about the location and the school district?

No doubt.

Given that array of contributing factors, appraisers most often turn to comparable home sales to generate an idea of the property's market value. The appraiser will start by tracking down similar nearby properties that have sold recently. The VA recommends finding **comparable sales**, or "comps," from within the past six months and never more than the previous 12 months.

Obviously, the more similarities they have with the property being appraised the better. It's also important for appraisers to get the whole story behind each of those potentially comparable sales. Maybe the seller recently got divorced and was in a hurry to sell for cheap, or perhaps there was a crush of buyers and the winner wound up paying significantly above the asking price. Those are circumstances that shouldn't affect the market value of the property you hope to purchase.

In an ideal world, the appraiser would find three homes exactly like the one you're under contract to buy: the same number of bedrooms with the same architectural style and square footage all in the same neighborhood. But the real world is rarely that tidy.

What ultimately happens is that the appraiser makes adjustments and allowances to compensate for one comparable's smaller size or slightly less desirable location. VA appraisers must select what they believe are the three best comps and adjust the sales price of each for those recognized adjustments and differences. Appraisers have to issue detailed explanations if they rely on sales that strain compatibility with the other comps included in the report.

The VA appraisal also has to include other important items, like location maps, photographs of both the home in question and the comparables and perimeter sketches.

After an appraiser has pored over all the documentation and information, he or she will create an estimate of the home's market value. This estimate will eventually help the lender's **staff appraisal reviewer**, or SAR, issue a final **Notice of Value** for the home. The NOV is an industry term, and you might hear it called by its old name, the Certificate of Reasonable Value, or CRV.

Here's a simple expression to explain the acronym soup: NOV = CRV = market value.

No matter what you call it, the appraisal is a big deal. And here's why: This ultimately determines your final loan amount. It might also have a big say in whether you actually become a homeowner, at least with the property you had in mind.

We'll talk more about SARs and their role in the next chapter. It turns out they're just as important as the appraiser, if not more so.

For now, though, the most important issue here is the purchase price of the home versus its appraised value. On one hand, veterans are overjoyed when the home they agreed to purchase for $250,000 winds up appraised at $275,000.

That extra $25,000 isn't real equity and can't somehow turn into real dollars. But it's certainly a consideration down the road if the veteran ultimately decides to sell or refinance.

The flip side — the frightening side, really — is when the NOV is *lower than* the purchase price. This phenomenon triggers a new wave of concerns and issues for veterans and their families.

If the home you've agreed to purchase for $250,000 is appraised at $240,000, the lender isn't going to selflessly cover that $10,000 gap. Lenders are going to fund whatever is lowest between the sales price and the appraised value.

That means the buyer is on the hook for the difference.

This kind of devastating discrepancy does happen. And it's crushing to veterans and prospective homebuyers. Making up the difference between the sales price and the appraised value can be incredibly difficult if not downright impossible, especially for military borrowers, most of who come to the table with little in the way of liquidity.

Today, most purchase agreements include some type of "out clause" that allows the borrower to walk away from the purchase if the appraisal comes back lower than the sales price. This is where the VA Amendment to Contract document that borrowers sign during the loan application process comes into play.

Borrowers can also seek what's known as a "Reconsideration of Value" when there's a question about the Notice of Value. A reconsideration is basically an appeal to include additional comparable home sales not considered in the initial appraisal. Veterans have to make this appeal in writing and present compelling evidence of at least three other comparable home sales that weren't used in the appraisal.

Some lenders may be open to offsetting the difference in exchange for the borrower taking a higher interest rate.

Borrowers can always try to renegotiate with the seller, too. In fact, that's one of the more common solutions, especially in today's real estate environment. Often, sellers will lower their asking price to meet the appraised value and eliminate some of the concessions they would normally pay on the back end of the deal. Sellers asking $350,000 for a home valued at $315,000 certainly have diminished leverage when it comes to negotiating.

Appraisals are required in order for a loan to receive a VA guaranty. It's the only real way for the agency to ascertain the market value and to ensure that the veteran's prospective purchase is in an acceptable condition. But there are some conditions that make a property ineligible for a VA appraisal.

This is another area where having a VA-savvy Realtor can save borrowers time and money.

Properties Ineligible for a VA Appraisal

In most cases, veterans will have no problem securing a VA appraisal for the home they want to purchase. But there are some exceptions that knock a property into the "ineligible" category. The bulk of these ineligible properties are homes in potentially hazardous locations. According to the VA, a property isn't eligible for an appraisal if it's located in:

- Some Special Flood Hazard Areas (SFHA). These are federally designated areas in 100-year floodplains. In these locations, a property isn't eligible if there's no flood insurance available or if it's new construction where the lowest floor is below the 100-year flood level.

- Areas that flood routinely, no matter if they're listed as SFHA with the Federal Emergency Management Agency (FEMA). Regular flooding would violate the Minimum Property Requirements, which we'll get into shortly.

- An area within a Coastal Barrier Resources System. These barriers protect marine habitats and help protect the mainland against storms and erosion along the nation's coastline. Since the early 1980s, Congress has restricted new development and building in these areas, which include parts of the Eastern Seaboard, the Great Lakes and the Gulf Coast.

- Some especially loud airport noise zones.

- Some areas susceptible to problems with geological or soil instability, including earthquakes and landslides. This applies only to homes that are new, proposed or currently under construction. The property can be deemed eligible if the builder can adequately document that the site isn't affected or that the problem is addressed in the building's engineering and design.

Condominiums are another tricky spot. We talked earlier about how VA loans can only be used for condominium developments that are approved by the agency. Just because a condo complex isn't currently approved by the VA doesn't mean it won't be at the time of your purchase. Before paying for an appraisal, though, the veteran should have a pretty solid expectation that the VA or HUD will accept the condo development before closing day arrives.

Veterans can also wind up losing out because of someone else's past mistakes. The VA won't grant an appraisal on a property if the seller, builder or another stakeholder has somehow ran afoul of the VA Loan Guaranty program in the past. The VA can issue what it calls "sanctions" against people or parties that harm veterans. The type of bad acts that can result in sanctions include:

- Violating the Minimum Property Requirements
- Deviating from plans and specs without VA approval
- Failing to follow contracts on previous VA houses
- Using a sales or marketing practice that VA considers unfair or prejudicial

Again, these are relatively rare occurrences, but they do happen. It's important for borrowers to ask questions and work to ensure that everyone involved in their home purchase is in good standing with the VA.

Manufactured homes represent a unique situation. To be eligible for a 30-year VA loan (and the appraisal that comes with it), a manufactured home has to be rooted in a permanent foundation, taxed as real property and conform to building codes and the VA's Minimum Property Requirements. But, again, securing a VA loan for these is all but impossible in the current market.

Appraisal Costs

The VA has field stations across the country that farm out appraisals to independent appraisers who are experts in agency regulations and requirements. Those individual field stations set a maximum appraisal and inspection fee based on comparable costs.

The average cost is usually about $450 for a single-family home.

Minimum Property Requirements

This is the second, crucial part of the appraisal process.

MPRs cover basic issues that can affect the value of the property or its safety. These are mostly high-level concerns that present immediate or near-immediate problems for veterans and their families.

Again, a VA home appraisal is not a home inspection. Appraisers haven't devoted their lives to studying the art and science of wiring, plumbing and HVAC systems. This is more like a 100-foot view of the property, as opposed to the more detailed, at times microscopic view you get with a home inspection.

When it comes to a VA loan, appraisers are looking for potentially major issues that revolve around the three S's: safety, sanitation and structural integrity. Actually, let's make that four: the final "S" is salability. A home can be safe, sanitary and structurally sound but still prove problematic for appraisers if it isn't similar to any other comps or has other issues that could make it difficult to sell in the future.

In order to get a detailed picture of the home's condition, veterans should hire a home inspector to scour the property. For now, let's focus on MPRs.

Homes under construction or soon to be built are governed by Minimum Property Requirements that help ensure the property meets building codes and all applicable federal regulations. For existing homes or those recently built, the MPRs are there to make sure the veteran is purchasing a safe property that meets acceptable community standards.

There are 10 basic Minimum Property Requirements that VA appraisers consider. Each diffuses down into a series of specifics, so we'll start by looking at those banner headings:

- **Entity**

  This just ensures the property is a single structure ready to hit the market.

- **Nonresidential Use**

  VA loans can't be used to purchase investment properties or businesses. But veterans can purchase a home that has business or nonresidential space so long as it doesn't exceed 25 percent of the total floor space. Whether lenders will accept this type of structure can vary.

- **Space Requirements**

  The property has to have enough space for veterans and their families to live, sleep and cook and eat. It must also have proper sanitary facilities.

- **Mechanical Systems**

  All of the home's mechanical systems (heating, cooling, etc.) have to be safe, in working order and likely to remain in that shape.

- **Heating**

  The VA is concerned about heating beyond the Mechanical Systems category. There are rules and regulations governing properties that rely on wood-burning stoves and solar systems as primary heat sources. Homes with the former must have a traditional heating system in place to make sure pipes don't freeze. Solar heating systems also need a back-up heat source. There are some climates that allow the VA to waive requirements for mechanical heat systems.

- **Water Supply and Sanitary Facilities**

  This isn't much of a shocker, but the VA requires that veterans live somewhere with hot water, continually safe and potable drinking water and acceptable sanitary and sewage systems.

- **Roof Covering**

  The roof can't be defective, leaking or in bad shape.

- **Crawl Space**

  If the home has a crawl space, the area has to be free of debris and vented properly. There must be enough space for workers to access ductwork and plumbing. Any problems with excessive moisture will have to be remediated.

- **Ventilation**

  This is more for crawl spaces and attics. The property has to have adequate ventilation in these areas so that heat and moisture don't begin to cause structural damage or lead to conditions that can adversely affect human health.

- **Electricity**

  This one's pretty self-explanatory. A barren cabin in the woods isn't going to cut it.

Those are the 10 big ones. Major problems that can't be corrected or otherwise present a significant hazard can knock a property out of contention for a VA loan. But there's a series of more nuanced requirements that appraisers must consider when evaluating a prospective property, such as:

- **Property access**

  Typically, the most important element here is that veterans must be able to get to their living area without having to first pass through someone else's. Streets are required to have some type of all-weather surface. If the access comes via a private road, the borrower has to produce a private road agreement that spells out the access rights and maintenance responsibilities. The agreement must have the signature of every person on the road.

- **Defective conditions**

  These include problems with the home's construction or workmanship; clear evidence that the house is continuing to settle; and water problems like excessive dampness and leakage.

- **Termites**

  These little buggers can lead to huge headaches for both buyers and sellers. Appraisers are required to look for insects that eat away at wood, along with fungus growth and dry rot. A separate pest inspection is required for VA funding if it's clear there's a problem or if the home is located in a place likely to see an infestation. A termite problem has to be under control before a veteran can secure a VA loan. Borrowers are not allowed to pay for the termite inspection.

- **Lead-based paint**

  This is a big one with appraisers, mainly because lead-based paint represents such a health hazard, especially for veterans with young children. VA appraisers are required to assume that paint problems (like chipping, cracking or peeling) at any property built before 1978 involve lead paint. Unless further tests can show acceptable lead levels, the surface has to either be repainted or reconstructed.

- **Gas, Petroleum and High Voltage Electricity Lines**
  Utility and energy companies often hold easements on properties near these types of transmission lines. That easement essentially means the utility company can control the use of some private property in order to operate and maintain its facilities. The VA will not fund a loan for a home that's located in an easement for any of these three types of transmission lines.

- **Wells and Septic Systems**
  About 15 percent of the country gets its drinking water from private wells, according to the Environmental Protection Agency. The VA prefers a connection to a community water system. When that isn't feasible, properties with well water have to meet either local or federal safe drinking water standards. But the array of home-based treatment systems available today means even veterans with contaminated well water may still be able to receive a VA-guarantied loan. There's currently no inspection required of septic systems unless the appraisal documents a potential need.

- **Manufactured Homes**
  Again, these are relative rarities in today's lending climate. The stability of the home's foundation is typically the signature issue. In fact, there are more than a half-dozen ultra-specific requirements regarding the foundation alone.

Veterans under contract to purchase an existing home can request an exemption from the Minimum Property

Requirements. They have to do so in writing, along with their lender, and be able to show the property is habitable in terms of those three S's — safety, sanitation and structural soundness. The word "exemption" is a bit misleading, though. It's really more like an extension, because lenders and the VA will ultimately want to see the problems fixed.

For example, one of our borrowers had a problematic appraisal because of flaking paint on exterior windows that, at minimum, needed to be scraped and primed. But this was during the dead of winter and four-foot snowdrifts made painting impossible. We secured an exemption after the borrower put some money into escrow — the requirement is 1.5 times the cost of the repair estimate — to pay for the repairs once spring arrived.

Unlike in years past, veterans are now allowed to pay for repairs in order for the loan to close. That includes some minor MPR issues, such as installation of handrails, cracked tile or torn carpet. How this works in practice will likely depend on the lender.

We'll say it once more, because it's that important: The VA's Minimum Property Requirements do not replace the need for an independent home inspection. The home inspection is what's going to dredge up the real problems, if there are any, hidden behind the walls and in the floorboards.

But having a Realtor who knows the VA MPRs can certainly spare veterans some time, heartache and money. Just imagine, for example, that you're looking at a property experiencing subsidence and settling problems or that resides in a termite hot spot. The earlier a veteran understands the limitations and requirements, the sooner he or she can make a decision about whether to move forward with the property or to continue the home search.

Understanding the MPRs has also become increasingly important since the economic collapse flushed the housing market with foreclosures.

MPRs and Buying Foreclosures

The recent foreclosure environment has been a homebuyer's dream in some parts of the country. Of course, it's been a nightmare for those homeowners living through it.

Nearly 4 million homes entered foreclosure in 2010. A stuttering housing market slowly chipped away at the glut of distressed properties, but foreclosure inventory at the close of 2013 still hovered around 2 million homes, according to property research firm CoreLogic.

Buying a home that's been foreclosed on can be a great way to save money and get a good chunk of house at a reasonable price. Borrowers may find lenders willing to dangle lower interest rates and down payments in order to thin out their inventory of foreclosed properties.

But veterans in some parts of the country haven't been able to take advantage of these low-cost opportunities, at least to the degree their civilian counterparts have enjoyed. Part of that is because not all foreclosed properties return to the open market in great shape, which can be problematic once VA appraisers bring their MPR checklist to the front door.

Agency officials are out to ensure that a veteran's prospective home is "move-in ready," and not a work in progress that requires a few more months of elbow grease and devotion. Investors who bring cash to the table have also pushed veterans out of the market. All-cash transactions don't require underwriting, appraisals and other lending mechanisms.

This is just one more example of why having a VA-savvy Realtor can make all the difference for military homebuyers.

Foreclosures can be tough, but they're certainly not impossible for veterans to purchase, usually with a savings of at least 5 percent below the market value.

Because of the MPRs and the nature of the VA appraisal process, some foreclosures simply aren't going to work. And that's why expert knowledge can be so crucial. A real estate agent fluent in VA loans might be able to sniff out those major, deal-breaking problems in the early stages. The sooner the veteran knows there's potential trouble, the sooner he or she can adjust the purchasing game plan — and, if necessary, the time line.

Before we move forward, it's important to stop and drill down a bit more into what homebuying is like today on the front lines. Purchasing a home in distressed and recovering real estate markets can present some unique challenges for military buyers, not just in hard-hit states like Nevada and Florida but across the country.

Buying in a Distressed Market

Buying a home in a distressed market can be frustrating and complicated. Transactions can prove time consuming, often because they involve financial institutions and bureaucracies in no hurry to close a deal. Patience is at a premium in these markets.

Generally, there are three types of homes available in a distressed market:

- **Foreclosures/REO (real estate owned homes)**: These homes have returned to bank ownership after the borrower failed to make mortgage payments. This type of property is characterized by a lack of maintenance and can represent a good value. These homes are sold "as-is," and unless repairs are required to complete the financing, these sellers will not make any.

- **Short Sale Transaction**: A short sale is when the lender OKs the sale of a home for less than what is owed on the mortgage. The lender has to approve the sale and reduced payoff of the mortgage. Transactions can take 120 days or more.
- **Investor Flip**: This is when a private company buys and upgrades a foreclosure in order to sell it for a profit. Because of the time that the new seller has owned the home (usually less than 120 days), it can be challenging to obtain financing for these homes.

The traditional home sale can seem a relative rarity in many distressed markets. Foreclosing on a home takes time. Government agencies have also worked in recent years to help homeowners modify their mortgages and stave off fore-closure, which also slows the process. The end result in many of these distressed areas is a relatively low supply of homes for sale.

That, in turn, spurs fierce competition among sellers and their real estate agents. Home prices in these areas are often set at artificially low levels, as sellers anticipate a wave of offers that will ultimately drive up the price. In some respects, it isn't all that different from any eBay auction.

What makes matters worse, at least for veterans, is that banks and investors clamoring for profits are turning to cash buyers with open arms. A crush of cash buyers in distressed markets has pushed scores of veterans to the sidelines.

It's almost difficult to describe how much different the process is when it's an all-cash purchase. Paperwork and proce-dural hassles disappear. There are no eagle-eyed underwriters scouring financial records and tax returns. Banks and investors will sometimes accept all-cash offers significantly below the asking price, just because of the ease.

Nearly half of all home purchases in November 2013 were all-cash deals, according to real estate data firm RealtyTrac. The figure was above 50 percent in a handful of states, including Florida (63 percent), Georgia and Nevada (51 percent each).

Most prospective VA borrowers aren't able to engage in a bidding war that escalates well beyond the home's appraised value. Some banks that own foreclosures actually require prospective borrowers to seek loan prequalification from them before entertaining an offer.

Veterans who manage to secure financing and find a willing seller still have to contend with those pesky Minimum Property Requirements.

The bottom line is that veterans in distressed markets should latch on to a real estate agent and lender they trust. They should also prepare themselves for disappointment and delays. Many will see their "dream home" turned over to an investor with a wad of cash. Patience and preparation are the keys to success — or at least to survival.

Purchasing While Overseas

The transient nature of military life means that sometimes veterans can't perfect their timing when it comes to home buying. That's where Power of Attorney comes in. Most service members are at least familiar with the phrase. This is where you bestow upon a trusted confidant the ability to sign legally binding documents in your stead.

There are certainly situations where a service member can't be on hand, let alone on the same continent, when the time comes to sign purchase agreements or closing documents. Lenders and real estate attorneys don't exactly give a wink and a nod to spouses and allow them to sign for their deployed husband or wife. Lying, misrepresentation and forgery on federal loan documents is a felony. Probably not something you want to be facing while your better half is half a world away.

It's important in the early stages to determine whether your potential lender requires its own Power of Attorney documents. Don't just assume that a generic, catchall POA is going to work when the time comes to secure home financing. In many cases, you will need a specific Power of Attorney that covers a single property in question, giving a date and price range and an address.

Be sure to get these questions nailed down with your loan officer or your attorney before proceeding on a home purchase.

Specially Adapted Housing

Veterans and service members with service-connected disabilities can have distinct needs when it comes to housing. That can prove a challenge during the house-hunting stage. But the VA has a unique program that provides grants to help service members and veterans with disabilities modify or otherwise adapt properties to meet their needs.

The Specially Adapted Housing grant program allows qualified veterans to obtain up to $50,000 to retrofit a home. Veterans who suffer from lack of motion, blindness, loss of limbs or other disabilities that require home modifications may be eligible for Specially Adapted Housing. Modifications can include specially sized doorways; certain types of carpet; retrofitted faucets and showerheads; ramps and banisters; and a host of other important changes.

There's a separate program that offers grants of up to $10,000 for eligible veterans with blindness or the anatomical loss or loss of use in both hands.

Service members and their families should talk with their loan officer about the SAH program.

Borrower Spotlight: Jason Foster
Army Veteran Builds His Dream Home From 1,600 Miles Away

Colorado Springs, Colo. — Jason Foster served two tours in Iraq during his nearly 10 years in the Army. His time in the Mideast kept him away from friends and family for a combined 27 months.

Between his two deployments, Jason met his wife. He was stationed at Fort Carson when mutual friends introduced the pair. They connected instantly and eventually married in November 2004.

Jason and his new family were separated while he was deployed for his second tour in Iraq. But he returned home earlier than expected after getting injured. The family was living in Washington, D.C., when they received Jason's medical retirement papers. With those in hand, Jason and his wife began scouring the Internet in search of a home for their growing family.

"We love the Midwest, and my wife has family there," Jason said.

It wasn't long until all signs pointed toward Colorado.

A job opened in Fort Carson, and Jason found information on the nursing program at the University of Colorado at Colorado Springs. Jason and his wife concentrated their online search efforts on finding a rental property in the Colorado Springs area.

Then the couple discovered an option they never considered before: building a home. A local builder let them know building the home they wanted would actually prove cheaper than renting. That's when Jason got in touch with local real estate agent Kris Korinek.

Jason presented Kris with quite the challenge. He and his family were going to have to remain in Washington, D.C., through the building and buying process.

Kris pointed Jason to Alice Schneider and the Colorado Springs branch of Veterans United Home Loans. Alice would not only help Jason secure a VA loan, a benefit earned by his service, but she would also walk him through a long-distance loan.

"I agreed to work with Alice because of the way she greeted us, and she was able to work with us over long distance," Jason said. "She called every day to make sure everything was going OK on a personal level, since she knew we were stressed buying a home from Washington, D.C."

The distance wasn't the only thing between Jason's family and their new home. During his deployment, Jason had problems with one of his credit card companies. It was as if his home-building process hit a giant speed bump.

Alice explained how credit works and gave Jason the information he needed to responsibly pay off his debt and boost his score.

"We got it paid off only because Alice helped us out," he said.

Despite the obstacles and long distance, the paperwork and process moved quickly.

"I've owned a house before, and I've never had any customer service like that," Jason said.

Jason and his family were finally able to start a new chapter in their lives. In September 2011, they officially moved to Colorado and into their beautifully built dream home. No more deployments. No more speed bumps. Just Colorado living from then on.

"I'm looking forward to settling down and having stability in our lives," Jason said.

W e're privileged to work with some of the country's truly dynamic military leaders, from the most senior enlisted NCOs to a Silver Star recipient and other modern-day heroes.

We all share a common mission: ***Helping veterans, active military and their families achieve the American Dream they sacrificed to protect.***

We're committed to spreading awareness of this nearly 70-year-old loan program and the significant benefits available to qualified veterans and active military members. Meet some of the incredible veterans who stand with us and help to share the story of the long-cherished VA loan program.

Jack L. Tilley, 12th Sergeant Major of the U.S. Army

"A VA Loan isn't about the individual service member, it's about the family. It's about helping your family be better off than they are today and help them fulfill their dreams.

"Veterans United is an A+ organization. They're committed. They're dedicated and enthusiastic. But most importantly they really understand and appreciate their mission of serving veterans."

Years of Military Service: 36

Current: President of Jack Tilley, Inc., and founder of the American Freedom Foundation

Of Note: Tilley was sworn in as the 12th Sergeant Major of the Army on June 23, 2000, and served until Jan. 15, 2004. He previously held the senior enlisted position as Senior Enlisted Leader of the United States Central Command, MacDill Air Force Base, Fla.

James L. Herdt, 9th Master Chief Petty Officer of the U.S. Navy

"When you think about the GI Bill where the VA Loan comes from, it essentially built this country into the power-house that it is.

"When you work with Veterans United, you're dealing with someone whose only job is to help veterans obtain a VA Loan. You're dealing with people who have specialized experience."

Years of Military Service: 35

Current: CEO of Herdt Consulting, Inc.

Of Note: Herdt was appointed the Ninth Master Chief Petty Officer of the Navy in March 1998. He is "triple qualified" (authorized to wear the Enlisted Aviation Warfare Specialist, Enlisted Surface Warfare Specialist, and Enlisted Submarine Warfare Specialist breast insignias). Master Chief Herdt is also certified as a Master Training Specialist. He currently serves on the board of the U.S. Navy Memorial, the Association of the United States Navy (AUSN) Board and the Florida Institute of Technology (FIT) Alumni Board.

Alford L. McMichael, 14ᵗʰ Sergeant Major of the U.S. Marines Corps

"We miss the genuineness of Veterans United if we limit our thinking to just providing a home. It's not just about a home. It's about providing for a decent life to the people who have put their life on the line on the battlefield. Veterans United has your back when you come back to the society that you went off to defend."

Years of Military Service: 36
Current: Founder and president of The Drew Foundation
Of Note: McMichael was the 14ᵗʰ Sergeant Major of the Marine Corp (1999-2003) and was the first African American 1ˢᵗ Senior Non-Commissioned Officer for Allied Command Operations for NATO (2003-2006); McMichael is also the author of "Leadership: Achieving Life-Changing Success from Within."

Frederick "Jim" J. Finch, 13th Chief Master Sergeant of the U.S. Air Force

"I would tell any service member who was thinking about buying a house that they should explore their benefits and what they can save using the VA home loan.

"I am most impressed with the people who work at Veterans United Home Loans. I've met some men and women who genuinely care about the customers they are serving."

Years of Military Service: 28

Current: Speaker; consultant; ombudsman for active and retired Air Force personnel and their families

Of Note: Jim served as the personal advisor to the Secretary of the Air Force and the Air Force Chief of Staff on issues regarding the welfare, readiness, morale, proper utilization and training of the enlisted force. In 2000, he affectionately became known as the "voice" of the Air Force when he narrated nationally televised Air Force recruiting commercials.

Vincent W. Patton III, 8ᵗʰ Master Chief Petty Officer of the U.S. Coast Guard

"The VA Loan helps military service members get started. Not just in transition from leaving the military, but those who currently serve, the VA Loan gives you the opportunity to start setting your roots. Veterans United helps folks on the other end of the phone know that someone really does cares about you and wants to help you achieve the American dream."

Years of Military Service: 30
Current: Vice president of corporate outreach for AFCEA International
Of Note: Patton served as the eighth Master Chief Petty Officer of the Coast Guard from May 1998 to October 2002. He became the first African American selected as the service's senior-most enlisted ranking position. His career included staff and operational assignments both afloat and ashore throughout the United States, and a joint military service assignment in Cuba and Haiti.

Fighting for Homeownership: Silver Star Recipient and UFC Icon Brian Stann

Brian Stann earned one of the nation's highest honors for his bravery in Iraq.

The hulking Marine and commander of the 2nd Mobile Assault Platoon coordinated air and tank support during a six-day siege at a key bridge near insurgent strongholds. At one point, 1st Lt. Stann led a charge into the heart of an ambush to recover six severely wounded soldiers.

The platoon ultimately took the bridge. All 42 Marines survived.

The Pennsylvania native and former Navy linebacker was awarded the Silver Star in 2006.

His mission was recreated for the History Channel. President Bush even referenced Brian's valor in a couple speeches.

The honors and accolades cemented his status as an American hero.

Today, with his military career behind him, Brian is dedicated to helping his comrades in a different way — by working to reduce veteran unemployment.

Brian is president of Hire Heroes USA, a nonprofit organization that offers transition and job search assistance and job placement to those who have honorably served our country. Hire Heroes helps thousands of veterans and their spouses secure the education and opportunities necessary to support themselves and their families.

The agency targets veterans who are most likely to be unemployed: Those who proudly served as part of Operations Iraqi Freedom and Enduring Freedom and veterans with disabilities. Hire Heroes USA also works to educate employers about this deserving demographic.

"The veteran unemployment rate is twice the general unemployment rate and service members are being denied the American Dream they fought to preserve," Brian said. "Employers owe it to these warriors to get educated and to better understand the skill sets and unique needs of our returning service members."

Brian has traveled the country meeting with Congressional representatives and corporate executives. He's even taken to the airwaves, talking about the difficulties facing returning veterans on programs like C-Span's "Washington Journal."

But he has also garnered support for the cause in a less traditional way: by becoming one of the leading faces of mixed martial arts.

Brian began his fighting career in 2006 while still on active duty. He was a natural, to put it mildly.

Within two years, he became the World Extreme Cagefighting Light Heavyweight champion. He moved to the sport's top tier, Ultimate Fighting Championship, or UFC, in 2009.

Brian became known as the "All-American," and was soon one of UFC's brightest stars.

Brian knows firsthand the power of the VA loan. He refinanced his mortgage with Veterans United and saw his monthly payment fall a whopping $450.

"I couldn't believe how simple the process was and how much Veterans United was able to save us," he said. "I was proud to take advantage of my VA benefits, and I urge other veterans to do the same."

Brian retired from UFC in July 2013 after eight years and 18 professional fights. He now provides TV commentary for UFC and for ACC football games on Fox Sports South.

"The team at Veterans United is dedicated to helping service members take full advantage of the benefits earned by their sacrifice and dedication to our country," Brian said. "Building wealth through homeownership is part of the American dream. Who deserves that more than our nation's heroes?"

Marcus Luttrell, former Navy SEAL and New York Times best-selling author

"Veterans United Home Loans truly appreciates the sacrifices service members and their veterans make in order to serve our country. That's why I'm proud to support Veterans United. The impact the company has on its customers is truly inspiring."

Quick briefing:
Marcus Luttrell was the sole survivor of a four-man Navy SEAL reconnaissance team ambushed hours after inserting into Afghanistan's Kunar Province during Operation Redwing, a month-long military campaign in 2006.

That firefight and subsequent rescue attempt in which 16 service members were killed generated headlines across the globe. Luttrell's harrowing account of the operation became a best-selling book that was made into a Hollywood movie starring Mark Wahlberg, Taylor Kitsch and Emile Hirsch.

Five years after writing *Lone Survivor: The Eyewitness Account of Operation Redwing and the Lost Heroes of SEAL Team 10*, Luttrell crafted a follow-up that sheds additional light on the operation and chronicles his follow-up tour in Iraq with SEAL Team 5.

Service: A Navy SEAL at War was released in May 2012.

Mike Landers, president and CEO of Armed Services YMCA

"VA home loans have made a tremendous difference in the lives of service members and their families for more than 65 years. Veterans who might otherwise never have a shot at homeownership are achieving that dream because of this incredible program. We thank them for their ongoing support of the Armed Services YMCA and helping us make military life easier with no and low-cost programs and services nationwide."

Quick briefing:
Capt. Michael J. Landers has served as deputy national executive director for ASYMCA since 1999, following his retirement from the Navy in 1998. Prior to his retirement, Capt. Landers served as Deputy Chief of Legislative Affairs for the U.S. Navy.

His distinguished Naval career includes assignments as Commanding Officer, Naval Submarine Base Bangor, Washington; Executive Assistant to the Deputy Chief of Naval Personnel/ Assistant Deputy Chief of Naval Operations (Manpower and Personnel); Detailer for the Bureau of Naval Personnel in the Submarine Distribution Division; Commanding Officer, USS ORTOLAN (ASR-22); Executive Officer, USS PIGEON (ASR-21); and Navigation System Operations and Technical Evaluation Branch Head for the Strategic Systems Project Office in Washington, D.C.
Captain Landers has been awarded the Legion of Merit (5), Meritorious Service Medal (3), Navy Commendation Medal (3), and Navy/Marine Corps Achievement Medal (2).

CHAPTER 5 :
LOAN PROCESSING, RATES AND COSTS

At this point, you're entering the home stretch.

Once you've got a contract in hand, the first person you call — after friends and loved ones, perhaps — is your loan officer. At many mortgage companies, this is when your trusted LO would actually start to fade into the background. Consider it one of the ironies of the industry. Many companies turn their borrowers over to a **loan processor** once a purchase agreement is in place.

Processors have an important job. They're charged with shepherding your loan file through the remaining channels and bringing home your home loan.

Loan officers, meanwhile, typically go back to working the front lines, taking those initial calls and kick-starting the process for veterans.

That isn't a bad thing, and it's pretty much the mortgage industry's standard operating procedure. But we tend to do things a little differently.

We love our processors, and they certainly interact with borrowers from time to time, but their focus is burrowing into the details and gaps in your loan file. Our loan officers stay connected to their customers from start to finish. The goal is to maintain that relationship from initial conversation to closing day. The LO is still fielding your late-night phone calls and early-morning emails. The LO is still chasing down answers and solving problems. It's a concerted, team effort. Veterans United borrowers aren't simply cast into the loan processing pen once they sign a contract.

Their loan officer is with them every step of the way.

The Lender's SAR

When a copy of your contract finally lands on your loan officer's desk, its stay will be a fleeting one. That hunk of important paperwork will soon be in the hands of a processor. Not to get too poetic, but one way to think of the processor is as the central hub of a wheel. Spokes emanate from the center: appraiser, inspector, title agent, insurance agent, underwriter, loan closer and a few others. Each has its own unique role in helping the wheel go round.

But they're all tied to that central hub, the loan processor. It's the processor's job to pull together the information and documentation necessary to complete your loan file and get it to an underwriter. The lender's underwriting unit has a final thumbs-up or down on your loan. And in most cases, a veteran's loan file can't be sent to the underwriter for approval until it's complete.

The processor will ensure an appraisal is ordered for the property. He or she will also make sure the appraisal is reviewed by the lender's **staff appraisal reviewer, or SAR**.

The SAR's job is to carefully examine appraisals to ensure they are complete and conform to agency guidelines. More importantly, it's the lender's SAR who ultimately determines the property's value. The appraiser will include his or her estimation in the report, but the VA bases its guaranty on the appraisal reviewer's findings.

The final Notice of Value will contain the market value of the property, the estimated remaining economic life of the property and a rundown of any conditions and issues necessary for the home to obtain VA approval. In most cases, the lender has five business days to get the NOV and a copy of the appraisal report to the borrower. For a home that's already built, the NOV is good for six months. Homes that are either under construction or proposed have a 12-month window.

The VA will not release an appraisal until the SAR issues a final Notice of Value. Even your loan officer doesn't get to see or discuss it until that step.

Here's an example of the first two pages of a standard Notice of Value:

LENDER'S NOTICE OF VALUE

[date of notice]   LENDER LOAN NO.:   VA CASE NO.:
                                                          APPRAISAL REVIEWER:
[Mr. and/or Ms.] [purchaser's   PROPERTY ADDRESS:
name and current mailing address]

Dear [Mr. and/or Ms.]]:

The above property has been appraised by a fee appraiser assigned by the VA regional office in [city and state]. On [   ], our VA-authorized appraisal reviewer personally reviewed the fee appraiser's report and determined the property's estimated reasonable value to be $[   ]. The maximum repayment period for a loan to purchase this property is [fee appraiser's "economic life" estimate or 30, whichever is less] years.

The VA appraisal was made to determine the reasonable value of the property for loan purposes. It must not be considered a building inspection. Neither VA nor the lender can guarantee that the home will be satisfactory to you in all respects or that all equipment will operate properly. A thorough inspection of the property by you or a reputable inspection firm may help minimize any problems that could arise after loan closing. In an existing home, particular attention should be given to plumbing, heating, electrical and roofing components.

REMEMBER: VA GUARANTEES THE LOAN, NOT THE CONDITION OF THE PROPERTY.

THE CONDITIONS/REQUIREMENTS CHECKED BELOW APPLY TO THIS PROPERTY:

_____   1. **ENERGY CONSERVATION IMPROVEMENTS.** You may wish to contact the utility company or a reputable firm for a home energy audit to identify needed energy efficiency improvements to this previously occupied property. Lenders may increase the loan amount to allow buyers to make energy efficiency improvements such as: Solar or conventional heating/cooling systems, water heaters, insulation, weather-stripping/caulking and storm windows/doors. Other energy-related improvements may also be considered. The mortgage may be increased by up to $3,000 based solely on documented costs; or up to $6,000 provided the increase in monthly mortgage payment does not exceed the likely reduction in monthly utility costs; or more than $6,000 subject to a value determination by VA.

_____ 2. **WOOD-DESTROYING INSECT INFORMATION**

_____a. **Inspection Report (Existing Construction).** The property must be inspected at no cost to you by a qualified pest control operator using Form NPMA-33, or other form acceptable to VA. Any reported infestation or structural damage affecting the value of the property must be corrected to VA's satisfaction prior to loan settlement. You must acknowledge receipt of a copy of the inspection report in the space provided on the form.

_____b. **Soil Treatment Guarantee (Proposed or Under Construction).** A properly completed Form NPCA-99a is required. If the soil is treated with a termiticide, a properly completed Form NPCA-99b is also required. The lender will provide you with a copy.

_____3. **LIEN-SUPPORTED ASSESSMENT.** This property is located in a development with mandatory membership in a homeowners' association. The lender is responsible for ensuring that title meets VA requirements for such property and that homeowner association assessments are subordinate to the VA-guaranteed mortgage.

_____a. **Homeowner Association Fee.** Estimated fee of $[_____] per [____].
_____b. **Other.** _____

_____4. **CONDOMINIUM REQUIREMENTS.** Evidence that VA requirements have been met for this condominium. There are may be additional information in "Other Conditions/Requirements" below.

_____5. **WATER/SEWAGE SYSTEM ACCEPTABILITY.** Evidence from the local health authority or other source authorized by VA that the individual _____ **water supply,** _____**sewage disposal** system(s) is/are acceptable.

_____6. **CONNECTION TO PUBLIC WATER/SEWER.** Evidence of connection to _____ **public water,** _____ **public sewer,** if available, and that all related costs have been paid in full.

_____7. **PRIVATE ROAD/COMMON-USE DRIVEWAY.** Evidence that use of the private road or common-use driveway is protected by a recorded permanent easement or recorded right-of-way from the property to a public road, and that a provision exists for its continued maintenance.

_____8. **FLOOD INSURANCE.** Since improvements on this property are located in a FEMA Special Flood Hazard Area, flood insurance is required.

_____9. **"AIRPORT" ACKNOWLEDGEMENT.** Your written acknowledgement that you are aware that this property is located near an airport and that aircraft noise may affect the livability, value and marketability of the property.

_____10. **REPAIRS.** The _____ **lender** _____ **fee appraiser** (_____[name]_____)
_____ **fee compliance inspector** (_____[name]_____) is to certify that the following repairs have been satisfactorily completed. See the above second paragraph about your responsibility concerning the condition of the property.

_____
_____
_____l_____
_____

_____11. **LOCAL HOUSING/PLANNING AUTHORITY CODE REQUIREMENTS.** Evidence that local housing or planning authority code requirements, if any, have been met.

_____12. **"NOT INSPECTED" ACKNOWLEDGEMENT.** Your written Acknowledgement that, you are aware that since this new property was not inspected during construction by VA,
_____a. VA assistance with construction complaints will be limited to defects in equipment, material and workmanship reported during the one-year builder's warranty period.
_____b. VA will not intercede on your behalf in the processing of any construction complaints.

_____13. **TEN-YEAR INSURED PROTECTION PLAN.** Evidence of enrollment of this new property in a 10-year insured protection plan acceptable to the Department of Housing and Urban Development (HUD).

In all, there are currently 19 conditions and requirements that may apply to the veteran's property, covering those Minimum Property issues we looked at in the last chapter along with some conditions that apply to new and proposed construction. The SAR will go through and check off any conditions that apply to the property in question.

Altering the home's market value requires clear and compelling documentation and data. Veterans can't get a second VA appraisal on the same property, but they can get an independent one to use as supporting evidence, provided someone else picks up the tab. The VA won't even consider that second appraisal if the veteran had to spend money on it.

The Loan Processor

Ordering the VA appraisal is one of the first jobs of the loan processor. It's far from the last.

The processor will forward your contract to your insurance company, who in turn will get cranking on a policy for the home. Most lenders will recommend insurance companies and push borrowers to solicit multiple quotes. Rates for **homeowners insurance** can vary wildly depending on a number of factors. Borrowers should get at least three quotes from reputable companies.

The processor will do the same with a title company to ensure the property has proper title insurance.

Let's pause here for a brief segue into **title insurance**. It's a foreign term for many first-time buyers. That's understandable, as it's a foreign concept outside the mortgage industry. In essence, title insurance protects the borrower against claims that the property belongs to someone else.

Think of it this way: A 100-year-old home may have had a string of owners in the last century. Title insurance companies scour public records to determine if there are any legitimate claims or rights to the property. Title insurance can protect homebuyers against any lingering problems and any unforeseen hidden risks that could arise. Say, for a rare but possible example, that a title transfer decades ago was predicated upon forged documents and someone claiming to be the "rightful owner" comes knocking on the door two weeks after you move in.

This is where title insurance comes into play. It is mandatory and a necessary part of today's real estate environment. In most cases, the seller's agent will recommend a title company in the purchase agreement. But that doesn't mean you have to use that particular company. Title insurance is a one-time purchase. The premium is covered in one lump sum that must be paid at closing.

Like any other form of insurance, title insurance in many states comes with varying rates (there are a few where rates are set by the state Department of Insurance or a similar governmental agency). And there's no guarantee that the listing agent will recommend a title company with the best rates for military borrowers. Veterans should shop around or at least check with their lender to see what else is available.

At the same time, the loan processor will work to clear up any remaining documentation and paperwork needs related to your loan financing. Inspections need to be completed. Insurance policies must be drafted and signed. Veterans might need to gather up another year's worth of tax statements or have their bank balances verified.

It's hard to put a specific time frame on this, but generally you're looking at a week or two to nail down some of this financial information and take care of appraisals, inspections and the rest. Once the processor is confident that the loan package looks complete, it will make its way to arguably the most important person in the chain: the underwriter.

This step can seem a bit confusing and needless to first-time buyers, many of whom will quickly note that their loan was already approved by the Automated Underwriting System. There's already a green light, right?

Sort of.

A lot can change during the course of the purchasing process. Financial statements and credit reports can get stale. Prospective borrowers lose their jobs. Spouses file for divorce.

Issues arise with the property. For these and countless other reasons, the initial verdict of an automated system can't possibly be the final word on a home loan. There's just too much potential for things to change.

That's why lenders like to turn to human beings as the process nears culmination. Some employ underwriters in-house, while others use outside firms. Either way, the underwriter is the person who makes the ultimate determination regarding your loan. And that's why an AUS approval isn't necessarily a green light.

Veterans must have their loan package approved by a real person. It's also important to remember that an AUS approval often comes with a list of conditions the borrower must meet. The underwriting office is the crucible for all those conditions.

For example, the veteran might have received AUS approval on the condition that two years worth of tax returns be supplied. In the best of all possible worlds, the veteran supplies those documents, the loan processor tosses them into the file and the underwriter gives the loan a big thumbs-up.

The underwriter is also there to ensure the loan follows VA guidelines and requirements. Most often, that's going to involve another hard look at the borrower's debt-to-income ratio and residual income figures. A lender's self-interest drives the process. Given that there's no down payment, the lender is on the hook for the entire amount if a loan defaults and the VA determines the company ignored or somehow skirted agency guidelines. In other words, the VA guaranty evaporates if a lender fails to follow the rules.

Needless to say, that's a scary thought for lenders who would otherwise be somewhat insulated against a borrower who goes belly up. That means underwriters are charged with an important task, and it's one they don't take lightly.

Despite the hard work of loan processors, most loan files aren't slam dunks. Tax returns may be slow in coming from the IRS. Pay stubs can become outdated if shopping for a home takes longer than expected. The same can be true of credit reports.

But those aren't deal breakers. The underwriter takes it on faith, to a degree, that the documentation and proof will be forthcoming. When that happens, the underwriter will issue **conditional approval** of the loan, which means exactly what it sounds like. The veteran's loan will be good to go on the condition that certain pieces of information or other requirements come together. The converse is to suspend the file, which happens less frequently and is typically triggered by some red flags that signal potential disaster.

Getting conditional approval for a loan is perfectly common. It's also commonly frustrating for veterans, who often wonder why they're being incessantly bombarded for thousands of pieces of information — or, at least that's how it can feel — so close to the end.

Veterans with conditional approval will be back on the phone with their loan officer, working to supply whatever outstanding information and documentation is necessary to fulfill the underwriter's concerns. That can take some time, which may delay the projected loan closing and make sellers and borrowers alike a bit nervous.

Still, this is standard fare that in most cases gets resolved in a matter of days. Repeated requests for information can prove daunting for some borrowers. Rest assured, though, that the underwriter isn't out to get you or anyone else. The goal is to put together a complete loan file that satisfies all VA requirements, meets the necessary terms set forth by the lender and ultimately protects the best interests of the veteran.

It can't always be a perfect shot the first time through.

Once those conditions are met, the lender will draft a commitment letter that, well, commits the lender to follow through on the loan. You might hear this step called the **clear to close**, or CTC. With a commitment letter in hand, the veteran is nearing the final stages. The loan closing is really all that stands between the borrower and turning the key.

Before we talk about loan closings and the costs that come with them, let's pull back the curtains on another crucial part of this process: settling on an interest rate.

A Primer on Interest Rates

The interest rate on your home mortgage reflects a lot of things, not the least of which is simply the current cost of borrowing money.

It can be staggering for first-time buyers to stop and consider just how much they'll spend over the course of three decades. Depending on the rate, that $300,000 home can easily wind up costing more than twice that after 30 years of principal and interest payments. Such is the cost of borrowing a big pile of money.

For the first decade or so, the majority of a buyer's monthly mortgage payments are dedicated to paying down the interest. You don't start biting into the principal for years, which is why making an additional payment each month toward your principal can shave years and thousands of dollars off the life of your mortgage.

From Day One, the loan officer will probably start talking about the need to lock in at a certain interest rate. We'll talk about **rate locks** and how they work shortly. First, it's important to understand how interest rates are determined and what role loan officers play in issuing a final interest rate for borrowers.

One of the first things a loan officer will mention is that interest rates are constantly in flux. And that's certainly true. Interest rates change all the time based on a host of economic indicators and factors.

But lenders don't just randomly pick rates each day. Nor do they cause them to change. Instead, the ebb and flow of rates depends on a couple of key things, including:

- **The Federal Reserve**
  The Fed, as it's called, is charged with managing the nation's monetary policy and trying to spur maximum economic growth while curbing inflation. The body sets the federal funds rate, which dictates the cost of short-term lending among banks. The Fed adjusts the rate depending on the health and vitality of the national economy.

- **The Secondary Mortgage Market**
  Lenders sell some of their home loans to mortgage investors and government-sponsored enterprises in what's known as the secondary market. These investors pool together a bunch of loans into mortgage-backed securities or sometimes simply tuck the loans away among their holdings. Securities are sold to Wall Street investment firms and others.

- **Supply and Demand**
  Invariably it's bond market investors who wind up shaping interest rates. The rate of return on their bond investments, also known as a yield, depends in large part on the state of the economy. If the economy is booming, that probably means the rate of return will be better down the road than at present. That, in turn, drives down demand for low-yield loans. And that, in

turn, means lenders have to increase the rate of return to attract investors. They do that, of course, by passing on the cost to consumers. Run that whole scenario backward and that's how interest rates decline.

So, it's this swirling free market free-for-all that ultimately helps determine interest rates on a given day. Lenders set their rates based on what's happening in the bond market. In particular, rates for VA loans are tied to mortgage-backed securities guarantied by Ginnie Mae, a government-owned enterprise separate from Fannie Mae and Freddie Mac.

Mortgage lending is a competitive arena. Lenders employ folks who spend their days tracking bond prices and economic events that might influence pricing. It's here, in what's essentially the lender's rate department, that a rate sheet is compiled, sometimes more than once a day depending on what's happening in the markets.

With the start of the day, the rate department — you might hear it called the secondary department — will watch how Ginnie Mae bonds fare in the early going and adjust rates accordingly. They can shift rates again during the middle and at the end of each day depending on the market. Those rates are distributed to the lender's loan officers. In today's environment, many computerized loan programs showcase these rates on screen, giving the LO ready access to what's available.

Mortgage Industry Reforms

The conversation about interest rates and how borrowers encounter them looks a little different today than it did a few years ago.

The reason is that major changes continue to take root in the mortgage industry, the fruits of sweeping legislation passed in 2010. One change is a shift in the way mortgage brokers and loan officers are paid. Another big one is the creation of a new classification of mortgages, known as Qualified Mortgages, or QM, and a new regulatory body to oversee the industry (the Consumer Financial Protection Bureau).

Government regulators believe the changes will in part help consumers more accurately compare lenders and eliminate the practice of steering borrowers into less beneficial loans for the sake of higher commissions.

First, let's talk briefly about the new era of Qualified Mortgages.

This new class of mortgages is all about safety and affordability, two long-time hallmarks of the 70-year-old VA loan program. Throughout the 2000s, some lenders made a ton of money providing home loans to people with poor credit and no realistic chance of repaying the loan. Those subprime loans played a major role in the financial crisis and ensuing collapse of the housing market.

In the aftermath, Congress sought a way to protect consumers and the economy at large. One of the results was the creation of the Qualified Mortgage. These loans are devoid of riskier features and meet a set of requirements aimed at ensuring the borrower can afford the loan they're getting. Mortgages that meet the QM requirement will also help shield lenders from claims that they put a borrower into a bad loan all but destined for default.

Qualified Mortgages, by definition, can't include any of the following:

- A period where the borrower pays only interest on the loan and nothing toward the principal, known as an interest-only loan
- Something known as "**negative amortization**," which occurs when your payment fails to cover all of the interest due, leading your principal balance to actually increase over time
- Balloon payments, where you're required to pay off the loan in one lump sum payment after a certain number of years
- Loan terms beyond 30 years

In addition, regulators laid out a set of eight credit and underwriting requirements that must be met in order for a loan to obtain Qualified Mortgage status. These requirements are the heart of what's called the Ability to Repay (ATR) rule. Most lenders have been using some or all of these requirements for a long time.

The Ability to Repay's eight financial metrics are:
- Current income or assets
- Current employment status
- Credit history
- Monthly mortgage payment
- Monthly payments on other mortgages
- Monthly payments for mortgage-related expenses, such as property taxes
- Current debt obligations, including things like child support or alimony
- Your monthly debt-to-income (DTI) ratio

These are common sense requirements that reputable lenders have employed for a long time. Veterans United has utilized these eight requirements for years, long before a legislative call to make them mandatory. Thoroughly documenting all eight of these is one of the pillars of a Qualified Mortgage, along with the absence of the risky features mentioned above.

There are a handful of other requirements in order for a loan to be considered QM. In most cases, costs and fees can't exceed 3 percent of the loan amount. There's also a maximum DTI ratio, but for most loans — including those backed by the Department of Veterans Affairs — this cap won't be part of the equation, at least anytime soon. Loans that already qualify for purchase or guaranty by a government entity (Fannie Mae, Freddie Mac, FHA, USDA, VA) are presumed to be Qualified Mortgages.

Given that background, the question is: What's it all mean for VA home loans and military borrowers?

Overall, there really shouldn't be much impact. This kind of safe, prudent underwriting has been part of the VA program for years, and it shows. VA loans have had the lowest foreclosure rate of any loan on the market for nearly all of the last six years. The financial requirements you need to meet for most VA lenders won't change, because they're already taking a long, hard look at all eight of the Ability to Repay requirements.

Borrowers will get some added protections. Many lenders that weren't already using these requirements will likely adopt the safer course. There will also be limits on the costs and fees associated with obtaining a mortgage.

And here's where we finally circle back to interest rates.

The wave of new regulations has also altered the compensation landscape for mortgage brokers and loan officers who want to originate Qualified Mortgages. In short, they can no longer be paid based on the costs and fees they charge, the interest rate or the loan's overall profitability.

The discussion can quickly become complicated. Let's start with a basic rundown of how borrowers secure rates and how brokers are paid under the old model.

Yield Spread and the Old Way of Doing Business

Borrowers qualify for a certain "**par rate**" at a given lender based on their unique financial and credit situation. You might also hear it called a **base rate**.

But borrowers aren't going to hear words like "par rate" or "base rate" from a prospective lender. Instead, they will get a rate quote — probably well above the true par rate — that includes what is essentially a lender's mark-up.

As we talked about before, financial institutions may buy and sell loans on the secondary mortgage market. In that marketplace, mortgages with higher interest rates are worth more than those with lower rates.

The financial institution purchasing the loan actually compensates lenders that lock borrowers into interest rates above the par rate. That compensation, essentially a rebate, is known as **Yield Spread Premium,** or Yield Spread, and it's at the heart of some of these regulatory changes.

Let's stop for a second and look at a sample rate sheet, which should help illustrate the concept:

Rate	15 Day	30 Day
7.375	103.415	103.312
7.25	103.359	103.261
7.125	103.124	103.031
7	102.82	102.733
6.875	102.569	102.486
6.75	102.34	102.263
6.625	102.125	102.053

6.5	101.77	101.703
6.375	101.314	101.252
6.25	100.986	100.929
6.125	100.592	100.541
6	100.118	100.072
5.875	99.591	99.55
5.75	99.163	99.128
5.625	98.67	98.64
5.5	98.075	98.05
5.375	97.4	97.38
5.25	96.81	96.795

The 15-day and 30-day headings refer to rate locks, which we'll cover later in this chapter. Most rate locks involve 30-day terms, so we'll focus on that column. In this example, 6 percent is as close as we can get to a true par rate (100.072 at a 30-day rate lock).

Notice that for every interest rate above 6 percent, there's a corresponding (and higher) rate of compensation, or yield spread. As an example, let's use this rate sheet and say the borrower wants a $300,000 loan. A lender that quotes a rate of 6.125 percent stands to make 0.541 percent of the loan amount in yield spread. In dollars, that translates to $1,623 ($300,000 x 0.00541). At 6.5 percent, the yield spread jumps to 1.703, or $5,109 ($300,000 x 0.01703).

There's no hard and fast standard, but consumers can generally assume, at least under this old structure, that lenders are looking to make 2.0 to 2.5 percent in Yield Spread. On a $300,000 loan, that's about $6,000. The lender is free to quote the borrower any rate on the sheet, but the higher the rate, the greater the compensation.

Borrowers don't pay Yield Spread Premium per se. Financial institutions that sell home loans to your VA lender are responsible for paying that cost. But borrowers wind up paying more in the form of a higher rate.

Taking a higher interest rate isn't necessarily a bad thing. Some borrowers may not have the cash on hand to cover up-front fees and costs associated with the loan closing. A borrower could elect to take a higher rate and have the lender use part of that yield spread rebate to pay those costs.

But what's to stop the loan officer from quoting every customer a 7.25 percent rate?

Nothing, at least in theory.

Mortgage lending is a hyper-competitive arena. Lenders and loan officers know that most borrowers are shopping around and comparing rates. Charging exorbitant rates to rack up huge yield spreads isn't much of a strategy for creating competitive advantage. Loan officers have to strike an appropriate balance between putting food on their tables and catering to the needs of choosy consumers.

And what about the rates below 6 percent?

Remember that the par rate is the breakeven point. Lenders *get paid* for a rate above par but *have to pay* for a rate below. Needless to say, lenders aren't in the habit of discounting mortgage loans or picking up the tab for a lower interest rate.

But that doesn't mean the borrower can't. We'll cover that shortly.

Changes to Broker Compensation and Rates

Under this type of compensation structure, loan officers would typically get a percentage of the total fees earned from the client and the Yield Spread. After the subprime mortgage debacle, housing regulators decided it was time to sever the link between what borrowers pay and what loan officers make.

The new Qualified Mortgage regulations no longer allow loan originators to make Yield Spread Premium. There's no longer any direct financial incentive for them to lock borrowers into higher interest rates.

Now, it's increasingly common to see loan originators paid a base salary, with commissions possible depending on the size of the loan, their overall production and other factors. Lenders who sell their loans on the secondary market can still earn a rebate, but that money cannot trickle down to individual loan officers.

Understanding yield spread and loan originator compensation is important for service members on a couple different levels.

The first is that mortgage lending is a specialized, service-oriented business. It's easy for consumers to get riled up when they first learn about yield spread and the concept of compensation. Perhaps our natural inclination is to look at rebates like this as something illicit.

But loan officers and other key employees have to earn a living, and the longstanding method for compensating industry folks is through commissions. It isn't a novel concept in the world of business. These dedicated people navigate borrowers through the sometimes-winding process of purchasing a home. They certainly deserve to be paid for it.

The second reason this is important: Yield Spread and this old compensation structure didn't just disappear. Loan officers originating loans that aren't classified as Qualified Mortgages can still utilize these rebates. QM loans are becoming the norm, but there will certainly be companies making non-QM loans to borrowers who need or want them.

So what does this all mean for interest rates?

Borrowers might be less likely to see wide variation moving forward. Lenders are going to quote you a rate based on a host of factors, which can include your credit score, a down payment if you're making one and their own in-house guidelines. But loan officers won't be looking to lock you into a higher rate to boost their own payday.

Negotiating a Rate

Now you're armed with a basic understanding of how rates and costs work. The question then becomes: What can I do with it?

You can't call up a lender and order a rate. It's not exactly a drive-through window. Veterans and service members should take the time to shop around and compare rates. While individual lenders aren't going to give you the par rate, you can probably come up with a pretty good sense of it by gathering enough quotes. Feel free to push and prod when necessary. Remember that companies compete on rates and use that to your advantage.

Be specific when putting the question to mortgage folks. Instead of asking, "What are your rates today?" be more pointed: "What is today's rate on a 30-year fixed-rate VA loan with no buydown points?"

Look for any inch of leverage you can find. If you've got great credit, this is the time to trumpet your top-tier score. Does Lender X have a better rate or lower up-front fees? Be sure to point that out to Lenders Y and Z. Some lenders are willing to come down and meet competitors on prices and fees — and even exceed them — in a tough market.

Be sure to compare the Annual Percentage Rate as well as the interest rate when you're soliciting quotes. As we mentioned earlier, the APR better reflects the true costs of borrowing.

There's another option for folks who would rather avoid the phone calls, the homework and the potential haggling. Retail banks, credit unions and similar lending institutions tend to operate on a non-negotiable level. They offer borrowers a flat, take-it-or-leave-it retail rate, which is typically higher than what you're able to get elsewhere. But not always.

The only hitch here is that VA loans can't be issued by just any institution. Veterans interested in securing financing through a neighborhood bank or similar retail outlet need to make sure it's approved by the VA. And don't let an institution that isn't VA-approved try to talk you out of considering your VA entitlement. No matter the sales pitch, there isn't another lending program that gives veterans this much financial flexibility and buying power.

Discount Points

One element of the old order of business that isn't supposed to change is that borrowers can shell out money up front to purchase a lower interest rate. This is the concept of paying **discount points**, or a purchasing a **permanent buydown**. A discount point is 1 percent of the total loan amount. One point on a $300,000 loan is $3,000.

Lenders are allowed to apply standard fees to most mortgage loans. On a VA loan, the lender can charge an **origination fee** of 1 point plus up to 2 additional discount points (as long as the lender isn't earning Yield Spread).

For an example, let's return to the sample rate sheet.

Let's say the lender gave you the option of a 6.25 percent rate with no points or a rate of 5.75 percent with 2 points. On a $300,000 mortgage, 2 points would cost the borrower $6,000. It's important to note this isn't a cost that can be rolled into the loan. You have to pay points up front. Or the seller can pay.

So are the points worth it? There's a relatively simple way to find out.

The monthly mortgage payment (without taxes and insurance) at 6.25 percent is $1,847. At a 5.75 percent interest rate, the monthly payment dips to $1,751. That's a difference of $96 per month, which is no small sum for many homebuyers, especially veterans with families.

Then again, $6,000 isn't exactly a small sum either. Here's a better way to gauge the investment: Divide the $6,000 in points by the $96 in monthly savings. That gives you 62.5, which is the number of months it will take you to "pay off" those points. So, in this example, it would take the veteran a little over five years to recoup that up-front investment.

Paying points isn't a common occurrence for many military homebuyers. VA borrowers typically come to the table without the kind of resources it takes to muster a big, one-time payment to buy down an interest rate. These are no-down payment loans that maximize buying power and help service members without significant financial resources become thriving homeowners. In many cases, coming up with the cash necessary to pay points is all but impossible. Veterans who have cash reserves can certainly crunch the numbers and consider whether the up-front cost of paying points is worth the monthly savings over the life of the loan.

Temporary Buydown

Veterans can also pay points to temporarily buy down their interest rate. The two most common **temporary buydowns** are the 3-2-1 buydown and the 2-1 buydown.

With a 3-2-1 buydown, the borrower's interest rate drops 3 percent below the note rate for the first year, 2 percent for the second year and 1 percent for the third year. The start of the fourth year marks the first year the borrower pays at the regular, full note rate.

Temporary buydowns can be a good option for borrowers on the edge. A lower initial interest rate means borrowers have more cash to pay down debt or take other steps to strengthen their financial position. That extra income can also allow borrowers with a higher debt-to-income ratio to qualify for a home they might not otherwise be able to land.

Of course, temporary buydowns come with a cost. Here's a quick example of how to calculate it.

Let's assume you're considering a 2-1 buy down on a 30-year, $200,000 mortgage at 6.5 percent interest. Find an online mortgage calculator that gives you a full amortization breakdown for your loan. Brett Whissel maintains an excellent one at www.bretwhissel.net/cgi-bin/amortize. Plug in the numbers and add up how much interest you'll pay in the first year (at 4.5 percent), in the second year (at 5.5 percent) and in the third and remaining years (at 6.5 percent). It should look something like this:

Interest Rate	Interest Costs
4.5 percent	$8,934
5.5 percent	$10,932
6.5 percent	$12,934

After just a quick glance, you can already see that the lender is losing money by allowing you to buy down the rate for the first two years. A borrower with a regular fixed-rate mortgage at 6.5 percent would pay $25,718 during those first two years. Instead, with a temporary buy down the borrower is paying only $19,866 in interest ($8,934 + $10,932). Here's where the cost to the borrower comes in.

Looking at the numbers, the lender effectively loses out on $5,852 in interest because of the temporary buydown ($25,718-19,866).

But lenders don't like to lose money. So they take that difference ($5,852) and divide it into the overall loan amount (which, in this case, is $200,000). That gives you 0.2926, which becomes 2.93 points that the borrower has to pay the lender to receive the buydown. On a $200,000 loan, that comes out to $5,840 that the borrower has to come up with to close the loan.

Borrowers without that kind of cash on hand can ask the lender to kick up the interest rate a bit and roll those costs into the life of the loan.

Either way, it's not as if the borrower is getting a huge financial break with a buydown. They still pay. It's just a question of how and when.

Temporary buydowns aren't incredibly commonplace among VA borrowers. They will likely become increasingly rare because of the new Qualified Mortgage regulations, which limit costs and fees.

Conventional Rates v. VA Rates

Way back in Chapter One, we declared that VA loans represent a better financial fit for the vast majority of military borrowers. Folks on the conventional financing side of the aisle might beg to differ and point out that some military borrowers can get a lower base rate on a conventional loan.

But that's rarely the whole story.

It's certainly true that conventional base rates can be lower than VA rates. But the borrower's final rate doesn't usually stay low for long. And that's because conventional mortgage lenders have to pay a premium on the loans they purchase from the secondary mortgage market. This premium is known as a **loan-to-value adjustment**, and it's essentially a fee based on a borrower's credit score and down payment.

Borrowers with excellent credit and a sizable down payment may cost the lender a small adjustment, if at all. There's often no adjustment for borrowers with a credit score of 740 or higher. The same goes for borrowers with sizable down payments. So a veteran with those kinds of credentials might snare an interest rate equivalent to a VA rate and, more importantly, avoid paying the VA Funding Fee.

But not every borrower has top-tier credit and a down payment nest egg. So once those adjustments are factored in, conventional lenders will typically offer the borrower a higher interest rate in order to recoup what they paid in adjustments.

Locking a Rate

Loan officers will talk a lot at the outset about locking into a great rate. But what exactly does that mean?

Well, it's not just an expression. A rate lock is a legal commitment that binds a borrower to a specific interest rate. Borrowers can typically lock their interest rate as soon as they sign a purchase agreement and up to five days before the loan closing. Rate locks are good for specific blocks of time. The most common lock periods are for 15 days, 30 days, 45 days and 60 days.

Getting locked into an interest rate is a serious step. It can also prove to be a savvy and wise decision if interest rates climb as your closing date nears.

There's no mathematical formula or chart to consult to help veterans determine when they should lock an interest rate. Just as rates can climb before a closing, they can also fall. Talk about a frustrating feeling.

This is another area where having a trusted lender is key. So is doing some homework on your own. Look at how rates have performed the previous few months. Dig around online and garner predictions and information from credible outlets about what rates are likely to do in the coming weeks and months.

You've ultimately got two choices: Lock or **float**. To float means you're going to hold off and watch rates as your closing nears. Some lenders will charge borrowers to lock in a rate, especially if it's for a lock term beyond 30 days. But not every lender charges a **lock fee**. It's a good question to ask your loan officer up front.

Borrowers who decide to float can count on a good loan officer keeping them abreast of rate news and predictions. Loan officers who sense that rates are on the verge of rising will usually contact their borrowers to let them know it might be time to lock. Other times, borrowers basically give their loan officer the freedom to lock a rate at his or her discretion, typically when rates appear headed for a notable increase.

No matter what, getting something in writing is crucial when it comes to rate locks. Conversations and oral commitments are about as useful as an umbrella in a hurricane. Once you decide on a rate, you should receive written confirmation that includes all the pertinent information you need: the rate, the dates and length of the lock, any fees and points and anything else that's relevant to your loan. Check the fine print with these rate commitments, too. Make sure the lender hasn't included any shady provisions that allow it to increase the rate or toss out the rate lock entirely. Borrowers can also purchase extensions on their rate locks if delays occurring during the closing process. Rate lock extensions usually come with a minimal cost that, again, depends on the duration.

Now, you might have to agree to a **rate cap** depending on the lender. Some borrowers would certainly argue that these are shady provisions by another name. But rate caps are relatively common tools that lenders use to insulate themselves. Basically, a rate cap gives the lender the right to give you a slightly higher interest rate if they rise before your closing.

New laws passed in 2010 require full disclosure to the borrower if the rate changes by more than an eighth of a point from the time of initial disclosure to closing.

You can also try to get an option added to your rate lock commitment that allows you to take advantage of a decrease in rates. Not all lenders allow these conditional commitments, and those that do tend to charge a premium for the service. And, in some cases, this option can backfire on a borrower if rates increase.

Any talk about rate locks inevitably leads to a single word: When?

Unfortunately, it doesn't come with a one-word answer. Obsessing over a rate lock can drive borrowers crazy. It's tough on loan officers, too.

Be an informed consumer. Stay in constant contact with your loan officer. Other than that, when to lock your rate depends on a host of factors that are often unique to the individual buyer. Look at your finances and crunch the numbers on an array of interest rates. You might decide it's worth floating if interest rates appear to be headed down (and you can afford a slightly higher payment if they don't).

Perhaps the best advice is simple common sense: Lock when you're completely comfortable with the rate environment and don't look back. Second guessing and obsessing isn't going to help anyone, and the days and weeks leading to a home closing can be stressful enough as it is. If something weird happens and rates take a huge nosedive, call your loan officer for a frank discussion. There's no guarantee they'll cut you a break, mainly because you're cutting into their commission.

One tactic that isn't recommended: Abandoning ship for another lender. It's a risky, last-minute gambit that could cost you that dream home. It would likely jeopardize your closing and any goodwill you established with the seller. Your credit score might also take a hit when a new lender pulls your credit.

Borrowers certainly do it from time to time if the rate drop is that dramatic. But it's an incredibly risky move that could delay, if not completely derail, your home purchase.

Fixed v. ARM

Borrowers have to consider more than just discount points and rate locks. One of the most important elements is the type of loan.

In all but a few instances, a **fixed-rate loan** is going to represent the safest and most reliable option for veterans and service members. Fixed-rate loans have a set-in-stone interest rate for the duration of the term. The most common fixed-rate term is the long haul, 30 years. But borrowers can opt for the shorter, 15-year term and typically land a slightly lower interest rate. A shorter term also means higher monthly payments.

Here's a quick example. The monthly mortgage payment on a 30-year, fixed loan at $300,000 and 5.75 percent is about $1,750. Drop the loan term to 15 years and that payment jumps to $2,491, an increase of almost $750 per month. That's a tremendous difference for most working families.

But there is another path for veterans who are bent on paying off their mortgage before the 30-year mark. We touched on it earlier in this chapter, but it's worth revisiting. One of the most underrated benefits of the VA loan is the borrower's ability to prepay without penalty. In layman's terms, that means you can make additional payments to your principal each month on top of your regular mortgage payment.

Those extra payments can quickly add up and artificially shorten your loan term and the interest you pay over the life of the loan. Here's another example, and let's stick with the same terms: a 30-year fixed-rate $300,000 mortgage at 5.75 percent interest. In this case, a veteran who can scrounge up an additional $300 each month will shave nine years and almost $113,000 from the life of the mortgage.

A fixed-rate mortgage is as close to certainty as most borrowers can get. It's also far and away the preferred vehicle for veterans and military borrowers using a VA loan.

That isn't to say that an **adjustable-rate mortgage** is out of the question. ARMs can represent a smart financial opportunity under the right set of circumstances. These are mortgages that can experience an interest rate hike based on what's happening in the greater economic landscape.

Rates on most ARMs can change once a year, and they're tied to a couple different economic indices, the most common being the one-year Treasury bill index. The way it typically works is that a borrower gets an ARM at a low initial rate, maybe a point or even two below average fixed rates. That rate will remain constant for a pre-determined period of time. Once that period expires, a new rate is calculated annually based on the Treasury index. Lenders will also add on percentage points in what's known as the margin.

Most ARMs come with an interest rate cap that protects borrowers against an astronomical rate hike.

Today, the most common ARM for VA borrowers is either a 3/1 or 5/1 Hybrid. The borrower gets a fixed interest rate for the first three or five years of the loan term (hence, the "hybrid" in the title). Hybrid VA ARMs feature what's known as a 1/1/5 cap:

- 1 percentage point is the highest your rate can increase on the first adjustment
- 1 percentage point is the most your rate can increase on each subsequent annual adjustment
- 5 percentage points is the most your rate can increase over the life of the loan

A low interest rate during those first few years can make a huge difference for veterans who might need cash to pay off other debts or obligations. ARMs are also a potential option for service members who only plan to stay in their homes for three to five years. The hybrid ARM options are a much safer route than some traditional ARMs, which can come with significant rate increases.

Not every VA-approved lender offers ARMs. Many states require lenders to have additional compliance disclosures and counseling initiatives in order to satisfy government requirements. Veterans United currently offers a 5/1 Hybrid VA ARM.

In terms of deciding between a fixed-rate mortgage and an ARM, consider your unique financial situation and what you can afford. If you're planning to move in a few years or expecting a big salary increase, a hybrid ARM may be the right option. Veterans who crave more stability and certainty may want to play it safer and stick with the set-in-stone rate.

Other Mortgage Types

Fixed-rate and adjustable-rate mortgages are the most commonly known, but they're not the only options veterans and military members have to choose from. We'll look at three in particular: Graduated Payment Mortgages, or GPMs; Growing Equity Mortgages, or GEMs; and Energy Efficient Mortgages, or EEMs.

A **Graduated Payment Mortgage** is a specialized, fixed-rate loan geared toward borrowers who plan to see an increase in income as homeownership progresses. Borrowers with a GPM begin by paying lower monthly mortgage payments than other borrowers with a fixed-rate mortgage but see a gradual increase in costs for a given time period.

Loan payments for VA borrowers increase at a rate of 7.5 percent each year for the first five years of the loan term. They then level off with the start of year No. 6 and stay at that plateau for the remainder of the loan.

In the civilian world, young professionals who anticipate a significant boost in earnings over time often express an interest in GPMs. If there's a shred of doubt about your ability to handle higher payments down the road, a GPM may not be the best option. They're slightly more predictable than ARMs because the rate of increase is hammered out before the borrower closes on the loan.

It's worth noting that veterans can't get a temporary buydown with a GPM. These also can't be used to refinance a loan (we'll cover refinance loans in the next chapter).

A second cousin to the GPM is the GEM, or **Growing Equity Mortgage**. This is another fixed-rate mortgage with payments that increase over time. But in this case, the extra payments are applied directly to the loan principal. These extra payments mean borrowers build equity faster and often pay off a 30-year mortgage in half the time.

Monthly payments on a GEM are tied to a fixed rate of increase (3 percent each year for the first 10 years) or to an economic index. While they may seem nearly identical, there are two major differences between a GPM and a GEM.

With a Graduated Payment Mortgage, the monthly payments can be so low that they don't quite cover the interest that's accrued during that period. That unpaid interest gets added to the loan balance and ultimately boosts the total amount you owe. Mortgage and financial folks call this negative amortization. Veterans who stay in their homes long enough will see this process basically reverse and erase that built-up interest in time to hit the loan's target payoff date. That's sort of the bargain borrowers have to strike with a GPM. The loan winds up costing more because of the negative amortization, but those low initial payments mean they can afford to get into a home sooner. The potential wrinkle here is that, as mentioned earlier, loans with negative amortization cannot be considered Qualified Mortgages.

The third alternative loan type is the **Energy Efficient Mortgage**, or EEM. This is a specialized mortgage that allows veterans to make energy-efficient improvements to a home they're purchasing or refinancing. An EEM can be a solid investment for veterans and their families, especially those planning to stay in the home for a while. Spending money at the outset on energy improvements can ultimately lower heating, cooling and other related energy costs for years to come. That monthly savings can be funneled into additional payments to the mortgage principal or dozens of other household necessities.

Veterans can't use an EEM to install an energy-efficient swimming pool or make cosmetic upgrades to the property. But there are more than a dozen acceptable improvements, including:

- Thermal windows and doors
- Insulation for walls, ceilings, attics, floors and water heaters
- Solar heating and cooling systems
- Furnace modifications (but not an entirely new furnace)

- Heat pumps
- Vapor barriers

There's standard language on all Notices of Value that explains to veterans their ability to secure an Energy Efficient Mortgage. That same section also notes that the buyer may want to consider paying for a home energy audit, a key step that kick-starts the process.

EEMs allow the lender to tack on $3,000 to the loan amount as long as the veteran can verify the cost of improvements through bids, contracts and other documents. For veterans who want to spend from $3,000 to $6,000 on improvements, the lender has to make sure the energy improvements generate enough savings to offset the new, higher monthly mortgage payment. In other words, it makes no sense to boost your monthly payment by $150 if the energy improvements only save you $15 in utility costs.

Improvements that cost more than $6,000 require special consideration by the lender and the VA. This is a relatively rare occurrence.

The veteran typically has six months after closing to get the improvements completed. Small fixes can be taken care of before closing, otherwise the lender may decide to open an escrow account for the improvement funding.

EEMs aren't exceptionally common with VA loans. Veterans can check with their local utility companies to see if there are free or reduced-cost energy audits available. Private firms may also offer discounts for military members, veterans and their families. As with any in-home service like this, make sure you hire a legitimate company with a proven track record.

Closing Costs

Governmental and industry officials have worked diligently over the last few decades to ensure borrowers don't get fleeced by unscrupulous lenders. Fees, costs and charges shouldn't be a mystery to borrowers. But there's a sordid history of bait-and-switch tactics and under-the-table kickbacks that spring unexpected costs on homebuyers just before their deal gets done.

Thankfully, those days are over, mostly because of new regulations and updated disclosure rules regarding fees and charges. There are always going to be costs and fees associated with your loan. Loan officers, loan processors, receptionists, executives and anyone else who works for a mortgage company expects to get paid. But homebuyers have a right to know, up front, exactly how much they're expected to pay and for what.

To that end, the U.S. Department of Housing and Urban Development recently decided to try and streamline the disclosure process for fees, costs and charges. The changes took effect in January 2010 and involve the Good Faith Estimate and its counterpart, the **HUD-1 settlement statement**.

As we talked about earlier, the Good Faith Estimate is an estimate of the costs and fees associated with your loan. A lender has three days to provide you with a GFE once you have a purchase agreement. But this is simply an estimate, and the costs aren't written in stone.

On the other hand, the HUD-1 comes at the end of your journey, just before the loan closing. This statement reflects the costs and fees you will be paying. These are set in stone. Beyond that, the updated versions of these documents put a premium on comprehension. Terms and concepts remain the same throughout so borrowers can make realistic comparisons. There are some fees and charges that can't change from the GFE to the HUD-1.

The VA limits what veterans can pay in closing costs to reasonable discount points, that flat 1 percent charge by the lender and other reasonable and standard fees and charges designated by the VA.

Those reasonable fees and charges can include things like VA appraisals, credit reports, title and insurance and pre-paid items like taxes and assessments. The lender's flat fee is meant to help them recoup costs they can't itemize as fees and charges, and there's a laundry list of things the lender *cannot* charge you for individually. Instead, the lender has to use that 1 percent flat fee to cover things such as:

- Their own inspection and appraisals
- Document prep costs
- Interest rate lock fees
- Notary costs
- Processing fees
- Loan closing costs
- And more

You can already get a feel for the array of costs by looking at the Initial Fees Worksheet that comes in your loan application packet. Now, we'll take a closer look at the Good Faith Estimate, a three-page document that brings all of that information up to date.

Good Faith Estimate

As clear and straightforward as it looks, there has been much consternation and controversy surrounding this document, at least in mortgage industry circles. This version became standard on Jan. 1, 2010, replacing a decades-old design that had long outlived its usefulness. Confusion and uncertainty reigned in the buildup to the unveiling. Mortgage insiders worried that the new document actually made things more confusing and difficult for industry folks, which could have major implications for borrower and lenders. So far, though, it seems most of the hubbub was hot air.

The new, more streamlined GFE was designed to make it easier for borrowers to understand fees and charges and effectively compare them against competing offers. And, by most accounts, that's exactly what it's done.

We'll quickly go over the most important sections, one page at a time. The first page of the GFE provides borrowers with a more high-level snapshot of their lending and fee situation. It includes information on how long the interest rate is available and how rate locks will affect your window to settle.

Here's a look at the big stuff from Page 1:

Summary of your loan		
Your initial loan amount is	$	
Your loan term is	years	
Your initial interest rate is	%	
Your initial monthly amount owed for principal, interest, and any mortgage insurance is	$ per month	
Can your interest rate rise?	☐ No ☐ Yes, it can rise to a maximum of % The first change will be in	
Even if you make payments on time, can your loan balance rise?	☐ No ☐ Yes, it can rise to a maximum of $	
Even if you make payments on time, can your monthly amount owed for principal, interest, and any mortgage insurance rise?	☐ No ☐ Yes, the first increase can be in and the monthly amount owed can rise to $ The maximum it can ever rise to is $	
Does your loan have a prepayment penalty?	☐ No ☐ Yes, your maximum prepayment penalty is $	
Does your loan have a balloon payment?	☐ No ☐ Yes, you have a balloon payment of $ due in years	

This is the loan summary. It spells out the terms of your loan, your interest rate and other key information. Unless you're pursuing an adjustable-rate mortgage, all of the questions should be checked "No."

Escrow account information	
	Some lenders require an escrow account to hold funds for paying property taxes or other property-related charges in addition to your monthly amount owed of $. Do we require you to have an escrow account for your loan? ☐ No, you do not have an escrow account. You must pay these charges directly when due. ☐ Yes, you have an escrow account. It may or may not cover all of these charges. Ask us.

Escrow is the money set aside to pay for future homeowner's insurance premiums and real estate taxes. This section details exactly how much, if any, the borrower should set aside in escrow.

Summary of your settlement charges

Good Faith Estimate (HUD-GFE) 1

This is the first time you see a total estimate of your closing costs. It's still an estimate at this point, as some charges are subject to change (we'll talk about that shortly). Field A represents the origination charge, which is the fee the lender charges for procuring the loan. This charge has to be separated out from the others. There's a whole lot more that goes into Field B, which is the sum of a host of charges and fees. Added together they represent an estimate — made, of course, in good faith — of your closing costs.

Now, on to Page 2. This is where the detail comes in.

Understanding your estimated settlement charges

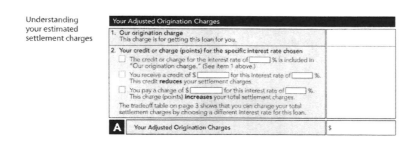

This first section relates explicitly to the lender's origination charge. Borrowers who are paying points will be able to track those exact costs. The origination charge cannot change between the time you get the GFE and your loan closing. Neither can the amount you pay for points once you've locked in your interest rate.

Some of these charges can change at settlement. See the top of page 3 for more information.

3. **Required services that we select**
These charges are for services we require to complete your settlement. We will choose the providers of these services.
Service — Charge

4. **Title services and lender's title insurance**
This charge includes the services of a title or settlement agent, for example, and title insurance to protect the lender, if required.

5. **Owner's title insurance**
You may purchase an owner's title insurance policy to protect your interest in the property.

6. **Required services that you can shop for**
These charges are for other services that are required to complete your settlement. We can identify providers of these services or you can shop for them yourself. Our estimates for providing these services are below.
Service — Charge

7. **Government recording charges**
These charges are for state and local fees to record your loan and title documents.

8. **Transfer taxes**
These charges are for state and local fees on mortgages and home sales.

9. **Initial deposit for your escrow account**
This charge is held in an escrow account to pay future recurring charges on your property and includes ☐ all property taxes, ☐ all insurance, and ☐ other _____.

10. **Daily interest charges**
This charge is for the daily interest on your loan from the day of your settlement until the first day of the next month or the first day of your normal mortgage payment cycle. This amount is $____ per day for ____ days (if your settlement is ____).

11. **Homeowner's insurance**
This charge is for the insurance you must buy for the property to protect from a loss, such as fire.
Policy — Charge

B Your Charges for All Other Settlement Services $

A + **B** Total Estimated Settlement Charges $

Good Faith Estimate (HUD-GFE) 2

The second section is the beast of the pair. But it's a far sight better than the old GFE. The first part, which is considered No. 3, is for charges that the lender requires in order to issue a loan, such as the VA Funding Fee, appraisal fees and, if necessary, appraisal re-inspection costs.

The next two parts, Nos. 4-5, relate to title information. Borrowers can shop around for title services and insurance. The number here will be an estimate that reflects rates for a title firm recommended by the lender.

The rest are relatively self-explanatory, which, again, is a testament to the readability of the new GFE. The "Daily interest charges" is more important than many borrowers realize. It also explains why so many borrowers look to close on their homes at the end of each month rather than the beginning. The reason is because you pay a mortgage in arrears. That is, when Month 2 starts, you write a check to pay for the privilege of having lived in your home during Month 1. Borrowers are on the hook for prepaid interest costs from the time they sign the closing papers until the first day of the next month. Their first month's payment is essentially those prepaid costs paid at the time of closing. So, if you can close at the end of June, you'll pay just a few days worth of interest costs and not write a check again until the beginning of August.

For example, on a $350,000 mortgage at 30 years and 5.25 percent, the per diem charge would be about $49. Closing on June 25 leaves just a five-day window of interest charges for the veteran to cover. Five days times $49 per day comes out to $245 the borrower must come up with at closing. On the other hand, the veteran who closes on June 5 has to come up with 25 days worth of prepaid interest costs, or $1,225 (25 x $49/ day). That's a significant difference and the main reason why so many borrowers try to close toward the end of the month.

Now, this isn't exactly a secret, which means scores of borrowers are hoping for a late-month closing date. Some months are typically busier than others, but it's always a good idea to scale back. Closing on the last day of the month invites major headaches if something goes wrong with your closing paperwork. And then you're stuck somewhere you really don't want to be. A couple days before the end of the month usually provides a comfortable enough window that lenders can correct problems and take care of last-minute issues while still saving the borrower a good deal of money.

The last line, No. 11, gives the borrower a good idea of the monthly cost for **homeowners insurance**. Most lenders mandate that borrowers obtain insurance to at least cover the amount owed on the property.

The third page of the GFE is all about making comparisons. The first section explains to the borrower what charges can and cannot increase at the time of the loan closing. Here's a look:

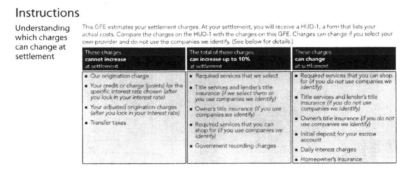

The next part is what the government has come to call a "tradeoff table." Essentially, it's a breakdown that allows borrowers to see how costs change if they take a higher interest rate to enable their lender to pay closing costs or if they decide to buy down the interest rate.

Using the tradeoff table

In this GFE, we offered you this loan with a particular interest rate and estimated settlement charges. However:
- If you want to choose this same loan with **lower settlement charges**, then you will have a **higher interest rate**.
- If you want to choose this same loan with a **lower interest rate**, then you will have **higher settlement charges**.

If you would like to choose an available option, you must ask us for a new GFE.

Loan originators have the option to complete this table. Please ask for additional information if the table is not completed.

	The loan in this GFE	The same loan with lower settlement charges	The same loan with a lower interest rate
Your initial loan amount	$	$	$
Your initial interest rate[1]	%	%	%
Your initial monthly amount owed	$	$	$
Change in the monthly amount owed from this GFE	No change	You will pay $ **more** every month	You will pay $ **less** every month
Change in the amount you will pay at settlement with this interest rate	No change	Your settlement charges will be **reduced** by $	Your settlement charges will **increase** by $
How much your total estimated settlement charges will be	$	$	$

[1] For an adjustable rate loan, the comparisons above are for the initial interest rate before adjustments are made

The third and final section is called the "shopping chart," not to be confused with shopping cart. Although one can certainly make a case. This is a consumer-focused tool meant to aid in comparative shopping. Here's a look at the chart:

Using the shopping chart

Use this chart to compare GFEs from different loan originators. Fill in the information by using a different column for each GFE you receive. By comparing loan offers, you can shop for the best loan.

	This loan	Loan 2	Loan 3	Loan 4
Loan originator name				
Initial loan amount				
Loan term				
Initial interest rate				
Initial monthly amount owed				
Rate lock period				
Can interest rate rise?				
Can loan balance rise?				
Can monthly amount owed rise?				
Prepayment penalty?				
Balloon payment?				
Total Estimated Settlement Charges				

If your loan is sold in the future

Some lenders may sell your loan after settlement. Any fees lenders receive in the future cannot change the loan you receive or the charges you paid at settlement.

 Good Faith Estimate (HUD-GFE) 3

Again, it's certainly a good idea to be cost-conscious and shop around when the time comes to purchase a home. This is a major investment with life-long financial repercussions. This chart was crafted to make it easier to compare the rates, terms

and conditions of multiple loan offers. But veterans should not expect to see a Good Faith Estimate until they have a purchase agreement in hand. That's why we issue borrowers that Initial Fees Worksheet mentioned in Chapter 2. That worksheet is essentially the old GFE and gives borrowers a pretty good idea of costs and charges in the early going.

New regulations mean lenders must disclose GFEs down to the dime when it comes to loan terms, amounts and rates. Many of the fees cannot vary, but some can as long as there is an acceptable "change of circumstance" and the GFE is re-disclosed to the borrower.

Some acceptable changes include circumstances like a change of property or a borrower requesting a lower rate, which leads to higher fees. Essentially, as long as it's legitimate and the borrower is made aware, some GFE fees can change. But the bulk will not.

It's also important for veterans to understand some of the limitations and omissions that are part of the new Good Faith Estimate. For example, the new GFE does not give borrowers an estimate of the total amount of cash they will need on hand to close their loan, only the total estimated settlement charges. Those two figures can vary greatly, sometimes by more than $10,000. The new GFE also fails to include an estimate of the borrower's total monthly **PITI** payment, which includes the mortgage principal along with insurance, taxes and escrow. There's also nothing in there about seller-financed closing costs, which is a big deal in the world of VA loans.

In many cases lenders themselves will supplement the GFE with additional documents to help borrowers get a more holistic financial picture. But it's up to the individual lender.

HUD-1 Settlement Statement

The Good Faith Estimate wasn't the only important lending document to get a makeover in recent years. Government officials also decided to revamp the HUD-1 settlement statement to help boost consumer understanding and comparative shopping.

The original HUD-1 grew out of the Real Estate Settlement and Procedures Act of 1974, or RESPA. The law increased transparency and disclosures within the mortgage industry. It also helped boost consumer protection and provide homeowners with a clearer accounting of costs and fees associated with their potential home purchase.

At the time, there wasn't a standard document that clearly spelled out closing and settlement costs for borrowers. That made it difficult to compare loans and to determine whether the mortgage was padded with unnecessary costs.

After 36 years, the original HUD-1 was replaced in 2010 by a new, three-page model. Much like the new GFE, there's been mixed reviews about the new settlement statement, although it often depends on whom you ask and on which side of the transaction they sit.

The settlement statement is designed to give consumers a detailed accounting of the pending transaction, from closing costs to how much both the seller and the buyer shell out and receive. We'll briefly take a look at each page to give you an idea of what awaits:

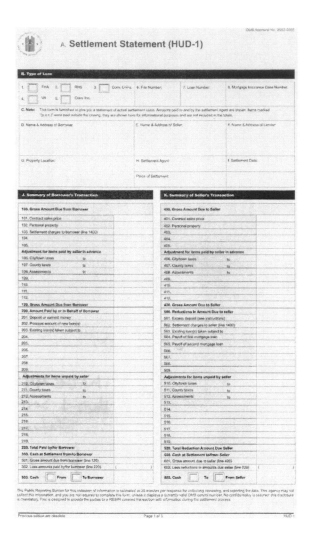

The primary focus of page 1 is to show consumers both sides of the transaction. Borrowers see their total settlement charges and their final payment amount. They also get to see what the seller is making on the deal. Section 300 details how much cash, if any, the borrower has to bring to the closing table. For many VA borrowers, this section will simply show that they're getting back their earnest money.

L. Settlement Charges

700. Total Real Estate Broker Fees			Paid From Borrower's Funds at Settlement	Paid From Seller's Funds at Settlement
Division of commission (line 700) as follows:				
701. $	to			
702. $	to			
703. Commission paid at settlement				
704.				

800. Items Payable in Connection with Loan				
801. Our origination charge	$	(from GFE #1)		
802. Your credit or charge (points) for the specific interest rate chosen	$	(from GFE #2)		
803. Your adjusted origination charges		(from GFE #A)		
804. Appraisal fee to		(from GFE #3)		
805. Credit report to		(from GFE #3)		
806. Tax service to		(from GFE #3)		
807. Flood certification to		(from GFE #3)		
808.				
809.				
810.				
811.				

900. Items Required by Lender to be Paid in Advance				
901. Daily interest charges from	to	@ $	/day	(from GFE #10)
902. Mortgage insurance premium for	months to			(from GFE #3)
903. Homeowner's insurance for	years to			(from GFE #11)
904.				

1000. Reserves Deposited with Lender				
1001. Initial deposit for your escrow account			(from GFE #9)	
1002. Homeowner's insurance	months @ $	per month $		
1003. Mortgage insurance	months @ $	per month $		
1004. Property Taxes	months @ $	per month $		
1005.	months @ $	per month $		
1006.	months @ $	per month $		
1007. Aggregate Adjustment		-$		

1100. Title Charges				
1101. Title services and lender's title insurance			(from GFE #4)	
1102. Settlement or closing fee	$			
1103. Owner's title insurance			(from GFE #5)	
1104. Lender's title insurance	$			
1105. Lender's title policy limit $				
1106. Owner's title policy limit $				
1107. Agent's portion of the total title insurance premium to	$			
1108. Underwriter's portion of the total title insurance premium to	$			
1109.				
1110.				
1111.				

1200. Government Recording and Transfer Charges				
1201. Government recording charges			(from GFE #7)	
1202. Deed $	Mortgage $	Release $		
1203. Transfer taxes			(from GFE #8)	
1204. City/County tax/stamps	Deed $	Mortgage $		
1205. State tax/stamps	Deed $	Mortgage $		
1206.				

1300. Additional Settlement Charges				
1301. Required services that you can shop for			(from GFE #6)	
1302.	$			
1303.	$			
1304.				
1305.				

1400. Total Settlement Charges (enter on lines 103, Section J and 502, Section K)				

Previous edition are obsolete   Page 2 of 3   HUD-1

The second page delves deeper into the borrower's total settlement charges. There's a simple reference on the relevant lines that shows consumers how the charge on the HUD-1 corresponds to the Good Faith Estimate. In Section 700, you see exactly how much the real estate agents are making on the transaction, a sum that's going to come from the seller's pocket and not your own. Section 800 provides a specific breakdown of the costs and charges. This is one section in particular you want to compare to your GFE.

Section 900 details up-front costs like interest charges and homeowners insurance that borrowers often have to pay at closing. This is where you'll see the final figures for those "daily interest charges" you may be required to pay. Sellers can pay these costs, too. In fact, most of our transactions involve the seller paying closing costs and pre-paid items.

Section 1100 covers titles and title insurance. There are two different types of coverage, lender's and owner's. The main difference is lender's coverage protects the lender against title claims up to the total remaining balance of the mortgage. Owner's insurance protects you, the homebuyer, against title claims up to the full purchase price of the property, plus equity. You can also see the settlement agent's commission on the title insurance premium in line 1107.

Section 1200 shows borrowers what the government gets out of the deal. These are all basically taxes and levies that help generate revenue for municipalities, counties and states. These costs have to be paid at closing and can't be rolled into the loan. If the seller is paying closing costs and pre-paid items, they're probably raising their sales price to cover the cost.

The third page of the new HUD-1 is a total departure from its predecessor. This page was designed as an easy-to-use comparison sheet between the GFE and the settlement statement. As we mentioned earlier, there are some costs that cannot legally increase from the GFE to the HUD-1. Those are examined more closely in the first section. It's not uncommon to see many of these charges decrease. Lenders tend to err on the side of caution and overestimate costs like origination charges and transfer fees. A lowball estimate can ultimately put the lender on the hot seat.

There are other charges that can only increase up to 10 percent. Those are spelled out in the second section. The lender is required to calculate both the dollar and percent increase from the GFE to the HUD-1 and drop those tallies in the last line of the box. It's important to note that this 10-percent cap only holds if the lender selected the service providers. Veterans who hire their own can see costs increase more than 10 percent from the GFE.

Otherwise, veterans needn't worry if something goes haywire with the numbers. If one or more of the "charges that cannot increase" actually increases or if the "charges that in total cannot increase more than 10%" wind up exceeding that threshold, the show still goes on. Veterans simply pay the higher charges and get a reimbursement from their lender within 30 days.

The final section of Page 3 is a basic summary of your loan.

Borrowers typically review the HUD-1 settlement statement the day of or the day before closing. Scour these pages for mistakes, as they do happen. At the same time, make sure you get full and complete answers to all of your questions about this document and how it relates to the Good Faith Estimate you received.

VA Loans and Closing Costs

Now it's time for a deep breath and some good news: Veterans typically pay only a fraction of those costs, if any. This is one of the most dynamic aspects of a VA loan. Sellers can pay all of the buyer's loan-related closing costs. They can also pay up to 4 percent of the home's value in what are called **seller concessions**, which can include things like:

- Paying the borrower's property taxes and insurance for a set number of months
- Paying the VA Funding Fee (which we'll cover in the next section)
- Paying additional points for a permanent buydown
- Paying off credit balances or judgments
- Providing gifts like furniture or electronics

It's difficult to talk averages when it comes to closing costs, but, generally speaking, VA borrowers can expect closing costs to be about 3 percent to 4 percent of the loan amount.

Why would a seller shell out that kind of money to pay a veteran's closing costs? Because they want to sell their home. How much a seller will pay often depends on the state of the real estate market. Paying costs and concessions can give sellers a competitive edge in a slow market.

But not every seller will bite. In fact, some industry observers argue that this benefit actually pushes sellers away from veterans and VA borrowers. That can certainly be the case in individual situations in different markets across the country. But seller concessions are certainly a part of the world of conventional financing, too.

There's another major reason sellers often agree to pay closing costs on a VA loan: Because they're not actually parting with their money. Here's how it works:

Say the veteran agrees to purchase a home for $150,000 and the closing costs come out to $5,000. If the seller balks at paying closing costs out of pocket, the veteran can produce a counteroffer for $155,000. Then, the seller simply turns around and pays that $5,000 back to cover the veteran's closing costs.

There are two big rubs with this scenario: The first is that a lender can't magically boost the loan amount. The home has to appraise for that higher value in order to make this work. The second issue revolves around the veteran, who is essentially footing the bill for these closing costs by agreeing to a slightly higher loan amount. That's going to mean higher monthly payments for the life of the loan.

For example, on a 30-year $150,000 mortgage at 6 percent, the monthly payment is $899. Bump up the loan amount to $155,000 and the payment increases to $929, a difference of $30 each month.

In many cases, it's about weighing pros, cons and outcomes. You can't argue with the math — you will pay more each month to make this maneuver possible. And, over 30 years, you're going to pay more than what you owed in closing costs. But for many borrowers that's the price of getting into a home now.

It's not uncommon for first-time buyers and folks with borderline credit to have only a couple thousand dollars in savings, if that. This type of closing arrangement can make a big difference for many veterans and their families.

Lenders can also "cover" the costs of closing by ratcheting up the borrower's interest rate. It's similar to the seller-financed scenario, in that the veteran winds up paying a little more each month but shells out nothing up front. For example, on that same $150,000 mortgage, increasing the interest rate from 6 percent to 6.5 percent increases the monthly mortgage payment by $49. A higher rate means a higher Yield Spread for the lender, who in turn uses some of that excess to cover your closing costs.

This set-up is how most companies that claim to have "No Fee" or "No Closing Cost" loans operate. Certainly sounds too good to be true, and this explains why it is. Getting a home loan "without fees" doesn't mean you've found a great deal.

It means the lender has simply taken a different path to the same payday.

VA Funding Fee

This is an unavoidable closing cost for most VA borrowers. You can't negotiate or sweet talk your way out of paying it. That's mostly because it's one of the keys to keeping the entire loan program afloat.

The VA Funding Fee is a set fee applied to every purchase loan or refinance. The proceeds go directly to the VA and help cover losses on the loans that go into default. The fee changes slightly depending on the down payment amount, whether the borrower has a prior VA loan and the nature of the borrower's service. There are exemptions for borrowers with service-connected disabilities and for qualifying surviving spouses. Otherwise, here's the breakdown for regular military:

Down payment	Funding Fee (1st use)	Funding Fee (2nd use)
None	2.15 percent	3.3 percent
5-10 percent	1.5 percent	1.5 percent
10 and up	1.25 percent	1.25 percent

The percentages shift slightly for members of the Reserves and the National Guard:

Down payment	Funding Fee (1st use)	Funding Fee (2nd use)
None	2.4 percent	3.3 percent
5-10 percent	1.75 percent	1.75 percent
10 and up	1.5 percent	1.5 percent

Veterans aren't required to come up with the Funding Fee from their own pocket. Most roll the cost into their loan amount, which adds a few dollars to their monthly mortgage payment. For example, the 2.5 percent funding fee on a $200,000 mortgage comes out to $5,000. On a fixed-rate loan at 30 years and 6 percent, rolling in the funding fee adds $30 per month.

The only downside to including the VA Funding Fee in the overall loan is that the borrower essentially pays it twice. With the above example, the borrower will pay off that $5,000 in about 14 years ($30 per month x 166 months). But that extra $30 per month doesn't end once the Funding Fee is paid off, and another 16 years worth of mortgage payments means another $5,900 or so that the lender gets in additional principal and interest payments.

Such is the price of convenience.

To get an estimate of your Funding Fee costs, visit VA Funding Fee.com

Occupancy

As we've talked about throughout, the veteran is required to use the property as a primary residence. The VA essentially gives veterans and their families 60 days to move in after the loan closing. That two-month threshold is the agency's definition of "reasonable time" for occupancy, but there are exceptions in cases where both of these occur:

- The veteran certifies that occupancy will occur on a specific date, and
- There is a particular reason why this will be possible

The VA allows for a spouse to fulfill the occupancy requirement for a military member who is deployed or who cannot otherwise live at the property within a reasonable time. Recent legislation also now allows military dependents to fulfill the occupancy requirement for their parent.

There are also some unique situations where the spouse of a veteran can fulfill the requirement if employment issues are making reasonable occupancy difficult. But both single and married service members can provide what the VA considers "valid intent" to occupy when they're deployed from their permanent duty station. This provides a degree of breathing room for homeowners who are still actively serving our nation both at home and abroad. It's important to note that VA lenders are required to factor in the cost of a couple's separate living arrangement. That means any rental costs or other expenses associated with the separate housing situations can be factored into the overall debt-to-income ratio and other key metrics.

Borrower spotlight: John Clark

Hawaiian Homecoming for Naval Commander

Pearl Harbor, Hawaii — Career has always come first for Naval Commander John H. Clark III.

The son and grandson of General Motors workers, John sought a life beyond the factory towns of Michigan. He enlisted at 18, and, after senior personnel spotted his exemplary academic record, he was eventually selected to attend the Navy's officer selection and training school in California.

He got his bachelor's degree soon after and received his officer commission in 1993. His expertise in contracting and logistics took him from Guam and South Texas to Iraq and Washington, D.C. But what stuck with him amid all the military moves was the month he spent in Hawaii early in his career.

A midshipman tour aboard the USS Sam Houston introduced him to the island and its rich culture and genuine people. Hawaii was always there, in the back of his mind, as he and his family jumped from assignment to assignment.

Over the years, he tried unsuccessfully to secure an assignment there. Finally, in 2008, as he was nearing the end of his stint with the Navy's Strategic Systems Programs in Washington, John got the good news: He was being reassigned to the Fleet and Industrial Supply Center at Pearl Harbor.

Elated, John and his wife, Delia, decided they were tired of renting and had little desire to return to base housing. The couple wanted to buy their own home in Hawaii, one of the nation's costliest real estate markets.

As first-time buyers, they scoured online listings from 5,500 miles away. John spoke with friends and colleagues in Hawaii and found a trusted real estate agent. He also knew he was eligible for a VA loan but didn't know a lot about the process or details.

Hearing of his interest in VA financing, John's agent pointed him to a mortgage lender she had never actually met: Tony Dias.

A Marine Corps veteran, Tony is a VA loan specialist renown on the island for his free seminars on this long-cherished home loan program. He also runs Veterans United Home Loans of Hawaii. John's real estate agent had attended one of Tony's seminars and recommended him on reputation alone.

John, who had scores of questions, wasted little time in calling.

He got the context and expertise for which he was searching.

"Tony was down to earth, he was not high pressure," John said. "This was someone who was going to walk me through the VA process."

Tony did just that, explaining the program's key benefits and what John and his wife were likely to encounter at each step.

As their moving date came closer, the couple found a house they loved in their price range. They put down earnest money but soon discovered the property was owned by government-sponsored enterprise Freddie Mac. Concerned that could lead to delays, they quickly changed gears.

Delia hopped back online and found a great house fresh to the market. The couple jumped at the listing and put down an offer. The seller accepted, and the Clarks made a nearly $700,000 purchase from thousands of miles away.

They finally had a place to call home.

"As with most things in life, it's all about relationships," John said. "My family and I were so blessed to have developed a relationship with Tony. The more questions I asked, the more he put me at ease."

This story does not represent an endorsement of Veterans United Home Loans by the Department of Defense, the Department of the Navy or any other governmental agency.

CHAPTER 6:
VA REFINANCE LOANS

Military borrowers have access to the most powerful home purchasing program on the market. So it certainly stands to reason that the same would hold true when it comes to a refinance loan.

There are two major VA refinance options, an Interest Rate Reduction Refinance Loan, also known as an IRRRL or a **VA Streamline**, and a **VA Cash-Out Refinance**. We'll look at each one separately. First, though, let's talk about refinancing in general.

Much like the "When should I lock my rate?" dilemma, the question of "When should I refinance?" is one of those lingering issues that haunts homebuyers and loan officers alike. And, of course, there's no formula or simple way to answer the question. Refinancing every couple of years just to refinance probably isn't the smartest tactic. It's important that veterans and military borrowers *know why* they want to refinance. The most obvious and likely reason is that interest rates have dropped and you want to save some money on that monthly mortgage payment.

But there may be other considerations. Maybe you've worked hard to improve your credit profile and your score has finally climbed, meaning you're eligible for a better rate.

Or perhaps you got a promotion or took a new job and the monthly household income is higher, making it possible to convert that 30-year mortgage into a 15-year one. Maybe — and we hope not — the converse is true and you need to adjust to a smaller income level.

Or maybe you need to make home improvements or pay off revolving debts and can capitalize on the equity built up in your home. Or you're tired of worrying about your ARM and want to refinance into a fixed-rate mortgage.

There are scores of potential reasons why a veteran should consider refinancing a mortgage. Offering up "Because someone told me I should" isn't typically the best answer. A VA refinance will almost always result in lower monthly payments (there are a few exceptions we'll look at later in the chapter). But they also come with a price. As with a VA purchase loan, borrowers have to pay closing costs every time they refinance. Part of deciding when to refinance is determining whether those added costs are worth the investment.

It's also important to note that veterans and military borrowers with conventional loans can refinance into a VA loan. This, as you'll soon see, is a pretty incredible opportunity.

VA Streamline

The "Streamline" moniker isn't just a clever marketing ploy. The VA Streamline is a no-frills, low-impact refinance loan that features almost none of the hassle and paperwork that accompanies a conventional refinance.

But, in today's lending environment, VA Streamlines aren't quite as streamlined as they once were.

The VA does not require appraisals, credit checks or any significant underwriting for an existing VA borrower to qualify for a Streamline. But be careful with semantics here. While the

VA may not require those things, you better believe a lender is certainly interested in your credit score and the value of your home. Remember, the Department of Veterans Affairs isn't in the business of actually issuing loans.

You should expect the lender to require both. Unlike years past, veterans are now finding themselves subject to credit checks and appraisal costs when applying for a VA Streamline. Given the widespread drop in home values across the country, most lenders are turning away refinance applications when the new loan amount exceeds the value of the home.

Despite the more cautious approach, we're still able to process some VA Streamlines without an appraisal. Previous customers have minimal paperwork because we already have their loan documents on file. That helps keep refinancing costs down, and we typically refrain from charging an origination fee.

The VA Streamline exists to get veterans into a lower-rate mortgage with lower monthly costs. In fact, that's one of the loan's primary requirements. Unless the borrower is refinancing an Adjustable Rate Mortgage, the Streamline has to lower the interest rate.

Refinancing would seem to be a no-brainer. In fact, why not refinance every time there's a halfway decent rate decrease? Because it isn't free.

Here are some of the closing costs likely to be a part of your VA Streamline:
- The VA Funding Fee of 0.5 percent
- An Origination Fee, which can't exceed 1 percent of the loan amount
- Up to 2 discount points
- Title exam and insurance fees
- Recording and mailing fees
- Flood Zone Determination

Those origination fees typically include things like rate lock fees, processing costs and loan settlement fees. The VA allows acceptable closing costs (veterans can pay additional discount points out of pocket, for example) to be rolled into the overall loan amount. Veterans can also add up to $6,000 in energy efficiency improvements.

While they're not closing costs, borrowers also have to come up with tax and insurance escrow reserves for a refinance.

Of course, veterans can pay all of these closing costs and fees out of pocket, but they seldom do. The lender can add those charges to the loan amount or increase the interest rate to cover the additional cost.

That means veterans might actually see their principal balance *increase* after a VA Streamline. No need to worry, though, as that's perfectly normal. What's more important is determining how long those payments will be higher and if the refinance is truly worth it over the long haul.

Looking at some numbers might help. Let's say the closing costs come out to $4,000 and the Streamline is going to lower your monthly payment by $100. If you're folding those closing costs in the loan, divide the amount by the monthly savings of your Streamline. In this case, $4,000/$100 = 40. That means it will take you 40 months, or 3¼ years, to recoup those closing costs. Depending on how many years are remaining on your loan term, that's probably a pretty solid investment.

On the other hand, imagine that rates aren't quite as low and that closing costs are a bit higher. With closing costs of $4,500 and a monthly savings of $50, it would take the borrower 90 months, or 7.5 years, to recover those additional costs. That might be too long of a wait for some homeowners, especially service members who may have another move or two ahead of them.

The VA requires veterans to go through the credit and underwriting process if the refinance is going to increase their monthly PITI payment by 20 percent or more. In those cases, there's an onus on the lender to satisfy the VA's concern about whether the veteran can afford this new, higher payment.

This is why it's important for veterans to do their homework and shop around when the time comes to refinance. You can certainly start with your original lender, but by no means are you bound to them. Veterans can and should hunt for the best deal possible, on both interest rates and costs and fees. At times, that might mean a VA loan isn't the best option for a refinance. The main reason is the VA Funding Fee, which isn't a part of the conventional financing picture. Veterans with equity in their homes and some cash on hand may opt to avoid the VA Funding Fee and seek out a conventional refinance.

A capable VA loan specialist will help borrowers do the math and compare a VA refinance to a conventional refinance loan. VA Streamlines are available only to existing VA borrowers. But veterans with conventional mortgages can refinance into a VA loan. They can even take out cash while doing so.

Cash-Out Refinance Loans

The VA Streamline is inherently flexible, but there's one major thing you can't do with it: Get cash back. No worries, though. There's a loan for that.

The VA's Cash-Out Refinance loan allows qualified veterans — with conventional or VA loans — to refinance to a lower rate while extracting cash from their home's equity. Essentially, you're getting a new mortgage at a value higher than what you owe and taking the difference in a cash lump.

Remember that two things are happening in the background: Your interest rate is likely lower but your loan amount is higher. That means a flux in monthly mortgage payments.

Borrowers have traditionally used Cash-Out Refinance loans to pay off high-interest debts or make home improvements. But there aren't any concrete constraints on how you spend the money. Have a teenager getting ready to start college? Always wanted a motorcycle? Either could be acceptable, but underwriters may require a letter of explanation from the borrower.

The VA and the lender are mostly concerned with making sure you can afford the new mortgage payment. Unlike on a Streamline, the VA mandates that borrowers pursuing a Cash-Out Refinance loan submit to the standard credit and underwriting process. The loan processing for a Cash-Out Refinance is basically identical to the original VA purchase loan, from the income verification and debt-to-income ratio to a home appraisal.

In the fall of 2008, President Bush signed the Veterans Benefits Improvement Act, a piece of legislation that boosted home loan benefits for qualified veterans and their families. One of the provisions of the act increased the maximum loan amount available to VA borrowers on a Cash-Out Refinance. Today, veterans can get a Cash-Out Refinance for up to 100 percent of the home's appraised value, plus the VA Funding Fee and any costs from energy-efficiency improvements.

Veterans who want a Cash-Out Refinance pay a higher VA Funding Fee than their Streamline counterparts. The current fee for a first refinance is 2.15 percent of the loan amount for regular military and 2.4 percent for Reserves and National Guard members. The fee jumps to 3.3 percent for both demographics for each subsequent refinance.

A Cash-Out Refinance shouldn't be confused with a home equity loan, which is a second loan that runs alongside your current mortgage. A refinance loan replaces that existing mortgage instead of complementing it. Depending on rates, a home equity loan may actually be a better option for some veterans. These come with minimal, if any, closing costs but tend to have higher rates than what you'll find with a VA Cash-Out Refinance. The key is to keep a close eye on rates and shop comparatively.

Veterans with conventional loans can refinance into a VA loan only by using the cash-out option. Strange as it might sound, those borrowers don't actually have to take out any money. But they are subject to the same credit, underwriting and appraisal guidelines that the VA has in place for Cash-Out Refinance loans.

Streamline v. Cash-Out Refinance

To help give borrowers a more high-level view of the two refinancing options, the VA maintains a helpful comparison table. Here's a shorter version of it that includes key features for prospective borrowers. Remember that what the VA mandates and what VA-approved lenders will demand can be two different things, especially when it comes to credit, underwriting and appraisals:

Feature	IRRRL	Cash-Out Refinance
Purpose	To refinance an existing VA loan at a lower interest rate	To pay off lien(s) of any type; can also provide cash to borrower
Interest Rate	Rate must be lower than on existing VA loan (unless existing loan is an ARM)	Any negotiated rate
Monthly Payment Amount	Payment must be lower than that on an existing VA loan (unless the ARM is being refinanced, a term is shortened, or energy efficiency improvements are being included)	No requirement
Discount Points	Reasonable points can be paid; only two of these points can be included in the loan amount	Reasonable points can be paid if source is loan proceeds
Maximum Loan	Existing VA loan balance, plus allowable fees and charges, plus up to two discount points, plus the cost of any energy efficiency improvements, plus the VA Funding Fee	100 percent of the reasonable value of the property indicated on the NOV, plus the cost of any energy efficiency improvements, plus the VA Funding Fee

Maximum Guaranty	Guaranty is at least 25 percent in all cases	Maximum guaranty is the same as for purchases
Cash to Borrower	Not permitted	Borrower can receive cash for any purposes acceptable to the lender
Fees and Charges in the Loan	All allowable fees and charges, including up to two discount points, may be included in the loan	Allowable fees and charges and points may be paid from the loan proceeds
Refinance of Other Liens	Cannot refinance other liens; can only refinance the existing VA loan	Can refinance any type of lien(s)
Maximum Loan Term	Existing VA loan term plus 10 years, not to exceed 30 years + 32 days	30 years + 32 days
Occupancy	Veteran or spouse of an active duty servicemember must certify to prior occupancy	Veteran or spouse of an active duty service-member must certify as to intent to occupy
Appraisal	Appraisal is required by most lenders	Appraisal is required
Credit Under-writing	Lenders will now examine credit score and financial information	Full credit information and underwriting are always required
Automatic Authority	All lenders can close IRRRLs automatically except if the loan being refinanced is 30 days or more past due	Only lenders with automatic authority can close these loans automatically

Some borrowers who go into the process thinking Stream-line ultimately decide they would rather opt for a Cash-Out Refinance. Each has its own benefits and drawbacks. There also isn't any sort of rule that veterans have to get a VA refinance. In fact, a conventional refinance loan may be attractive to borrowers who have cultivated a decent chunk of equity. Veterans will pay standard closing costs with a conventional refinance, but there isn't a VA Funding Fee to contend with.

Remember, though, that credit, income and underwriting standards will likely be more stringent with a conventional loan than a VA refinance. Pursuing a refinance means veterans again have to consider that most frustrating of questions: When should I lock my rate? The rules of the road aren't much different when it comes to a refinance. But one of the luxuries of a refinance loan is that there's no real deadline or pressure to push forward. You can watch rates for weeks before deciding to jumpstart the process. At the same time, good loan officers are going to be doing the same thing for their past clients.

Construction-to-Permanent Refinance Loans

We first mentioned these way back in Chapter 2, part of a small section on construction loans and the all-but-impossible uses of a VA program. Again, service members in today's lending climate will be hard-pressed to find a VA lender willing to finance new home construction. But that doesn't mean they can't ultimately reap the rewards of their VA entitlement. The key is knowing how and when to bring the VA Loan Guaranty program into the picture.

Construction loans are by their nature short-term loans. Since most VA lenders shy away from financing the actual construction of the home, service members typically obtain financing from either a local lender or the builder. But construction loans tend to have relatively unfavorable terms and rates for borrowers because they're meant to be temporary. That means service members need to be able to refinance the construction loan into a more traditional loan upon completion of the home.

One option for qualified borrowers is to refinance that construction loan into a VA loan, using what's called a construction-to-permanent refinance. For the most part, the requirements and underwriting are virtually identical to other VA refinance options (you'll need new things like builder documents and a certificate of occupancy).

It's in the borrower's best interest to get preapproved for a VA refinance loan before seeking the construction financing from local sources. But here's the wrinkle, and it's one that's affecting service members looking for all types of VA refinance loans: the refinance climate has tightened. That tightening is having an impact on scores of service members, from those looking for construction-to-permanent refinance loans to folks seeking a straightforward VA Streamline.

Current Refinancing Challenges

Low interest interest rates have spurred significant interest in refinance loans. At the same time, lenders have put a renewed emphasis on credit scores, home values and limiting their exposure to risk. The result is that borrowers with a 620 credit score are struggling to secure a refinance loan.

Unlike years past, most borrowers are now going to have to shell out money for appraisals. Lenders want to ensure the value of the home reflects current market conditions. Many veterans are going to face another long, hard look at credit and their overall financial profile.

Veterans United is one of the few lenders able to process some Streamlines without an appraisal and offer up to 100 percent financing on Cash-Out Refinance loans.

Borrower spotlight: Matthew Tammen

Navy Veteran, Mountaineer Uses VA Refinance to Scale His Dream

Bremerton, Wash. — 26,906 feet.

That's as tall as 178 Statues of Liberty or 48 Washington Monuments stacked on top of each other. That's as high as most commercial airliners fly – over 5 miles up – where the minus 30 degree air is too thin to breathe.

That's the height of Cho Oyu, the world's sixth-tallest mountain. A few thousand feet shorter than nearby Mount Everest, the peak rises nearly 27,000 feet above the Nepal-Tibet border, and dares even the most experienced climbers to reach its tip.

Summiting the mountain takes an incredible combination of patience, physical endurance and training. Leave it to a Navy veteran to overcome all obstacles and make it to the top.

Matthew Tammen began his career in the U.S. Navy in 1979, graduated from the Naval Academy four years later and served 20 years as a submarine officer. He retired as a Lieutenant Commander, and settled down with his wife, Jennifer, and their three kids in Puget Sound, Wash.

They later purchased their dream home, which overlooks Mount Rainier. The family loves the outdoors, and the proximity to the beauty of nature was critical for them.

"We love the mountains and sea," Jennifer said. They take trips to the mountain for skiing and hiking, and enjoy taking their kayaks out on Puget Sound.

Matthew loves the outdoors, too, but takes a more adventurous angle. An avid climber, he has summited mountains like Mount Aconcogua in Argentina and Mount McKinley in Alaska.

But looking at Mount Rainier every day kept nagging at Matthew, reminding him of the dream climb he still hadn't made. That challenge was Cho Oyu.

The strength and determination he gained from the military could take him to the top, but his finances could barely get him to the foot of the mountain.

That's when Veterans United Home Loans threw Matthew a rope.

Climbing one of the world's tallest peaks takes tenacity – and a lot of money. Hiring guides, buying gear and traveling to some of the most remote places on earth can set mountaineers back tens of thousands of dollars.

With kids and a mortgage, the financial burden for the Tammens would be too much to bear. But their house, which they had purchased in 2004, was ripe for a refinancing, and a lower interest rate could save them a mountain of money.

As Matthew and Jennifer shopped for lenders, they felt stranded and alone. The Tammens couldn't obtain a refinance because the value of their house had fallen because of the recession.

"In my opinion, they just didn't try very hard to help us," Jennifer said.

But Veterans United Home Loans stepped in to work with them when other lenders wouldn't. With the help of Veterans United loan officer Kody Gilbow, the Tammens were able to refinance their mortgage and save a significant chunk of change.

"Our mortgage payment went down by $1,000 per month," Jennifer said.

The price tag for Matthew's expedition was set at $25,000. Pocketing an extra $1,000 per month thanks to the refinance, Matthew would have to wait two years to make the attempt to summit. He trained four hours per day for 14 months to have the physical stamina to summit.

No stranger to tough challenges, Matthew persevered. In fall 2013, he and his team flew into Kathmandu, Nepal, and then crossed into Tibet to begin a six-week trip. After struggling up the 8,200 meters for weeks, they finally reached the summit.

After two years of hard work, he reached his goal. On the morning of Oct. 1, 2013, Mathew saw the sun rise from the summit of Cho Oyu. Just 12 miles away, Mount Everest glowed in the morning light.

Matthew accomplished his goal, and the whole family came out on top by getting a better deal on their dream home.

"When you refinance, you may not think about big mountains and life-long dreams, but you should," Jennifer said. "He couldn't have made it without Veterans United."

CHAPTER 7 :
THE FUTURE OF VA LOANS

Purchasing a home today isn't the same as it was just a few years ago. The collapse of the housing market in the wake of the subprime mortgage meltdown has created a more restrictive and cautious lending environment.

That's a good thing in many respects, although talking about lessons learned provides little comfort to veterans who are now on the edge. Securing a home loan today is generally more difficult, with lenders looking for greater certainty that an applicant can and will handle the financial burden. The days of so-called no-paper loans, which allowed borrowers to secure a home loan with scant evidence of their ability to pay for it, are gone. Regulations that took effect in early 2014 have added further layers of protection to the process.

Still, one of the lingering questions is whether these new, cautious underwriting standards will become the new normal. It's difficult to imagine otherwise. Lenders might start to loosen up a bit in the coming years, but in most cases a more conservative approach to lending will continue to define the industry and govern the path to homeownership in the United States.

What does that mean for VA loans?

Well, veterans nationwide have already felt the effects. Despite the low foreclosure rate of VA loans, lenders across the country have tightened credit and underwriting standards. Today, veterans with a credit score below 620 have relatively few financing options. That's why building a solid credit profile is only going to become more important in the months and years ahead.

Refinance policies have also become more restrictive in the last couple of years. Credit checks and appraisals were never a real element of a VA Streamline until this latest bubble burst. Now scores of veterans are paying for home appraisals and seeing their credit scrutinized.

More than ever before, military members and veterans have to keep close watch of their credit profiles, debt-to-income levels and discretionary spending. That can add new layers of stress during deployments, permanent changes of station and other challenging phases that civilian borrowers don't have to contend with. Increasingly, discipline and responsible financial decisions are going to serve as the keys to landing a home loan.

The VA Loan Guaranty program itself is stronger than ever. Not only does it remain a refuge for military borrowers, but the VA home loan program also continues to provide qualified borrowers with better rates and greater buying power than any loan program out there. Veterans with a credit score right at 620 can get rates on a 30-year fixed-rate loan that are just a hair above the national average. Good luck getting that kind of deal on a conventional loan.

Today, VA loans are absolutely booming. The huge gains we mentioned in Chapter 1 (a 372 percent increase since 2007) come as lenders have tightened their lending requirements and as interest rates have hit rock bottom. There's no telling how long this combination will last, but the tougher standards are likely here to stay.

The history of the VA Loan Guaranty program is marked in many ways by evolutionary change. That course has led to today's more streamlined VA loan process, which complements existing technology rather than fighting against it. The VA Loan Guaranty program has been a constant in the lives of military members and their families since 1944. The agency has helped level the playing field for those who have served our country, making homeownership more accessible and more affordable.

That isn't going to change. But mortgage laws, lender regulations and underwriting expectations all do. That's why veterans and service members with any interest in homeownership — not to mention those who already own homes — need to make sure they understand the process and what's available to them.

The mortgage industry has always been one that rewards informed, educated consumers, and that's even truer today. So, whether you're in the market for your first home or looking to refinance an existing mortgage, do as much homework as possible. Ask questions, demand honest, thoughtful answers and don't be afraid to get a second or third opinion. Veterans who come to the process with a solid knowledge base have an immediate leg up on other buyers.

At some point, though, you're ultimately entrusting the process to someone on the other side. And that can be a scary proposition, especially for first-time buyers. Telling the world you're a prospective homebuyer can be like tossing chum in a shark tank. Mortgage folks will emerge from the shadows with deals, special financing and an array of other potential offers that sound a little too good to be true.

The best advice is to go with your gut. Sometimes your gut might simply point you to the lowest rate, which certainly isn't a terrible strategy.

Perhaps think of it this way: VA loans were created to honor and reward the hard work and sacrifices of our nation's veterans.

Gravitate to the loan officers, mortgage companies and real estate agents who genuinely embrace that spirit.

ACKNOWLEDGEMENTS

I am indebted to the entire team at Veterans United for helping make this book possible.

I want to thank our executive leadership for their relentless support, especially co-founders Brant and Brock Bukowsky; Chief Executive Officer Nate Long; Chief Marketing Officer Kris Farmer; and Chief Production Officer Gardell Powell.

Mr. Powell, in particular, deserves special thanks. Gardell graciously responded to every question, every clarification and every lengthy email, offering his expertise and insight from the planning stages through a final read. His commitment to this project was integral and invaluable.

A host of other Veterans United colleagues made significant contributions, including John Meyer, Zane Corn, Winsor Cooper III, John Lyman, Chris Lunn, Scott Schaefer, Pam Swan, Megan Sievers, Lisa O'Bannon, Lauren Okruch and Jon Galloway.

Mortgage industry sages Peter G. Miller and Justin McHood provided encouragement along the way. And William White at the Department of Veterans Affairs patiently fulfilled data requests.

I would also like to thank the Veterans United borrowers who made time to share their stories. We have the privilege of helping some amazing people capitalize on benefits earned through service and sacrifice. They are the kind of people who relish the opportunity to help those who will one day be in their shoes.

Last, I would like to thank my family, my friends and, most especially, my wife, Michela.

GLOSSARY

Adjustable-rate mortgage (ARM): These are mortgages where the interest rates can fluctuate based on what's happening in the greater economic landscape. Most ARMs allow for an annual rate change based on the one-year Treasury bill index.

Annual Percentage Rate (APR): This rate reflects the total cost of borrowing money, including the interest rate and other costs built into the loan amount. The interest rate and the APR are typically different, and veterans should look at both when comparing VA lenders. Two loans can have similar interest rates, but the one with a higher APR will cost more.

Automated Underwriting System (AUS): This computer system utilized by select VA-approved lenders allows for an automatic approval on a borrower's loan application. Loan officers can tweak loan amounts in the AUS to help secure approval.

Basic Allowance for Housing: A service member's BAH can be included as monthly income. Housing allowances can help defray or entirely cover monthly mortgage payments.

Buyer's agent: This is the real estate agent who represents the homebuyer.

Cash-Out Refinance: This refinance loan allows veterans to refinance to a lower interest rate and tap into their equity. Borrowers can obtain a Cash-Out Refinance for up to 100 percent of the home's appraised value, plus the VA Funding Fee and any costs from energy-efficiency improvements.

Certificate of Eligibility: This is a formal VA document that delineates what entitlement a prospective borrower has available. It is the only acceptable method to document entitlement.

Clear to close: This means that all loan conditions have been met to the underwriter's satisfaction and the borrower is ready to formally close on the home purchase.

Closing costs: These are charges and fees associated with finalizing a loan. The VA limits what veterans can pay in closing costs to a 1 percent lender origination fee, reasonable discount points and other reasonable and standard fees and charges.

Comparable sales: They're better known as "comps." These are recently sold properties that are similar in size, location and other key facets to a home being purchased.

Compensating factors: These are strengths on a loan application that can help offset lender concerns about a borrower's credit or financial weaknesses. Low debt, great credit history and liquidity are all examples. Compensating factors must go above and beyond what would be considered a normal program requirement.

Conditional approval: A loan with conditional approval will be issued as long as the veteran meets the requirements and stipulations — the conditions — spelled out by the underwriter.

Conforming loan limit: Fannie Mae and Freddie Mac can only purchase mortgages below what's known as the conforming loan limit. This limit, which is subject to change, is currently $417,000.

Construction-to-Permanent Refinance Loan: This allows qualified borrowers to refinance a construction loan into a VA loan. Requirements and underwriting are nearly identical to other VA refinance options.

Conventional loan: These loans feature no government guaranties and adhere to the standards and requirements of government-sponsored enterprises Fannie Mae and Freddie Mac.

DD-214: This is an official VA document that explains a veteran's discharge information. Reservists and National Guard members, who don't have a single discharge certificate like the DD-214, should procure their latest annual retirement points summary along with evidence of their honorable service.

Debt-to-income ratio (DTI ratio): This is the ratio of your total monthly debt payments to your gross monthly income. VA-approved lenders use 41 percent as a benchmark. Your DTI ratio can change depending on the loan amount you seek.

Deed-in-lieu of foreclosure: An alternative to straightforward foreclosure. The borrower basically returns the house to the bank. A deed-in-lieu will negatively affect your credit score.

Discount points: A point is equal to 1 percent of the loan amount. Borrowers can pay points to buy down their interest rate. Paying points is relatively infrequent among most VA borrowers.

Earnest money: Borrowers put this into an escrow account when the time comes to purchase a home. These good faith funds can be put toward closing costs or refunded to the borrower. The amount depends on several factors, including geography and the property.

Energy Efficient Mortgage (EEM): This specialized mortgage allows veterans to make energy-efficient improvements to a home they're purchasing or refinancing. Veterans can add up to $6,000 to the loan amount provided they can verify the cost of improvements or prove the efficiencies will result in savings.

Entitlement: The VA uses the word to mean the amount of money it will guaranty on a given loan. The primary entitlement is $36,000, with a secondary entitlement of $68,250.

FICO score: FICO stands for Fair Isaac Corp., a California-based company that created the first-ever credit score. FICO scores run from 300 to 850.

Fixed-rate mortgage: Interest rates cannot fluctuate on a fixed-rate mortgage. The most common fixed-rate terms are 15 years and 30 years.

Float: Borrowers can either float or lock when it comes to an interest rate. Float is the default setting until a purchase agreement is in place.

Foreclosure: This basically means the lender takes back its house because you failed to keep up with mortgage payments. There are restrictions on foreclosures against service members through the Servicemembers Civil Relief Act.

Good Faith Estimate (GFE): This recently streamlined document gives borrowers an estimate of their closing costs and settlement fees. Some charges cannot change from the Good Faith Estimate to the final settlement statement. The GFE gives borrowers a good feel for their closing costs, origination fees, points and other charges.

Government-sponsored enterprises (GSEs): These are federal financial services corporations, with Fannie Mae and Freddie Mac being the most familiar. Fannie Mae securitizes mortgages in the secondary market. Freddie Mac purchases, pools and sells mortgages to investors.

Graduated Payment Mortgage (GPM): A fixed-rate mortgage where borrowers start with a low monthly payment that rises a fixed percent each year for the first five years of the loan before leveling off. GPMs are aimed at borrowers who anticipate income gains as the loan term progresses. These also require veterans to come up with a down payment and generate negative amortization.

Growing Equity Mortgage (GEM): Another fixed-rate mortgage where borrowers have higher monthly payments over time. There is no negative amortization with a GEM. As the payments increase, borrowers begin to pay off the principal directly, shaving interest and years off the loan term.

Homeowners insurance: Lenders require borrowers to secure a home insurance policy to cover at least the value of their mortgage. Homeowners insurance isn't included in the mortgage.

Hybrid adjustable-rate mortgage (ARM): Borrowers with a hybrid ARM have a fixed interest rate for the first three or five years of the loan term. After that, rates can fluctuate but are capped annually as well as over the life of the loan.

HUD-1 Settlement Statement: This recently revamped document comes just before closing and breaks down final closing and settlement costs for borrowers, who also get to see what the seller makes on the sale. The HUD-1 also spells out which charges can and cannot change from the Good Faith Estimate.

Interest Rate Reduction Refinance Loan (IRRRL): This is also known as a VA Streamline. This is a no-frills refinance designed to get veterans into a lower-rate mortgage. Borrowers cannot take cash out with an IRRRL.

Lender Appraisal Processing Program (LAPP): This computer system allows authorized lenders to directly order and process VA appraisals, which are conducted by independent VA-approved appraisers.

Leave and Earnings statement: This is basically the Verification of Employment document for service members. Prospective borrowers can obtain their LES online by using the MyPay portal at https://mypay.dfas.mil/mypay.aspx.

Lighthouse Program: This special wing of Veterans United Home Loans helps teach veterans and military borrowers about credit and what it takes to improve their score.

Loan officer: On a lender's front lines, loan officers help veterans get qualified for a loan and navigate the entire process.

Loan processor: This person pulls together outstanding documents and information once a borrower has signed a purchase contact. Their job is to piece together loan applications for an underwriter.

Loan-to-value adjustment: A mark-up on conventional loan rates based on a borrower's credit score and down payment.

Lock fee: Some lenders charge borrowers for rate locks, depending on the time period, the rate and other factors. Veterans should ask lenders about lock fees when comparison shopping.

Listing agent: This is the real estate agent representing a home seller.

Manual underwriting: This occurs when a borrower cannot get AUS approval. Underwriters evaluate the loan file manually and make a determination without the computer automation. Veterans who can't secure AUS approval tend to need great credit in order to get manual approval.

Minimum Property Requirements: These are basic health and safety conditions that a property must meet to satisfy the VA. They're also the conditions that make the home sellable. The VA in most cases requires homes to be "move-in ready."

Multiple Listing Service (MLS): Real estate databases and software that allow agents and brokers to look at transactions, home listings and a suite of other information tools. These are private systems unavailable to the general public.

Negative amortization: This is essentially unpaid interest that gets added to the loan balance. Negative amortization occurs on a Graduated Payment Mortgage, where the initial monthly payments are so low that they don't cover the accrued interest. This makes a loan ineligible for Qualified Mortgage status.

Negative compensating factor: Compensating factors are strengths on a loan application that can help borrowers secure a loan. Negative compensating factors can do the opposite. Bankruptcies, foreclosures, late payments can all be considered negative compensating factors.

Note rate: This is your interest rate.

Notice of Value (NOV): This is the VA appraisal, which spells out the independent expert's assessment of the property's value. Ultimately, it's up to a lender's staff appraisal reviewer to issue the final notice of value.

Origination fee: The VA allows lenders to charge borrowers a flat fee of up to 1 percent of the loan amount to cover in-house costs and services.

Permanent buydown: Veterans can pay reasonable discount points to buy down their interest rate. A discount point is

1 percent of the loan amount. Borrowers have to pay this cost up front.

PITI: The acronym stands for Principal, Interest, Taxes and Insurance. These are the four pillars of a veteran's monthly mortgage payment.

Power of Attorney: A surrogate with Power of Attorney can sign contracts and other documents on behalf of an absent service member. Many lenders require a unique Power of Attorney document.

Preapproval: This is a more serious step than prequalification. Real estate agents and sellers put significant stock into loan preapproval. But this is not a guarantee from a lender or any kind of binding document for the borrower.

Prequalification: This introductory step involves an unverified, cursory discussion about a borrower's finances. Prequalification helps veterans get a sense of what they can afford but it means little to sellers and real estate agents, who are looking for preapproval letters.

Prime: This essentially means borrowers or loans at or above an accepted credit standard, typically around 620. Some loans and borrowers beneath that are considered greater risks and classified as subprime.

Private mortgage insurance (PMI): On most mortgages, borrowers who can't put down 20 percent of the loan amount are required to pay insurance. It protects lenders against borrowers who default and also helps borrowers who can't muster a large down payment. There is no PMI on a VA loan.

Rate lock: A binding commitment that locks a borrower to a specific interest rate. Borrowers can typically lock their interest rate as soon as they sign a purchase agreement and up to five days before the loan closing. Rate locks are good for specific blocks of time. The most common lock periods are for 15 days, 30 days, 45 days and 60 days.

Realtor: A real estate agent who is a member of the National Association of Realtors.

Rate cap: Some lenders include a rate cap with their rate locks. These caps give lenders the ability to give borrowers a slightly higher interest rate if rates rise considerably before closing.

Reserves: This is cash set aside to cover costs and expenses. Having additional money set aside can help strengthen a loan application.

Retail rate: This is a flat, non-negotiable mortgage rate offered by banks, credit unions and other lending institutions. The retail institution must be VA-approved in order to offer VA purchase loans.

Residual income: This is a lending standard unique to VA loans. Residual income is the amount of money a borrower retains each month after covering all monthly debts and obligations. Veterans must hit a minimum level of residual income (depending on geography and family size) in order to satisfy VA requirements.

Seller concessions: Sellers can pay a range of costs and charges for VA borrowers, including closing costs, property taxes, the VA Funding Fee and other items. But the VA caps seller concessions at 4 percent of the loan amount.

Staff Appraisal Reviewer (SAR): A lender's staff appraisal reviewer, or SAR, examines a property's independent VA appraisal and issues the final Notice of Value.

Second-tier entitlement: This additional entitlement ($68,250) helps boost the VA guaranty on qualified loans. Borrowers can secure a loan solely with their second-tier entitlement, as long as the loan amount is at least $144,001.

Secondary mortgage market: Lenders sell mortgages, often packaged into mortgage-backed securities, in this marketplace. Private investors and government-sponsored enterprises buy loans in the secondary market. Proceeds help fuel the lending industry.

Short sale: An alternative to straightforward foreclosure. This is when the bank agrees to let you sell your home for less than the balance owed. A short sale will negatively affect your credit score.

Special Adapted Housing (SAH): This VA program provides grants for veterans with service-connected disabilities to retrofit properties to meet their needs.

Streamline: A VA Streamline is another name for the Interest Rate Reduction Refinance Loan (IRRRL).

Subprime: This essentially means borrowers or loans below an accepted credit standard, typically around 620. Subprime borrowers carry greater risks and now have trouble securing financing.

Temporary buydown: Borrowers can pay discount points to buy down their rate for a limited time instead of permanently. On a 3-2-1 buydown, the borrower's interest rate drops 3 percent below the note rate for the first year, 2 percent for the second year and 1 percent for the third year. The start of the fourth year marks the first year the borrower pays at the regular, full note rate.

Title insurance: This is mandatory insurance that protects borrowers, sellers and lenders against previous ownership claims on a property. Title insurance is a one-time cost that must be paid at closing. Buyers can shop around for the best price.

Underwriter: These trained experts review a borrower's loan file and give an ultimate thumbs-up or down. They act as the lender's gatekeeper.

Uniform Residential Loan Application: This is the five-page loan application for almost all home mortgages.

Verification of Employment: This is an important document that lenders send to a veteran's employer(s). The VOE, as it's known, helps lenders verify employment, tenure, salary and any bonuses or raises.

Yield Spread Premium: Wholesale lenders pay this rebate to lenders for higher-rate loans.

APPENDIX A

OMB Control No. 2900-0086
Respondent Burden: 15 minutes

Ⓥ Department of Veterans Affairs			TO	Department of Veterans Affairs Eligibility Center P.O. Box 20729 Winston-Salem, NC 27120
REQUEST FOR A CERTIFICATE OF ELIGIBILITY				

NOTE: Please read information on reverse before completing this form. If additional space is required, attach a separate sheet.

1. FIRST-MIDDLE-LAST NAME OF VETERAN	2. DATE OF BIRTH	3. VETERAN'S DAYTIME TELEPHONE NO.

4A. ADDRESS OF VETERAN *(No., street or rural route, city or P.O., State and ZIP Code)*	5. MAIL CERTIFICATE OF ELIGIBILITY TO: *(Complete ONLY if the Certificate is to be mailed to an address different from the one listed in Item 4A)*
4B. E-MAIL ADDRESS OF VETERAN *(If applicable)*	

6. MILITARY SERVICE DATA *(ATTACH PROOF OF SERVICE - SEE PARAGRAPH "D" ON REVERSE)*

A. ITEM	B. PERIODS OF ACTIVE SERVICE		C. NAME *(Show your name exactly as it appears on your separation papers or Statement of Service)*	D. SOCIAL SECURITY NUMBER	E. SERVICE NUMBER *(If different from Social Security No.)*	F. BRANCH OF SERVICE
	DATE FROM	DATE TO				
1.						
2.						
3.						
4.						

7A. WERE YOU DISCHARGED, RETIRED OR SEPARATED FROM SERVICE BECAUSE OF DISABILITY OR DO YOU NOW HAVE ANY SERVICE-CONNECTED DISABILITIES? ☐ YES ☐ NO *(If "Yes," complete Item 7B)*	7B. VA CLAIM FILE NUMBER C-

8. PREVIOUS VA LOANS *(Must answer N/A if no previous VA home loan. DO NOT LEAVE BLANK)*

A. ITEM	B. TYPE *(Home, Refinance, Manufactured Home, or Direct)*	C. ADDRESS OF PROPERTY	D. DATE OF LOAN	E. DO YOU STILL OWN THE PROPERTY? *(YES/NO)*	F. DATE PROPERTY WAS SOLD *(Submit a copy of HUD-1, Settlement Statement, if available)*	G. VA LOAN NUMBER *(If known)*
1.						
2.						
3.						
4.						
5.						
6.						

I CERTIFY THAT the statements herein are true to the best of my knowledge and belief.

9. SIGNATURE OF VETERAN *(Do NOT print)*	10. DATE SIGNED

FEDERAL STATUTES PROVIDE SEVERE PENALTIES FOR FRAUD, INTENTIONAL MISREPRESENTATION, CRIMINAL CONNIVANCE OR CONSPIRACY PURPOSED TO INFLUENCE THE ISSUANCE OF ANY GUARANTY OR INSURANCE BY THE SECRETARY OF VETERANS AFFAIRS.

FOR VA USE ONLY

11A. DATE CERTIFICATE ISSUED	11B. SIGNATURE OF VA AGENT

VA FORM APR 2008   **26-1880**   EXISTING STOCKS OF VA FORM 26-1880, JAN 2006, WILL BE USED.

APPENDIX B

Department of Veterans Affairs
USDA, Department of Agriculture

VA OMB Approval No. 2900-0521
USDA OMB Approval No. 0575-0009
Respondent Burden: 10 minutes

Department of Veterans Affairs — REQUEST FOR VERIFICATION OF EMPLOYMENT

Privacy Act Notice: VA will not disclose information collected on this form to any source other than what has been authorized under the Privacy Act of 1974 or Title 38, Code of Federal Regulations 1.576 for routine uses (i.e., information verifying an applicant's employment may be disclosed to a prospective mortgagee proposing to make a guaranteed loan on the veteran applicant's behalf) as identified in the VA system of records, 55VA26, Loan Guaranty Home, Condominium and Manufactured Home Loan Applicant Records, Specially Adapted Housing Applicant Records and Vendee Loan Applicant Records - VA, and published in the Federal Register. Your obligation to respond is voluntary, but failure to provide requested information could impede processing.

Respondent Burden: We need this information to help determine a veteran's qualifications for a VA-guaranteed loan. Title 38, United States Code, allows us to ask for this information. We estimate that you will need an average of 10 minutes to review the instructions, find the information, and complete this form. VA cannot conduct or sponsor a collection of information unless a valid OMB control number is displayed. You are not required to respond to a collection of information if this number is not displayed. Valid OMB control numbers can be located on the OMB Internet Page at www.whitehouse.gov/omb/library/OMBINV.VA.EPA.html#VA. If desired, you can call 1-800-827-1000 to get information on where to send comments or suggestions about this form.

Lender or Local Processing Agency (LPA) completes Items 1 through 6 and has the applicant sign in Item 7. Forward the completed form directly to the employer named in Item 1.
Employer completes either parts II and IV or parts III and IV. Return the form directly to the lender or local processing agency named in Item 3 of part I.

PART I - REQUEST CERTIFICATION

1. NAME AND ADDRESS OF EMPLOYER

2. NAME AND ADDRESS OF APPLICANT

3. NAME AND ADDRESS OF LENDER OR LOCAL PROCESSING AGENT (LPA)

I CERTIFY THAT this verification has been sent directly to the employer and has not passed through the hands of the applicant or any other interested party.

4A. SIGNATURE OF LENDER, OFFICIAL OF LPA, OR USDA LOAN PACKAGER
X

4B. TITLE OF LENDER, OFFICIAL OF LPA, OR USDA LOAN PACKAGER

5. DATE

6. VA OR USDA NO.

I have applied for a mortgage loan or rehabilitation loan and stated that I am/was employed by you. My signature in the block authorizes verification of my employment information.

7. APPLICANT'S SIGNATURE AND EMPLOYEE IDENTIFICATION
X

PART II - VERIFICATION OF PRESENT EMPLOYMENT

8. PRESENT POSITION

9. DATE OF EMPLOYMENT

10. PROBABILITY OF CONTINUED EMPLOYMENT

11A. PAID BY: SALARY [ ]YES [ ]NO COMMISSION [ ]YES [ ]NO OVERTIME [ ]YES [ ]NO

11B. IS OVERTIME/BONUS LIKELY TO CONTINUE? BONUS [ ]YES [ ]NO

12. CURRENT BASE PAY ▶ [ ]ANNUAL [ ]MONTHLY [ ]WEEKLY [ ]HOURLY [ ]OTHER (Specify)

14A. MONTHLY TAXABLE PAY (For Military Personnel Only)

	BASE PAY	CAREER C PAY	PRO PAY
13A. BASE EARNINGS YEAR-TO-DATE $ / PAST YEAR $	$	$	$
13B. OVERTIME YEAR-TO-DATE $ / PAST YEAR $	FLIGHT PAY $	OTHER (Specify) $	

14B. MONTHLY NONTAXABLE PAY (For Military Personnel Only)

	QUARTERS	VHA	CLOTHING
13C. COMMISSION YEAR-TO-DATE $ / PAST YEAR $	$	$	$
13D. BONUSES YEAR-TO-DATE $ / PAST YEAR $	RATIONS $	OTHER (Specify) $	

15. REMARKS: IF PAID HOURLY, PLEASE INDICATE AVERAGE HOURS WORKED EACH WEEK DURING CURRENT AND PAST YEAR

PART III - VERIFICATION OF PREVIOUS EMPLOYMENT

16. SALARY/WAGE AT TERMINATION: [ ]YEARLY [ ]MONTHLY [ ]WEEKLY BASE PAY $ OVERTIME $ COMMISSIONS $ BONUS $

17. DATES OF EMPLOYMENT FROM / TO

18. REASONS FOR LEAVING

19. POSITION HELD

PART IV - CERTIFICATION
Federal statutes provide severe penalties for any fraud, intentional misrepresentation, or criminal connivance or conspiracy purposed to influence the issuance of any guaranty or insurance by VA or USDA Administrators.

20. SIGNATURE
X

21. TITLE OF EMPLOYER

22. EMPLOYER'S TELEPHONE NO. (Include Area Code)

23. DATE

VA FORM DEC 2007 **26-8497** USDA Form 410-5   SUPERSEDES VA FORM 26-8497, OCT 2004, WHICH WILL NOT BE USED.

APPENDIX C

Uniform Residential Loan Application

This application is designed to be completed by the applicant(s) with the Lender's assistance. Applicants should complete this form as "Borrower" or "Co-Borrower," as applicable. Co-Borrower information must also be provided (and the appropriate box checked) when □ the income or assets of a person other than the Borrower (including the Borrower's spouse) will be used as a basis for loan qualification or □ the income or assets of the Borrower's spouse or other person who has community property rights pursuant to state law will not be used as a basis for loan qualification, but his or her liabilities must be considered because the spouse or other person has community property rights pursuant to applicable law and Borrower resides in a community property state, the security property is located in a community property state, or the Borrower is relying on other property located in a community property state as a basis for repayment of the loan.

If this is an application for joint credit, Borrower and Co-Borrower each agree that we intend to apply for joint credit (sign below):

_____ _____
Borrower   Co-Borrower

I. TYPE OF MORTGAGE AND TERMS OF LOAN

Mortgage Applied for:	□ VA □ FHA	□ Conventional □ USDA/Rural Housing Service	□ Other (explain):	Agency Case Number	Lender Case Number
Amount $	Interest Rate %	No. of Months	Amortization Type:	□ Fixed Rate □ GPM	□ Other (explain): □ ARM (type):

II. PROPERTY INFORMATION AND PURPOSE OF LOAN

Subject Property Address (street, city, state & ZIP)					No. of Units
Legal Description of Subject Property (attach description if necessary)					Year Built

Purpose of Loan	□ Purchase □ Refinance	□ Construction □ Construction-Permanent	□ Other (explain):	Property will be: □ Primary Residence □ Secondary Residence	□ Investment

Complete this line if construction or construction-permanent loan.

Year Lot Acquired	Original Cost $	Amount Existing Liens $	(a) Present Value of Lot $	(b) Cost of Improvements $	Total (a + b) $

Complete this line if this is a refinance loan.

Year Acquired	Original Cost $	Amount Existing Liens $	Purpose of Refinance	Describe Improvements □ made □ to be made Cost: $	

Title will be held in what Name(s)	Manner in which Title will be held	Estate will be held in: □ Fee Simple □ Leasehold (show expiration date)
Source of Down Payment, Settlement Charges, and/or Subordinate Financing (explain)		

III. BORROWER INFORMATION

Borrower				Co-Borrower			
Borrower's Name (include Jr. or Sr. if applicable)				Co-Borrower's Name (include Jr. or Sr. if applicable)			
Social Security Number	Home Phone (incl. area code)	DOB (mm/dd/yyyy)	Yrs. School	Social Security Number	Home Phone (incl. area code)	DOB (mm/dd/yyyy)	Yrs. School
□ Married □ Separated □ Unmarried (include single, divorced, widowed)	Dependents (not listed by Co-Borrower) no. ages			□ Married □ Separated □ Unmarried (include single, divorced, widowed)	Dependents (not listed by Borrower) no. ages		
Present Address (street, city, state, ZIP) □ Own □ Rent ___ No. Yrs.				Present Address (street, city, state, ZIP) □ Own □ Rent ___ No. Yrs.			
Mailing Address, if different from Present Address				Mailing Address, if different from Present Address			

If residing at present address for less than two years, complete the following:

Former Address (street, city, state, ZIP) □ Own □ Rent ___ No. Yrs.				Former Address (street, city, state, ZIP) □ Own □ Rent ___ No. Yrs.			

IV. EMPLOYMENT INFORMATION

Borrower			Co-Borrower		
Name & Address of Employer	□ Self Employed	Yrs. on this job	Name & Address of Employer	□ Self Employed	Yrs. on this job
		Yrs. employed in this line of work/profession			Yrs. employed in this line of work/profession
Position/Title/Type of Business	Business Phone (incl. area code)		Position/Title/Type of Business	Business Phone (incl. area code)	

If employed in current position for less than two years or if currently employed in more than one position, complete the following:

Borrower		IV. EMPLOYMENT INFORMATION (cont'd)	Co-Borrower	
Name & Address of Employer	☐ Self Employed	Dates (from – to)	Name & Address of Employer	☐ Self Employed	Dates (from – to)
		Monthly Income $			Monthly Income $
Position/Title/Type of Business		Business Phone (incl. area code)	Position/Title/Type of Business		Business Phone (incl. area code)
Name & Address of Employer	☐ Self Employed	Dates (from – to)	Name & Address of Employer	☐ Self Employed	Dates (from – to)
		Monthly Income $			Monthly Income $
Position/Title/Type of Business		Business Phone (incl. area code)	Position/Title/Type of Business		Business Phone (incl. area code)

V. MONTHLY INCOME AND COMBINED HOUSING EXPENSE INFORMATION

Gross Monthly Income	Borrower	Co-Borrower	Total	Combined Monthly Housing Expense	Present	Proposed
Base Empl. Income*	$	$	$	Rent	$	
Overtime				First Mortgage (P&I)		$
Bonuses				Other Financing (P&I)		
Commissions				Hazard Insurance		
Dividends/Interest				Real Estate Taxes		
Net Rental Income				Mortgage Insurance		
Other (before completing, see the notice in "describe other income," below)				Homeowner Assn. Dues		
				Other:		
Total	$	$	$	Total	$	$

* Self Employed Borrower(s) may be required to provide additional documentation such as tax returns and financial statements.

Describe Other Income

Notice: Alimony, child support, or separate maintenance income need not be revealed if the Borrower (B) or Co-Borrower (C) does not choose to have it considered for repaying this loan.

B/C		Monthly Amount
		$

VI. ASSETS AND LIABILITIES

This Statement and any applicable supporting schedules may be completed jointly by both married and unmarried Co-Borrowers if their assets and liabilities are sufficiently joined so that the Statement can be meaningfully and fairly presented on a combined basis; otherwise, separate Statements and Schedules are required. If the Co-Borrower section was completed about a non-applicant spouse or other person, this Statement and supporting schedules must be completed about that spouse or other person also.

Completed ☐ Jointly ☐ Not Jointly

ASSETS Description	Cash or Market Value	Liabilities and Pledged Assets. List the creditor's name, address, and account number for all outstanding debts, including automobile loans, revolving charge accounts, real estate loans, alimony, child support, stock pledges, etc. Use continuation sheet, if necessary. Indicate by (*) those liabilities, which will be satisfied upon sale of real estate owned or upon refinancing of the subject property.		
Cash deposit toward purchase held by:	$			
List checking and savings accounts below		LIABILITIES	Monthly Payment & Months Left to Pay	Unpaid Balance
Name and address of Bank, S&L, or Credit Union		Name and address of Company	$ Payment/Months	$
Acct. no.	$	Acct. no.		
Name and address of Bank, S&L, or Credit Union		Name and address of Company	$ Payment/Months	$
Acct. no.	$	Acct. no.		
Name and address of Bank, S&L, or Credit Union		Name and address of Company	$ Payment/Months	$
Acct. no.	$	Acct. no.		

Freddie Mac Form 65   7/05   Page 2 of 5   Fannie Mae Form 1003   7/05

VI. ASSETS AND LIABILITIES (cont'd)

Name and address of Bank, S&L, or Credit Union		Name and address of Company	$ Payment/Months	$
Acct. no.	$	Acct. no.		
Stocks & Bonds (Company name/ number & description)	$	Name and address of Company	$ Payments/Months	$
		Acct. no.		
Life insurance net cash value	$	Name and address of Company	$ Payment/Months	$
Face amount: $				
Subtotal Liquid Assets	$			
Real estate owned (enter market value from schedule of real estate owned)	$			
Vested interest in retirement fund	$			
Net worth of business(es) owned (attach financial statement)	$	Acct. no.		
Automobiles owned (make and year)	$	Alimony/Child Support/Separate Maintenance Payments Owed to:	$	
Other Assets (itemize)	$	Job-Related Expense (child care, union dues, etc.)	$	
		Total Monthly Payments	$	
Total Assets a.	$	**Net Worth** (a minus b) ▶	$	**Total Liabilities b.** $

Schedule of Real Estate Owned (If additional properties are owned, use continuation sheet.)

Property Address (enter S if sold, PS if pending sale or R if rental being held for income) ▼	Type of Property	Present Market Value	Amount of Mortgages & Liens	Gross Rental Income	Mortgage Payments	Insurance, Maintenance, Taxes & Misc.	Net Rental Income
		$	$	$	$	$	$
Totals		$	$	$	$	$	$

List any additional names under which credit has previously been received and indicate appropriate creditor name(s) and account number(s):

Alternate Name	Creditor Name	Account Number

VII. DETAILS OF TRANSACTION

a.	Purchase price	$
b.	Alterations, improvements, repairs	
c.	Land (if acquired separately)	
d.	Refinance (incl. debts to be paid off)	
e.	Estimated prepaid items	
f.	Estimated closing costs	
g.	PMI, MIP, Funding Fee	
h.	Discount (if Borrower will pay)	
i.	Total costs (add items a through h)	

VIII. DECLARATIONS

If you answer "Yes" to any questions a through i, please use continuation sheet for explanation.

	Borrower Yes No	Co-Borrower Yes No
a. Are there any outstanding judgments against you?	☐ ☐	☐ ☐
b. Have you been declared bankrupt within the past 7 years?	☐ ☐	☐ ☐
c. Have you had property foreclosed upon or given title or deed in lieu thereof in the last 7 years?	☐ ☐	☐ ☐
d. Are you a party to a lawsuit?	☐ ☐	☐ ☐
e. Have you directly or indirectly been obligated on any loan which resulted in foreclosure, transfer of title in lieu of foreclosure, or judgment?	☐ ☐	☐ ☐

(This would include such loans as home mortgage loans, SBA loans, home improvement loans, educational loans, manufactured (mobile) home loans, any mortgage, financial obligation, bond, or loan guarantee. If "Yes," provide details, including date, name, and address of Lender, FHA or VA case number, if any, and reasons for the action.)

VII. DETAILS OF TRANSACTION		VIII. DECLARATIONS				
j.	Subordinate financing		If you answer "Yes" to any questions a through i, please use continuation sheet for explanation.	Borrower		Co-Borrower
				Yes No		Yes No
k.	Borrower's closing costs paid by Seller		a. Are you presently delinquent or in default on any Federal debt or any other loan, mortgage, financial obligation, bond, or loan guarantee? If "Yes," give details as described in the preceding question.	☐ ☐		☐ ☐
l.	Other Credits (explain)		g. Are you obligated to pay alimony, child support, or separate maintenance?	☐ ☐		☐ ☐
			h. Is any part of the down payment borrowed?	☐ ☐		☐ ☐
m.	Loan amount (exclude PMI, MIP, Funding Fee financed)		i. Are you a co-maker or endorser on a note?	☐ ☐		☐ ☐
			j. Are you a U.S. citizen?	☐ ☐		☐ ☐
n.	PMI, MIP, Funding Fee financed		k. Are you a permanent resident alien?	☐ ☐		☐ ☐
			l. Do you intend to occupy the property as your primary residence? If "Yes," complete question m below.	☐ ☐		☐ ☐
o.	Loan amount (add m & n)					
			m. Have you had an ownership interest in a property in the last three years?	☐ ☐		☐ ☐
p.	Cash from/to Borrower (subtract j, k, l & o from i)		(1) What type of property did you own—principal residence (PR), second home (SH), or investment property (IP)? (2) How did you hold title to the home—solely by yourself (S), jointly with your spouse (SP), or jointly with another person (O)?	_____		_____

IX. ACKNOWLEDGEMENT AND AGREEMENT

Each of the undersigned specifically represents to Lender and to Lender's actual or potential agents, brokers, processors, attorneys, insurers, servicers, successors and assigns and agrees and acknowledges that: (1) the information provided in this application is true and correct as of the date set forth opposite my signature and that any intentional or negligent misrepresentation of this information contained in this application may result in civil liability, including monetary damages, to any person who may suffer any loss due to reliance upon any misrepresentation that I have made on this application, and/or in criminal penalties including, but not limited to, fine or imprisonment or both under the provisions of Title 18, United States Code, Sec. 1001, et seq.; (2) the loan requested pursuant to this application (the "Loan") will be secured by a mortgage or deed of trust on the property described in this application; (3) the property will not be used for any illegal or prohibited purpose or use; (4) all statements made in this application are made for the purpose of obtaining a residential mortgage loan; (5) the property will be occupied as indicated in this application; (6) the Lender, its servicers, successors or assigns may retain the original and/or an electronic record of this application, whether or not the Loan is approved; (7) the Lender and its agents, brokers, insurers, servicers, successors, and assigns may continuously rely on the information contained in the application, and I am obligated to amend and/or supplement the information provided in this application if any of the material facts that I have represented herein should change prior to closing of the Loan; (8) in the event that my payments on the Loan become delinquent, the Lender, its servicers, successors or assigns may, in addition to any other rights and remedies that it may have relating to such delinquency, report my name and account information to one or more consumer reporting agencies; (9) ownership of the Loan and/or administration of the Loan account may be transferred with such notice as may be required by law; (10) neither Lender nor its agents, brokers, insurers, servicers, successors or assigns has made any representation or warranty, express or implied, to me regarding the property or the condition or value of the property; and (11) my transmission of this application as an "electronic record" containing my "electronic signature," as those terms are defined in applicable federal and/or state laws (excluding audio and video recordings), or my facsimile transmission of this application containing a facsimile of my signature, shall be as effective, enforceable and valid as if a paper version of this application were delivered containing my original written signature.

Acknowledgement. Each of the undersigned hereby acknowledges that any owner of the Loan, its servicers, successors and assigns, may verify or reverify any information contained in this application or obtain any information or data relating to the Loan, for any legitimate business purpose through any source, including a source named in this application or a consumer reporting agency.

Borrower's Signature	Date	Co-Borrower's Signature	Date
X		X	

X. INFORMATION FOR GOVERNMENT MONITORING PURPOSES

The following information is requested by the Federal Government for certain types of loans related to a dwelling in order to monitor the lender's compliance with equal credit opportunity, fair housing and home mortgage disclosure laws. You are not required to furnish this information, but are encouraged to do so. The law provides that a lender may not discriminate either on the basis of this information, or on whether you choose to furnish it. If you furnish the information, please provide both ethnicity and race. For race, you may check more than one designation. If you do not furnish ethnicity, race, or sex, under Federal regulations, this lender is required to note the information on the basis of visual observation and surname if you have made this application in person. If you do not wish to furnish the information, please check the box below. (Lender must review the above material to assure that the disclosures satisfy all requirements to which the lender is subject under applicable state law for the particular type of loan applied for.)

BORROWER ☐ I do not wish to furnish this information		CO-BORROWER ☐ I do not wish to furnish this information	
Ethnicity: ☐ Hispanic or Latino ☐ Not Hispanic or Latino		Ethnicity: ☐ Hispanic or Latino ☐ Not Hispanic or Latino	
Race: ☐ American Indian or Alaska Native ☐ Native Hawaiian or Other Pacific Islander	☐ Asian ☐ Black or African American ☐ White	Race: ☐ American Indian or Alaska Native ☐ Native Hawaiian or Other Pacific Islander	☐ Asian ☐ Black or African American ☐ White
Sex: ☐ Female ☐ Male		Sex: ☐ Female ☐ Male	
To be Completed by Interviewer This application was taken by: ☐ Face-to-face interview ☐ Mail ☐ Telephone ☐ Internet	Interviewer's Name (print or type)		Name and Address of Interviewer's Employer
	Interviewer's Signature	Date	
	Interviewer's Phone Number (incl. area code)		

Freddie Mac Form 65   7/05   Page 4 of 5   Fannie Mae Form 1003   7/05

APPENDIX C

CONTINUATION SHEET/RESIDENTIAL LOAN APPLICATION		
Use this continuation sheet if you need more space to complete the Residential Loan Application. Mark B for Borrower or C for Co-Borrower.	Borrower:	Agency Case Number:
	Co-Borrower:	Lender Case Number:

I/We fully understand that it is a Federal crime punishable by fine or imprisonment, or both, to knowingly make any false statements concerning any of the above facts as applicable under the provisions of Title 18, United States Code, Section 1001, et seq.

Borrower's Signature	Date	Co-Borrower's Signature	Date
X		X	

APPENDIX D

OMB Approval No. 2502-0265

Good Faith Estimate (GFE)

Name of Originator		Borrower	
Originator Address		Property Address	
Originator Phone Number			
Originator Email		Date of GFE	

Purpose

This GFE gives you an estimate of your settlement charges and loan terms if you are approved for this loan. For more information, see HUD's *Special Information Booklet* on settlement charges, your *Truth-in-Lending Disclosures*, and other consumer information at www.hud.gov/respa. If you decide you would like to proceed with this loan, contact us.

Shopping for your loan

Only you can shop for the best loan for you. Compare this GFE with other loan offers, so you can find the best loan. Use the shopping chart on page 3 to compare all the offers you receive.

Important dates

1. The interest rate for this GFE is available through _____. After this time, the interest rate, some of your loan Origination Charges, and the monthly payment shown below can change until you lock your interest rate.

2. This estimate for all other settlement charges is available through _____.

3. After you lock your interest rate, you must go to settlement within ☐ days (your rate lock period) to receive the locked interest rate.

4. You must lock the interest rate at least ☐ days before settlement.

Summary of your loan

Your initial loan amount is	$
Your loan term is	years
Your initial interest rate is	%
Your initial monthly amount owed for principal, interest, and any mortgage insurance is	$ per month
Can your interest rate rise?	☐ No ☐ Yes, it can rise to a maximum of %. The first change will be in
Even if you make payments on time, can your loan balance rise?	☐ No ☐ Yes, it can rise to a maximum of $
Even if you make payments on time, can your monthly amount owed for principal, interest, and any mortgage insurance rise?	☐ No ☐ Yes, the first increase can be in and the monthly amount owed can rise to $. The maximum it can ever rise to is $
Does your loan have a prepayment penalty?	☐ No ☐ Yes, your maximum prepayment penalty is $
Does your loan have a balloon payment?	☐ No ☐ Yes, you have a balloon payment of $ due in years.

Escrow account information

Some lenders require an escrow account to hold funds for paying property taxes or other property-related charges in addition to your monthly amount owed of $_____.
Do we require you to have an escrow account for your loan?
☐ No, you do not have an escrow account. You must pay these charges directly when due.
☐ Yes, you have an escrow account. It may or may not cover all of these charges. Ask us.

Summary of your settlement charges

A	Your Adjusted Origination Charges (See page 2)	$
B	Your Charges for All Other Settlement Services (See page 2)	$
A + B	**Total Estimated Settlement Charges**	$

Good Faith Estimate (HUD-GFE) 1

APPENDIX D

Understanding your estimated settlement charges

Some of these charges can change at settlement. See the top of page 3 for more information.

Your Adjusted Origination Charges

1. Our origination charge
This charge is for getting this loan for you.

2. Your credit or charge (points) for the specific interest rate chosen

☐ The credit or charge for the interest rate of ☐ % is included in "Our origination charge." (See item 1 above.)

☐ You receive a credit of $ ☐ for this interest rate of ☐ %. This credit **reduces** your settlement charges.

☐ You pay a charge of $ ☐ for this interest rate of ☐ %. This charge (points) **increases** your total settlement charges.

The tradeoff table on page 3 shows that you can change your total settlement charges by choosing a different interest rate for this loan.

A | Your Adjusted Origination Charges | $

Your Charges for All Other Settlement Services

3. Required services that we select
These charges are for services we require to complete your settlement. We will choose the providers of these services.

Service	Charge

4. Title services and lender's title insurance
This charge includes the services of a title or settlement agent, for example, and title insurance to protect the lender, if required.

5. Owner's title insurance
You may purchase an owner's title insurance policy to protect your interest in the property.

6. Required services that you can shop for
These charges are for other services that are required to complete your settlement. We can identify providers of these services or you can shop for them yourself. Our estimates for providing these services are below.

Service	Charge

7. Government recording charges
These charges are for state and local fees to record your loan and title documents.

8. Transfer taxes
These charges are for state and local fees on mortgages and home sales.

9. Initial deposit for your escrow account
This charge is held in an escrow account to pay future recurring charges on your property and includes ☐ all property taxes, ☐ all insurance, and ☐ other ☐.

10. Daily interest charges
This charge is for the daily interest on your loan from the day of your settlement until the first day of the next month or the first day of your normal mortgage payment cycle. This amount is $☐ per day for ☐ days (if your settlement is ☐).

11. Homeowner's insurance
This charge is for the insurance you must buy for the property to protect from a loss, such as fire.

Policy	Charge

B | Your Charges for All Other Settlement Services | $

A + B | Total Estimated Settlement Charges | $

 Good Faith Estimate (HUD-GFE) 2

281

Instructions

Understanding which charges can change at settlement

This GFE estimates your settlement charges. At your settlement, you will receive a HUD-1, a form that lists your actual costs. Compare the charges on the HUD-1 with the charges on this GFE. Charges can change if you select your own provider and do not use the companies we identify. (See below for details.)

These charges cannot increase at settlement.	The total of these charges can increase up to 10% at settlement.	These charges can change at settlement.
• Our origination charge • Your credit or charge (points) for the specific interest rate chosen (after you lock in your interest rate) • Your adjusted origination charges (after you lock in your interest rate) • Transfer taxes	• Required services that we select • Title services and lender's title insurance (if we select them or you use companies we identify) • Owner's title insurance (if you use companies we identify) • Required services that you can shop for (if you use companies we identify) • Government recording charges	• Required services that you can shop for (if you do not use companies we identify) • Title services and lender's title insurance (if you do not use companies we identify) • Owner's title insurance (if you do not use companies we identify) • Initial deposit for your escrow account • Daily interest charges • Homeowner's insurance

Using the tradeoff table

In this GFE, we offered you this loan with a particular interest rate and estimated settlement charges. However:
- If you want to choose this same loan with **lower settlement charges**, then you will have a **higher interest rate**.
- If you want to choose this same loan with a **lower interest rate**, then you will have **higher settlement charges**.

If you would like to choose an available option, you must ask us for a new GFE.

Loan originators have the option to complete this table. Please ask for additional information if the table is not completed.

	The loan in this GFE	The same loan with lower settlement charges	The same loan with a lower interest rate
Your initial loan amount	$	$	$
Your initial interest rate¹	%	%	%
Your initial monthly amount owed	$	$	$
Change in the monthly amount owed from this GFE	No change	You will pay $ **more** every month	You will pay $ **less** every month
Change in the amount you will pay at settlement with this interest rate	No change	Your settlement charges will be **reduced** by $	Your settlement charges will **increase** by $
How much your total estimated settlement charges will be	$	$	$

¹ For an adjustable rate loan, the comparisons above are for the initial interest rate before adjustments are made.

Using the shopping chart

Use this chart to compare GFEs from different loan originators. Fill in the information by using a different column for each GFE you receive. By comparing loan offers, you can shop for the best loan.

	This loan	Loan 2	Loan 3	Loan 4
Loan originator name				
Initial loan amount				
Loan term				
Initial interest rate				
Initial monthly amount owed				
Rate lock period				
Can interest rate rise?				
Can loan balance rise?				
Can monthly amount owed rise?				
Prepayment penalty?				
Balloon payment?				
Total Estimated Settlement Charges				

If your loan is sold in the future

Some lenders may sell your loan after settlement. Any fees lenders receive in the future cannot change the loan you receive or the charges you paid at settlement.

 Good Faith Estimate (HUD-GFE) 3

INDEX

Forms are indicated in italics

A
Ability to Repay (ATR) rule, 194
ACE (*Automated Certificate of Eligibility*) system, 31
active duty employment
    Certificate of Release or Discharge from Active Duty (DD-214), 29–30, 104
    Leave and Earnings Statement, 64–65
    MIA (missing in action), 27
    occupancy requirements, 232–33
    POW (prisoner of war), 27
    Power of Attorney, 155–56
    See also military borrowers; service members
adjustable-rate mortgages (ARMs)
    vs. fixed rate loans, 208–10, 216
    Hybrid ARMS, 209–10
    refinancing, 240, 241
    types of, 85
Air National Guard, 30
airport noise, 144
all-cash purchases, 152, 154–55

amortization
   finding tables online, 203
   how it works, 202–4, 211–12
   negative amortization, 194, 211–12
   and temporary buydown of interest rate, 202–4
   types of, 85
annual percentage rate (APR), 43, 108–9, 110–11, 200
appraisal. *See* VA appraisals
ARMs. *See* adjustable-rate mortgages (ARMs)
Army National Guard, 30
"as-is" sales, 153
assets and liabilities, 63, 69, 90–92, 187, 194
attorneys, 137, 139, 156
Automated Certificate of Eligibility (ACE), 30–32
   See also *Certificate of Eligibility* (COE); *Request for a Certificate of Eligibility* (Form 26-1880)
Automated Underwriting System (AUS)
   and loan approval, 187–88
   and loan preapproval, 117–18
   and loan prequalification, 83
   vs. manual underwriting, 83, 120–21, 187–88
   See also underwriting

B
bankruptcy, 52–55, 57
Basic Allowance for Housing, 65, 123–25
Borrowers Certification and Authorization, 96–97
business-use properties, 23–24, 147
buydown of interest rates, 201–4, 211, 229
buyer's agent. *See* Realtors

C
Cash-Out Refinance loan, 243–48, 249
cash-out refinancing
   Cash-Out Refinance loan vs. VA Streamline loan, 244, 246–47
   with VA loan, 22, 243–48, 249
   See also refinancing; VA loans; VA loans (specific loans)

Certificate of Eligibility (COE), 29–30, 34–35
   See also Automated Certificate of Eligibility (ACE); *Request for a*
     Certificate of Eligibility (Form 26-1880)
Certificate of Reasonable Value, 142
Certificate of Release or Discharge from Active Duty (DD-214), 29–30, 104
clear to close (CTC), 190
closing
  cash needed for, 222, 224, 229–31
  contingency removal and, 186–90
  and interest rate locks, 205–8
  timing of, 32, 133, 137, 219–20
closing costs
  comparison among lenders, 220–22
  consumer protections, 214–15, 223
  earnest money and, 91, 224
  Good Faith Estimate (GFE), 102, 111, 214, 215–22
  HUD-1 Settlement Statement, 214, 223–28
  Initial Fees Worksheet, 215, 222
  limits on for veterans, 132, 214, 228
  negotiating, 219–20, 228–31
  no fee/no cost loans, 230–31
  origination fee, 110–11, 201–2, 217, 241–42
  payment of, 110–11, 132, 137, 149, 228–31
  points, 201–2, 217–18, 229, 246–47
  refinancing and, 240, 241–42
  rolled into loan, 242
  seller concessions, 137, 222, 226, 228–30
  specific fees and charges, 215, 216–22, 226, 227–28
  total settlement charges, 224–25
  transfer fee, 228
  and VA loans, 11, 20, 228–31
  Veterans United Realty concessions, 134
  who pays, 110–11, 117, 137, 149
  See also purchase agreement; VA loans
co-borrowers, 41–42, 118
Coastal Barrier Resources system, 155
coastal properties, 144
commitment letter, 190

compensating factors, 69–71, 81–92
compensation of loan brokers, 116–17, 193–95, 196–98, 198–200
comps (comparable home values), 24, 141, 143, 146
conditional approval, 110, 189
condominiums, 21–23, 130, 145
conforming loan limits, 33–34
construction loans, 23, 24–25, 86, 137, 183, 185, 248–49
Construction-to-Permanent Refinance Loan, 25, 248–49
Consumer Financial Protection Bureau, 193
consumer protection
    and Adjustable Rate Mortgages (ARMs), 210
    closing costs, 214–15, 223
    credit clinics, 45–46
    credit report discrepancies, 47–49
    discrimination in housing, 95–96
    home purchase, 214, 223–28
    loan broker compensation, 193–96, 198–200
    mortgage industry reforms, 192–96, 207
    See also Good Faith Estimate; HUD-1 Settlement Statement
contingencies
    "out" clause, 143
    in preapproval letter, 120
    in purchase agreement, 137–38, 143
    removing, 186–90
conventional loans
    credit scores and, 5, 43
    vs. nonconventional loans, 9, 14–15
    overview, 13
    vs. VA loans, 3–5, 9–11, 14–15, 43, 78–79, 132–33, 204–5, 247–48
county loan limits, 34
crawl space, 148
credit bureaus. *See* credit history
credit clinics/counseling, 44–46
    See also Veterans United Lighthouse Program
credit/credit cards
    closing accounts, 40, 49
    conservative use as compensating factor, 70
    credit card balances, 39–40, 49–50, 92, 229
    payment history, 36–37, 39, 49, 58–59

prepaid credit cards, 59
secured credit cards, 59
student loans, 92
types of credit, 40
understanding credit, 36–37, 50
credit history
and Ability to Repay, 194
bankruptcy and foreclosure, 53, 120
as compensating factor, 69
and credit score, 40–41, 49–50
having no credit, 58–59
underwriting and, 83, 91, 97, 120
and VA loans, 3–4
credit market, 4
credit profile
of additional borrowers, 41
and credit checks, 40
effect of bankruptcy and foreclosure on, 52
explained, 36–37, 44
importance to lender, 59, 81, 256
and interest rate, 42–43, 50, 239
and Veterans United Lighthouse Program, 50
credit report
accessing, 37–38
on borrower's business, 63
closing fees for, 215
disputing errors, 47–49
free, 37–38
importance of checking, 47
overview, 37–38
and underwriting, 92, 189
credit score
accessing, 37–38, 41
amount of debt and, 49
as compensating factor, 70, 92
components of, 39–40
and conventional loans, 5, 13
Credit Score Information Disclosure, 100–101
disputing errors in credit reports, 47–49

  effect of bankruptcy and foreclosure on, 52, 54–55
  effect of multiple inquiries on, 40, 208
  effect on interest rate, 43, 200, 239–40
  effect on PMI, 10
  FICO score, 38–42
  improving, 42–44, 46–47, 51
  late payments and, 39
  loan-to-value adjustment, 204–5
  and risk to lender, 37, 42, 121, 249, 256
  subprime loans/borrowers, 42
  and VA loan requirements, 5, 81–82, 92
  and VA loans, 37, 42, 59
  VantageScore, 38
  and Veterans United Lighthouse Program, 44–46, 50, 51, 54, 81–82
  See also underwriting
Credit Score Information Disclosure, 100–101

D
DD-214 (*Certificate of Release or Discharge from Active Duty*), 29–30, 104
debt-to-income ratio (DTI ratio)
  and loan amount, 70–71, 118
  military spouses living separately, 233
  overview, 60, 66–67
  and Qualified Mortgages, 194, 195
  and residual income, 66–71
  and temporary buydowns of interest rate, 203–4
  and VA loans/underwriting, 5, 99, 117–18, 121, 124, 188, 256
deed-in-lieu of foreclosure, 54
defaulting on loans
  effect on interest rate and fees, 42
  as risk to lender, 64, 66–67, 121
  subprime mortgages, 42
  and VA Funding Fee, 231–32
  VA Loan Disclosures and, 115–16
  and VA Loan Guaranty program, 21, 33, 59, 115–16, 121, 188
defective conditions, 149
disabled veterans
  as borrowers, 57–58, 103, 116, 156–57, 231
  disability income, 66

surviving spouse eligibility, 28
Verification of VA Benefits, 103
discrimination in housing, 95–96
doors, 212
down payment
   conventional loans, 13, 14–15
   and FHA loans, 12, 14–15, 57–58
   and loan-to-value adjustment, 204–5
   no money down, 4, 10, 14, 20, 34, 124, 188, 201
   and non-eligible co-borrowers, 41–42
   and PMI (private mortgage insurance), 10
   and purchase agreement, 137
   and risk to lender, 188, 200
   USDA loans, 14–15
   and VA Funding Fee, 14, 231–32
   and VA loans, 4, 10, 14, 34, 55–58, 65
   See also earnest money
DTI ratio. *See* debt-to-income ratio (DTI ratio)

E
earnest money
   described, 91–92
   and the purchase agreement, 136
   return of at closing, 91, 106–7, 224
   See also down payment
earthquakes, 144
education, information for loan application, 88–89, 116
electricity, 148
electronic signatures, 83
eligibility for VA loans
   Automated Certificate of Eligibility (ACE), 30–32
   Certificate of Eligibility (COE), 29–30, 34–35
   co-borrowers, 41–42
   credit history, 59
   exceptions, 28–29
   persons, 25–29, 31–32, 41–42, 104
   properties ineligible for VA appraisal, 144–46
   property, 21–25, 86–87, 140, 146–53, 232–33
   Request for Certificate of Eligibility (Form 26-1880), 29–30, 104, 273

See also VA Loan Guaranty program; VA loans
Ellie Mae, 5
employment
  as compensating factor, 69
  current employment, 61, 187
  information for loan application, 69, 88–89, 99–100
  military employment, 29–30, 64–65
  new employment, 64
  and Qualified Mortgages, 194
  Request for Verification of Employment (VA Form 26-8497), 61, 274
  self-employment, 52–53, 62–63
  of spouses, 233
  two-year benchmark for stability, 61, 62, 82, 88
  Verification of Employment (VOE), 61
energy-efficient improvements, 22, 212–13, 242, 244, 246
Energy Efficient Mortgage (EEM), 116, 212–13
entitlement to VA loans, 25–26, 33–34, 55–58, 248
Environmental Protection Agency, 150
Equifax, 37, 38
equity
  and cash-out refinancing, 243–44
  home equity loans, 245
  and home value, 8, 241
  and PMI, 14
  type of loan considerations, 247
escrow
  earnest money, 91–92
  funds for repairs and improvements, 151, 213
  insurance payments, 217, 241–42
  real estate taxes, 217, 242
Experian, 37, 38

F
Fannie Mae, 84, 97, 192
Federal Emergency Management Agency (FEMA), 144
Federal Housing Administration (FHA) loans, 9, 11–12, 14–15, 57, 195
Federal Reserve, 8, 191
Federal Trade Commission, 45–46, 48

fees. *See* closing costs; finance charges

FEMA (Federal Emergency Management Agency), 144

FHA (Federal Housing Administration) loans, 9, 11–12, 14–15, 57, 195

FICO score, 38–42

    See also credit score

finance charges

    Good Faith Estimate (GFE), 217–18

    Initial Fees Worksheet, 110–11, 215

    paid outside of closing (POC), 110–11

    prepaid finance charges (PFC), 110–11

    See also VA Funding Fee

financial counseling, military borrowers, 44–46

financial statements. *See* assets and liabilities

fixed-rate loans

    vs. ARMs, 85, 208–10, 216

    and Graduated Payment Mortgage (GPM), 210–12

    monthly payments on, 43, 70

    negotiating, 200–201

    and refinancing, 240

    and VA Funding Fee, 231–32

flipping, 22, 154

float, 114–15, 206–8

flood zones, 120, 144, 241

foreclosed properties

    buying distressed properties, 153–55

    buying homes in foreclosure, 152–53

    REO owned homes, 153

    short sale transactions, 54, 154

foreclosure

    deed-in-lieu of, 54

    effect on credit score, 54–55

    effect on eligibility for VA loans, 31, 55–58, 120

    overview, 5–6

    rates of, 5–6, 152

    and second-tier entitlement, 55–56

    on VA loans, 5, 31, 55

    VA programs to prevent, 6

Freddie Mac, 97, 192

G

glossary of terms, 261–71
Good Faith Estimate (GFE), 102, 111, 215–22, 280–82
    vs. *HUD-1 Settlement Statement*, 214, 225, 227–28
    and rate locks, 216
    See also consumer protection
Good Faith Estimate Provider Relationship, 102
Graduated Payment Mortgage (GPM), 85, 210–12
Growing Equity Mortgage (GEM), 211–12

H

health and safety
    hazardous locations, 144
    Minimum Property Requirements (MPRs), 140, 146–53
    and VA appraisals, 133, 135–36
heating, 147–48, 212–13
home business, 23–24
home construction, 21, 24–25, 137, 144, 147, 159–60, 248–49
home energy audits, 213
home equity loans, 245
home improvement, 22, 240, 242
    and Energy Efficient Mortgages, 212–13
    and VA Cash-Out Refinance loan, 244, 246
home inspections
    and Minimum Property Requirements (MPRs), 146–53
    purchase agreement contingency, 138
    Realtor's knowledge about, 128, 130
    vs. VA appraisals, 146
    and VA loans, 135–36, 187
    who pays, 138
    wind mitigation, 125
home prices, 136, 140–43
    See also VA appraisals
home purchase
    condominiums, 21–23, 130, 145
    distressed properties, 153–55
    foreclosures, 152–53
    Internet listings, 128–29
    Multiple Listing Service (MLS), 128–29

Realtor's role, 127–29
starting the process, 77–79, 127
homeowner's insurance, 89, 111, 186, 217, 220, 222, 226, 229, 242
homeownership, 3–4, 7–8
honesty, 82, 86, 88
housing expenses, 60, 67, 89
housing market. *See* market influence
HUD-1 Settlement Statement, 223–28
closing costs and fees, 226–28
vs. *Good Faith Estimate* (GFE), 214, 225, 227–28
summary of loan, 228
title insurance charges, 226
total settlement charges, 224–25
See also consumer protection
HUD (U.S. Department of Housing and Urban Development), 145, 214
HUD/VA Addendum to Uniform Residential Loan Application, 105–6
hurricane-prone regions, 125
Hybrid ARM loans, 209–10

I

income
active duty employment, 64–65
debt-to-income ratio (DTI ratio), 5, 60, 66–71, 89, 99, 117–18,
    188, 256
disability, 66, 116
employment, 61–62, 64, 81–82
information for loan application, 89, 96–97, 113–14
military benefits, 69
and mortgage type, 210–11, 248
overview, 60
pension/retirement benefits, 66
requirements for VA loans, 61–64
residual, 60, 67–70, 188
self-employment, 62–63
sources other than employment, 66
of spouse, 65–66
stock dividends, 66
verification of, 61–64, 244
See also tax returns

Initial Fees Worksheet, 110–11, 222
inspections. *See* home inspections
insulation, 212
insurance. *See* homeowner's insurance; title insurance
Interest Rate Reduction Refinance Loan, 27, 239, 246–47
interest rates
    annual percentage rate (APR), 43, 108–9, 110–11, 200
    and appraised value, 143
    base rate, 196, 204
    buying down, 201–4, 220–21, 229
    conventional loans, 13, 14–15, 43
    and credit score, 43–44
    daily (per diem) interest charges, 219–20, 226
    determination of, 190–92, 256
    float, 114–15, 206–8
    fluctuation of, 117
    and Ginnie Mae bonds, 192
    Good Faith Estimate (GFE), 102, 111, 216, 220, 221–22
    HUD-1 Settlement Statement, 226
    HUD/VA Addendum to Uniform Residential Loan Application, 105–6
    Initial Fees Worksheet, 110–11
    Loan Pricing Agreement Defining Interest Rates and Terms, 114–15
    lock fee, 206
    locking a rate, 114–15, 190, 197, 205–8, 215, 216, 242, 248
    and margin, 209–10
    negative amortization, 194, 211–12
    negotiating, 200–201
    overview, 190–92
    par rate, 196–98, 200
    PITI, 89, 222
    and points, 201–2, 206–8, 215, 217–18, 229, 242, 246–47
    rate caps, 207, 209–10
    rate sheets, 192, 196–97, 201
    retail rate, 201
    and seller concessions, 111, 143, 228–31
    temporary buydown of, 202–4, 211
    tradeoff table, 220–21
    and Truth in Lending Act, 109
    VA loans vs. conventional, 10–11, 14, 43, 204–5

and Yield Spread, 191, 196–98, 198–200, 201, 230–31
investment properties, 22, 23–24, 86, 147

L
land purchases, 22
landslides, 144
lead-based paint, 149
Leave and Earnings Statement, 64–65
Lender Appraisal Processing Program (LAPP), 139–40
lenders
    Ability to Repay (ATR) rule, 194
    compensation to loan broker, 116–17, 193–95, 196–98, 198–200
    consequences of abandoning, 208
    flat fees, 215
    loan processors, 181–82, 186–90
    mortgage industry reforms, 192–96, 207
    and rate locks, 205–8
    relationship with borrowers, 91–92, 155–56, 208
    relationship with real estate agents, 78
    selection of service providers, 102, 228
    temporary buydowns of interest rate, 203–4, 211
    VA-approved, 9, 56, 59, 121, 133–34, 201, 210
    VA loans, 24–25, 78–79, 241
    See also loan application; loans; VA loans
length of service requirements, 28, 31
Lighthouse Program. *See* Veterans United Lighthouse Program
listing agent (seller's agent), 129, 131
loan amount
    appraisal and, 142–43
    Cash-Out Refinance loans, 244–45
    closing costs and, 228–31, 241–42, 244–45
    conforming loans, 33–34
    county loan limits, 34
    determination of, 33–34, 55–56, 70–71
    discount points and, 246
    Energy Efficient Mortgage (EEM), 212–13
    HUD/VA Addendum to Uniform Residential Loan Application, 105–6
    loan application and, 85

Loan Pricing Agreement Defining Interest Rates and Terms, 114–15
negative amortization, 194, 211–12
preapproval, 19, 117–20
prequalification, 19, 80, 83
and residual income, 68
and seller concessions, 228–31
and VA Funding Fee, 103, 231–32
VA loan limits, 32–34
loan application
accessing online, 85
declarations, 94–95
earnest money, 91
evaluation of, 44, 53, 67, 69–70, 82
financial information, 67, 90–92
form of ownership, 87
housing expenses, 89
HUD/VA Addendum to Uniform Residential Loan Application,
105–6
Initial Fees Worksheet, 215, 222
loan officer assistance with, 82–84, 85, 96, 105, 155–56
mortgage type, 85
occupancy, 86
personal information, 87, 96–97, 116
preparation of, 32–33, 85, 143
property and purpose, 86–87, 105–6
transaction details, 93–94
Uniform Residential Loan Application (Fannie Mae Form 1003),
84–96, 275–79
VA Amendment to Contract, 106–7, 143
See also lenders
loan approval
Automated Underwriting System, 83
clear to close (CTC), 190
commitment letter, 190
compensating factors, 69–71, 90–92
conditional approval, 110, 189–90
vs. loan preapproval, 119–20
manual underwrite, 83, 120–21
negative compensating factors, 53

preparation of paperwork, 82–84

starting the process, 25–26, 77–79

See also loan preapproval; loan prequalification; loans; underwriting

loan brokers. *See* mortgage brokers

loan comparison chart, 14–15

loan documents

Borrowers Certification and Authorization, 96–97

Certificate of Eligibility (COE), 29–30, 34–35

Credit Score Information Disclosure, 100–101

falsifying information on, 82, 86

Good Faith Estimate (GFE), 102, 111, 214

Good Faith Estimate Provider Relationship, 102

HUD-1 Settlement Statement, 214, 223–28

HUD/VA Addendum to Uniform Residential Loan Application, 105–6

Initial Fees Worksheet, 110–11

loan approval paperwork, 82–84

Loan Pricing Agreement Defining Interest Rates and Terms, 114–15

Mortgage Broker Fee Agreement and Disclosure, 116–17

Notice of Value (NOV), 142, 183–86

Patriot Act Information Disclosure, 101

Report and Certification of Loan Disbursement, 112

Request for Certificate of Eligibility (Form 26-1880), 29–30, 104, 273

Request for Transcript of Tax Returns (IRS Form 4506-T), 99–100

Servicing Disclosure Statement, 98

timely completion of, 117

Uniform Residential Loan Application (Fannie Mae Form 1003), 84–96, 275–79

VA Amendment to Contract, 106–7, 143

VA Loan Disclosures, 115–16

VA Loan Summary Sheet, 113–14

loan officers

assistance with credit bureaus, 48–49

compensation of, 193–95, 196–98, 198–200

determining amount and type of loan, 15, 118, 257

and loan application paperwork, 82–84, 85, 96, 105, 155–56

and locking interest rates, 207–8

relationship with borrower, 91, 182

and underwriting process, 121, 182, 189

loan preapproval
    contingency removal, 120
    vs. loan approval, 119–20
    necessity for, 78
    overview, 71, 117–20
    vs. prequalification, 79–80, 119
    sample letter, 119
    without a *Certificate of Eligibility*, 32
    See also loan approval; loan prequalification; loans
loan prequalification
    and the Automated Underwriting System (AUS), 83, 121
    and buying foreclosed properties, 155
    and credit score, 81, 100–101
    described, 80
    vs. loan approval, 119
    vs. preapproval, 79–80, 119
    and rate locking, 114–15
    underwriting, 19, 80, 82–84, 121
    See also loan preapproval
Loan Pricing Agreement Defining Interest Rates and Terms, 114–15
loan processors. *See* lenders
loan specialists (VA), 6, 9, 15
loan-to-value. *See* equity; loans
loans
    additional payments of principal, 208–9
    amortization, 85, 202–4
    balloon payments, 194
    co-borrowers, 41–42, 118
    conventional vs. VA, 3–5, 9–11, 14, 78–79, 132–33, 204–5
    costs and fees, 102, 108–11, 195, 214–15, 223–28, 247
    costs and fees in *Good Faith Estimate* (GFE), 214–22
    costs and fees in *HUD-1 Settlement Statement*, 214, 223–28
    delinquent, 116
    down payment, 10, 34, 57–58
    fixed vs. ARM, 85, 208–10, 216
    interest-only, 194
    interest rates, 10–11, 106, 108–9, 190–92
    loan-to-value adjustment, 204–5

negative amortization, 194, 211–12

"no fee", 230–31

prime borrowers, 42–43

sale of on secondary market, 96–97, 191, 199, 204–5

shopping for, 221–22

subprime borrowers/loans, 3, 42, 44, 81, 193, 255

term of loan, 194, 247

types of, 9–15

VA vs. other nonconventional loans, 9, 14–15

VA vs. conventional, 4, 9–11, 14, 78–79, 132–33, 204–5

See also lenders; loan approval; loan preapproval; loan
    prequalification; mortgages; refinancing; VA loans

locking an interest rate, 114–15, 190, 197, 205–8, 215, 216, 242,
    248

M

manual underwrite, 83, 120–21

manufactured homes, 24, 145, 150

market influence

    distressed market, 5, 152, 153–55

    mortgage industry reforms, 192–96, 207, 255–58

    and seller concessions, 229

    and subprime mortgages, 3, 42, 81, 193, 255

    "underwater" mortgages, 5, 252

market value

    appraised value vs. asking price, 142–43

    determination of, 140–43

    Notice of Value (NOV), 142, 183–86

    reconsideration of value, 143

married veterans, 65–66

mechanical systems, 147

merchant seamen, 28

military borrowers

    attorney review of documents, 139

    awareness of VA loan programs, 257

    buying distressed properties, 153–55

    character of, 6

    financial counseling, 44–46

and foreclosure rates, 5–6
loan preapproval, 118
and Realtors, 127, 130–36, 151
receiving disability benefits, 103, 116
refinance VA Funding Fee, 244–45
Verification of VA Benefits, 103
Veterans Benefits Improvement Act (2008), 244
See also active duty employment
military service academy cadets, 28
military spouses
    awareness of VA loan programs, 6–7
    credit history of, 52
    eligibility requirements, 27–28
    income of, 65–66
Minimum Property Requirements (MPRs), 140, 145, 146–53
    manufactured homes, 145
    and *Notice of Value* (NOV), 185
    properties in foreclosure, 152–53
    request for exemption, 150–51
    See also VA appraisals
MIP (mortgage insurance premiums), 12
moisture, 148
Mortgage Bankers Association, 3
Mortgage Broker Fee Agreement and Disclosure, 116–17
mortgage brokers
    compensation, 116–17, 193–95, 196–98, 198–200
    familiarity with VA loans, 79
mortgage calculators, 8, 203
mortgage companies. *See* lenders
mortgage financing. *See* loans
mortgage industry reforms, 192–96, 207
mortgage insurance premiums (MIP), 12
mortgage protection, 138
mortgages
    fixed vs. ARM, 85, 208–10
    loan payments, 98
    loan servicing, 98
    mortgage-backed securities, 191–92

negative amortization, 194, 211–12
Qualified Mortgages (QM), 193–96, 199, 204, 212
sale of in secondary market, 96–97, 191, 199, 204–5
Servicing Disclosure Statement, 98
summary of loan in *HUD-1 Settlement Statement*, 228
See also loans; VA loans (specific loans)
multi-unit properties, 23–24
Multiple Listing Service (MLS), 128–29

N
National Association of Realtors, 128
National Guard members, 27, 28, 29, 31
refinance VA Funding Fee, 245
National Oceanic and Atmospheric Administration officials, 28
negative compensating factors, 53
newly-built homes. *See* home construction
no-paper loans, 255
nonconventional loans
types of, 9, 14–15
See also conventional loans; VA loans
Notice of Value (NOV), 142, 183–86

O
occupancy requirement, 21–22, 23, 86–87, 232–33, 235, 247, 249
origination fee, 110–11, 201–2, 217, 227, 241–42
"out" clause, 143
See also contingencies
ownership, forms of, 87

P
partition, 23–24
Patriot Act Information Disclosure, 101
pension/retirement benefits, 66
permanent buydown. *See* buydown of interest rates
personal property, 138
PFC (prepaid finance charges), 110–11
PITI (principal, interest, taxes, and insurance), 89, 222, 243

PMI (private mortgage insurance), conventional loans, 10, 13, 14–15
POC (fees paid outside of closing), 110–11
points
    discount points, 201–4, 215, 229, 246
    Good Faith Estimate (GFE), 217–18
    as origination fee, 201–2, 217–18, 241–42
    overview, 201–2
    permanent buydown, 201–4, 229
    and rate locks, 206–7
    rolled into loan, 201, 241, 247
    as seller concession, 201, 229
    and temporary buydown of interest rate, 202–4, 211
    and VA Streamline loan, 241–42
Power of Attorney, 155–56
preapproval. *See* loan preapproval
prepaid finance charges (PFC), 110–11
prepayment penalties, 11, 209
prequalification. *See* loan prequalification
primary residence requirement, 21–22, 23, 86–87, 232–33, 235,
    247, 249
prime. *See* credit score; subprime mortgages/borrowers
private mortgage insurance (PMI). *See* PMI
property
    access to, 149
    characteristics of and value, 140
    and distressed markets, 5, 153–55
    eligibility requirements for VA loans, 21–25, 86–87, 140, 146–53,
        232–33
    ineligible for VA appraisal, 144–46
    inspections, 125, 130, 138, 146–53, 187
    Minimum Property Requirements (MPRs), 140, 145, 146–53,
        185
    multiple units, 23–24
    purchasing while overseas, 155–56
    title to, 87, 186–87
    transfer fee, 228
property tax, 217, 222, 229, 243
    PITI, 89, 243

property, value of. *See* market value; VA appraisals
Public Health Service officials, 28
purchase agreement
    attorney review, 137, 139
    closing costs, 137, 214–15, 216–22
    components of, 136–39
    contingencies, 137–38, 143
    Good Faith Estimate (GFE), 214, 221–22
    HUD-1 Settlement Statement, 214, 223–28
    purchase price, 137
    Realtor's role, 136
    See also closing costs
purchase price
    and affordability, 70–71
    asking price vs. appraised value, 142
    negotiating, 136, 143
    and *Notice of Value* (NOV), 142, 183–86
    in purchase agreement, 137
    See also VA appraisals
purchasing while overseas, 155–56

Q

Qualified Mortgages (QM), 193–96, 199, 204, 212
"qualified rural area", 12, 15
qualifying for a loan
    conventional loans, 13
    VA loans, 3–5, 13, 44
    VA loans vs. conventional, 3–5, 11, 43

R

real estate agents. *See* Realtors
real estate taxes. *See* property tax
Realtors
    areas of expertise, 128–29
    benefits of using, 127–30
    buyer's agent, 129, 130–32
    defined, 127–29

experience with military buyers, 127, 130–36, 151
  expertise with VA loans, 78–79, 127–36, 151, 152–53, 155, 258
  finding a Realtor, 130–36
  listing (seller's) agent, 129
  vs. real estate agents, 127–30
  relationship with mortgage lenders, 78
  sales commissions, 129, 225–26
  Veterans United Realty, 18–20, 134–35
RealtyTrac, 6, 155
reconsideration of value, 143
refinancing
  in challenging economy, 249, 252, 257
  closing costs, 240, 241–42, 248
  construction loans, 248–49
  interest rate locks, 114–15, 248
  reasons for, 239–40
  with VA loan, 6–7, 21–22
  See also cash-out refinancing; loans; VA refinance loans
relocation, 56
rental properties *See* investment properties
renting, vs. buying, 7–8
REO (real estate owned) homes, 153
Report and Certification of Loan Disbursement, 112
Report of Separation and Record of Service (NGB Form 22), 30
Request for Certificate of Eligibility (Form 26-1880), 29–30, 104, 273
  See also Automated Certificate of Eligibility (ACE); *Certificate of
    Eligibility* (COE)
*Request for Determination of Loan Guaranty Eligibility–Unmarried
    Surviving Spouse,* 104
Request Pertaining to Military Records (Form SF-180), 30
reserves (cash), 65, 91–92, 202
reserves (escrow), 151, 242
Reserves (members of), 27, 28, 29, 31
  refinance VA Funding Fee, 245
residual income
  described, 60, 67
  and DTI ratio, 69
  information for loan application, 89
  Table of Residual Incomes by Region, 68

and underwriting, 67–69, 188

VA loan guidelines, 67–69

RESPA (Real Estate Settlement and Procedures Act), 223

retail rate, 201

roof, 148

Rural Development loans, 12

S

safety. *See* health and safety

sanitation, 146, 148, 150

second-tier entitlement, 55–58

secondary entitlement, 33–34, 55

secondary market, sale of mortgages in, 96–97, 191, 199, 204–5

self-employment, 52–53, 62–63

seller's agent. *See* listing agent (seller's agent)

septic systems, 130, 148, 150

service members

awareness of VA loan programs, 6–7

discharge conditions, 26, 27, 28, 29–30, 31–32

recently discharged, 64–65

See also active duty employment; veterans

Servicing Disclosure Statement, 98

settlement. *See* closing

short sale, 54, 154

signatures/signing documents

electronically, 83

loan approval paperwork, 83–84, 95

Power of Attorney, 155–56

solar heating/cooling, 212

Special Flood Hazard Areas (SFHA), 144

Specially Adapted Housing program, 156–57

spouses of service members and veterans. *See* military spouses

staff appraisal reviewer (SAR), 142, 182–83, 185

stock dividend income, 66

structural integrity, 146, 147, 148, 149

student loans, 92

subprime mortgages/borrowers, 3, 42, 81, 193, 255

surviving spouses of veterans, 27–28, 32, 103, 104, 231

T

tax returns
  and loan approval, 84, 97
  Request for Transcript of Tax Returns (IRS Form 4506-T), 99–100
  underwriting requirement, 19, 63, 188, 189
  See also income
taxes
  as debt, 62, 67, 70
  local government, 226, 242
  PITI, 89, 222, 243
  property, 111, 215
termite inspection, 120, 130, 149
title, forms of ownership, 87
title fees
  Good Faith Estimate (GFE), 215, 218–19
  HUD-1 Settlement Statement, 226
  VA refinance loans, 241
title insurance, 120, 186–87, 218–19, 226
transfer fees, 228
TransUnion, 37, 38
Truth in Lending Act, 109
Truth-in-Lending Disclosure Statement (TIL), 107–9
two-year benchmark for stability
  employment, 61, 62, 82, 88
  following bankruptcy, 52–54
  following foreclosure, 56
  secondary sources of income, 66
  self-employment, 62–63

U

"underwater" homes, 5, 252
underwriting
  analysis of residual income, 68, 188
  Automated Underwriting System (AUS), 83, 117–18, 187–88
  bankruptcy's effect on, 53
  and cash-out refinancing, 244, 245
  and cash reserves, 65
  in challenging economy, 255–57
  clear to close (CTC), 190

compensating factors, 69–71

and conditional loan approval, 188–89

construction loans, 248–49

and credit history/score, 120–21, 187, 198, 244, 247

debt-to-income ratio (DTI ratio), 5, 60, 66–71, 99, 117–18, 121, 124, 188, 256

and down payment, 65

and employment history, 52–53, 61–64, 82, 187

and loan prequalification, 19, 80, 82–84, 121

manual underwriting, 83, 120–21

necessity for, 188–89

negative compensating factors, 53

overview, 35–36

and preapproval, 19, 83, 120

recently discharged service members, 64–65

and refinancing, 240, 243, 244, 245, 248–49

risk to lender, 59, 188

tax returns required for, 19, 63, 99–100, 189

See also Automated Underwriting System (AUS); credit score; loan approval; VA loans

Uniform Residential Loan Application (Fannie Mae Form 1003), 84–96, 275–79

United States Department of Agriculture (USDA) loans, 12, 14–15

U.S. Department of Housing and Urban Development (HUD), 214

U.S. Public Interest Research Group, 47

USDA (United States Department of Agriculture) loans, 12, 14–15, 195

utilities easements, 150

V

VA Amendment to Contract, 106–7, 143

VA appraisals

asking price vs. appraised value, 143

and Cash-Out Refinance loan, 244

Certificate of Reasonable Value, 142

comps (comparable home values), 24, 141, 143, 146

costs for, 146, 215, 218

vs. home inspections, 146

importance of, 133, 134, 135–36, 142–43, 256

independent appraisal, 185–86
Lender Appraisal Processing Program (LAPP), 139–40
as loan contingency, 106–7, 120, 143
market value determination, 140–43, 182–86
Minimum Property Requirements (MPRs), 140, 145, 146–53, 185
Notice of Value (NOV), 142, 183–86
overview, 133, 134, 135–36, 139–43
of properties in foreclosure, 153
properties ineligible for, 144–46
property characteristics, 140
reconsideration of value, 143
and refinancing, 240–41, 244, 247, 249, 256
sanctions, 145
second appraisals, 185–86
staff appraisal reviewer (SAR), 142, 182–83, 185
and VA Streamline loan, 240–41, 256
See also home prices; Minimum Property Requirements (MPRs); purchase price; VA loans
VA Cash-Out Refinance loan, 243–48, 249
VA entitlements. *See* entitlement to VA loans; VA Loan Guaranty program
VA Funding Fee
calculation of, 10, 231–32
and Cash-Out Refinance loan, 244–45, 246
and down payment, 231–32
exemptions, 103, 231
and *Good Faith Estimate* (GFE), 111, 218
and loan-to-value adjustment, 205
and loans in default, 231
overview, 231–32
payment of, 103, 111, 229
and seller concessions, 229
and VA Streamline loan, 241, 243, 246
See also finance charges; VA Loan Guaranty program
VA grant programs, Specially Adapted Housing, 156–57
VA Loan Disclosures, 115–16
VA Loan Guaranty program
amounts guaranteed, 26, 33–34

INDEX

appraisal requirement, 144

approved lenders, 56, 59, 121, 133–34, 201

Automated Certificate of Eligibility (ACE), 30–32

benefits of, 3–7, 255–58

Certificate of Eligibility (COE), 29–30, 34–35

and credit history, 3–4, 58, 59

described, 3–4, 18, 21, 34–36, 236

eligible persons, 25–29, 31–32, 41–42, 58, 104, 145

eligible properties, 21–25, 105, 144–45

eligible uses, 21–23

entitlement amounts, 33–34, 55–56

future of, 255–58

how it works, 21, 33, 59

ineligible uses, 23–25

loan limits, 32–34

occupancy requirement, 21–22, 23, 86–87, 232–33, 235, 247, 249

protection of borrowers, 21, 145, 193

Realtor's experience with, 131

and refinance, 247–48

and risk assessment, 35, 50, 64, 66 71, 121, 188

sanctions, 145

testimonials, 158–79

volume of loans, 4–5, 9, 256

See also eligibility for VA loans; VA Funding Fee; VA loans

VA Loan Summary Sheet, 113–14

VA loans

   approved lenders, 9, 56, 59, 121, 133–34, 201, 210

   availability of, 6–7

   and bankruptcy, 52–54, 120

   benefits of, 3–7, 9–10, 21

   and co-borrowers, 41–42, 118

   comparison chart, 14–15

   condominiums, 21–23, 145

   vs. conventional loans, 3–5, 9–11, 14–15, 78–79, 132–33, 204–5, 247–48

   credit requirements, 3–5, 11, 36, 44, 58, 59, 81

   down payment, 4, 10, 34, 57–58, 65

   Good Faith Estimate (GFE), 215–22, 280–82

and home construction, 23, 24–25, 137, 144, 159–60
HUD-1 Settlement Statement, 214–15, 223–28
income requirements, 60–71
misconceptions about, 31, 78–79, 132–33
multiple VA loans, 56, 86–87
no money down, 4, 10, 34, 124, 188, 201
vs. other nonconventional loans, 9, 14–15
overview, 9–10
and prior foreclosures, 55, 120
as Qualified Mortgages, 195
Realtors' knowledge about, 78–79, 127–36, 151, 152–53
Report and Certification of Loan Disbursement, 112
Request for Certificate of Eligibility (Form 26-1880), 29–30, 104
seller concessions, 228–31
VA Amendment to Contract, 106–7, 143
VA Loan Disclosures, 115–16
VA Loan Summary Sheet, 113–14
Verification of VA Benefits, 103
See also eligibility for VA loans; lenders; loans; underwriting; VA
    appraisals; VA Loan Guaranty program
VA loans (specific loans)
    Energy Efficient Mortgage, 116, 212–13
    Graduated Payment Mortgage (GPM), 210–12
    Growing Equity Mortgage (GEM), 211–12
    Hybrid ARM loans, 209–10
    Interest Rate Reduction Refinance Loan, 27, 239, 246–47
    VA Cash-Out Refinance loan, 243–45, 249
    VA Streamline loan, 239, 240–43, 244, 245–48, 256
    See also closing costs; mortgages
VA refinance loans
    closing costs, 240, 241–42, 248
    Construction-to-Permanent Refinance Loan, 25, 248–49
    from conventional loans, 240
    vs. conventional refinancing, 247–48
    Interest Rate Reduction Refinance Loan, 27, 239, 246–47
    overview, 239–40, 246–47
    VA Cash-Out Refinance loan, 243–48
    and VA Funding Fee, 241, 243

VA Streamline loan, 239, 240–43, 244, 245–48, 256

Veterans Benefits Improvement Act (2008), 244

See also refinancing

VA Streamline loan, 239, 240–43, 244, 245–48, 256

vs. Cash-Out Refinance loan, 244, 246–47

value. *See* market value; VA appraisals

vapor barriers, 213

ventilation, 148

Verification of VA Benefits, 103

veterans

awareness of VA loan programs, 6–7, 257

defined, 26–27

dependents of, 233

discharge conditions, 26, 27, 28, 29–30, 31–32

loan preapproval, 118

remarried spouses of deceased, 27

spouses of, 232–33

surviving spouses of deceased, 27–28

unmarried surviving spouses of, 32, 104

See also active duty employment; service members

Veterans Affairs, Department of, 29, 195, 241

Veterans Benefits Improvement Act (2008), 244

Veterans United Home Loans, 19–20, 57–58, 74, 79, 81, 124–25, 159–60, 235–36, 249, 252

credit and underwriting requirements, 194–95

and hybrid VA ARMs, 210

testimonials, 161–79

Veterans United Lighthouse Program, 45–46, 50, 51, 54, 81–82

See also credit clinics/counseling

Veterans United Realty, 18–20, 134–35

payment to buyer at closing, 134

testimonials, 161–79

W

water supply, 148, 150

wells, 130, 150

windows, 212

Y

Yield Spread
    and compensation of lender, 196–98, 198–200, 230–31
    and compensation of loan brokers, 198–200
    and interest rates, 191, 196–98, 198–200, 201, 230–31
    and Qualified Mortgages, 199

14027486R00183

Made in the USA
San Bernardino, CA
14 August 2014